-0. DEC.

C.

MARIE
WALEWSKA

MARIE WALEWSKA

Napoleon's Great Love

CHRISTINE SUTHERLAND

WEIDENFELD and NICOLSON
LONDON

© Christine Sutherland 1979
Weidenfeld and Nicolson
91 Clapham High Street, London sw4

ISBN 0 297 77626 6

Printed by Willmer Brothers Limited
Rock Ferry Industrial Estate Merseyside

TO DAVID

The life of Europe was centred on one man and all were trying to fill their lungs with the air he had breathed. Every year France presented him with three hundred thousand of her youth. . . . Never had there been so many sleepless nights as in the time of that man . . . never had there been such a nation of desolate mothers. And yet . . . there never was such joy, such life, such fanfares of war in all hearts. Never was there such pure sunlight as that which dried all this blood. God made the sun for this man, they said, and they called it the Sun of Austerlitz. . . .

It was the air of the spotless sky where shone so much glory, where glistened so many swords, that the youth of the time breathed. They well knew that they were destined for the hecatomb . . . but even if one must die what did it matter? Death itself was so beautiful, so noble, so illustrious in its battle-scarred purple . . . it became young and there was no more old age. All the cradles of France, as all its tombs, were armed with shield and buckler; there were no more old men, there were only corpses or demi-gods.

Alfred de Musset, *Confessions of a Child of the Century*

CONTENTS

ILLUSTRATIONS

AUTHOR'S NOTE

The first problem confronting Marie Walewska's biographer is the scarcity of personal documentation left by this intensely private and sensitive woman. In the course of her short life she wrote comparatively few letters, and her diary, hurriedly dictated to a secretary in the last three months before her death, when she knew that the end was approaching, was composed for the benefit of her three sons in order to explain and justify their mother's involvement with Napoleon. As a result, although it accurately describes her childhood and early youth, it errs on a number of historical details and generally overemphasizes the patriotic motives at the expense of her genuine love for the Emperor.

In addition, although the romance between Napoleon and the beautiful Polish Countess was widely known and talked about at the time, the majority of Napoleonic memoirs both in France and in Poland were not published until the mid-nineteenth century, under the reign of Napoleon III. At that time France's Minister of Foreign Affairs was none other than Alexander Colonna-Walewski, son of Napoleon and Marie Walewska. Intent on protecting his mother's reputation he actively discouraged references to the famous romance.

Having been acknowledged as a legitimate Walewski, Alexander insisted on maintaining this fiction. As Ambassador to the Court of St James, while attending a reception at Lady Holland's house in London, he once rebuked a well known lady guest, who had been enthusing about his striking resemblance to his 'distinguished father'. 'I had no idea, Madame,' he said, 'that you were acquainted with the late Count Walewski, my father.'

Such factors were considerable obstacles and not surprisingly the romantic nature of the subject gave birth to various fictionalized accounts of Marie's life. Luckily, however, there exists solid documentation, including fourteen letters from Napoleon to Marie, some of which have only recently been discovered and have never yet been translated, which makes it possible to piece together the various details of this extraordinary life. A meticulous examination of contemporary Polish sources – the daily newspapers and memoirs, particularly those relating to the years 1807, 1808 and 1812 – yields a rich harvest.

French sources take the story up where Polish leave off, and here the Archives du Quai d'Orsay, the Archives Nationales, Archives de la Seine and those of the Ministère de la Guerre are helpful. Of the published works I have consulted, as indicated in my bibliography, I owe a particular debt of gratitude to Mr Marian Brandys' study in Polish *Kłopoty z Panią Walewską* which the author most kindly sent me, and to the excellent *Napoleon's Campaign in Poland, 1806–7* by F. Loraine Petre. Of the infinite number of works pertaining to Napoleon I, I have found the two fairly recent biographies in English – Vincent Cronin's and Felix Markham's – and Professor Jean Tulard's in French, the most useful reference sources.

I do not claim to have produced a definitive biography of Marie Walewska. There may still be some documents locked in private collections in France, that have not yet come to light. What I have attempted to do, taking advantage of my knowledge of Polish and French, and having been fortunate to have been given access to the Walewski family archives, was to recreate for the benefit of the general reader the personality and the life of this unusual young woman, who through an accident of history found herself at the epicentre of the greatest military epic of all times.

Marie's story is inextricably bound up with Poland's involvement with Napoleon – a one-sided love affair, because for the great Emperor Poland was only the means to push back the frontiers of Russia and open a land route to the east. 'I like the Poles on the battlefield, they furnish it well', Napoleon used to say, but if the opportunity arose to trade off Poland for some concessions from the

Tsar, or use it to buy the goodwill of his uncertain ally Austria, he was perfectly prepared to do so.

I have tried to describe in my introduction the state of Poland in the latter part of the eighteenth century in order to explain how the partitions and the loss of national independence came about. This of course was the reason why the Poles so passionately espoused Napoleon's cause. Freedom meant everything to them, as it does now, and they thought that in Napoleon they had found its apostle. Though he let them down badly, the glory of the Napoleonic adventure was such that in Poland his legend lives on undiminished.

Throughout this book I have kept to the more familiar westernized form of spelling first names: Stanislaus for Stanislaw, Antonia instead of Antonina, Catherine instead of Katarzyna, Elizabeth instead of Elzbieta, etc. Marie's oldest brother Benedict-Joseph is variously referred to in contemporary sources as Benedict or sometimes Joseph; I have chosen to call him Benedict. Polish surnames sometimes end with an 'i' to indicate masculine gender and 'a' for the feminine (Walewski and Walewska), and I have felt it easier to retain this practice.

During Marie's lifetime the Napoleonic franc, the Germinal, established in 1803 (its value remained constant until 1914), was worth approximately six of today's francs (about $1.20) at current rates of exchange. Thus Marie's allowance from Napoleon of 10,000 francs a month would be equivalent to about $12,000 or £6,000 a month – a considerable sum, but difficult to compare with today's values.

I wish to express my thanks to Count Charles-André Walewski, who has kindly opened the family archives to me and given me much precious documentation. I also wish to thank Count Guillaume d'Ornano, a direct descendant of Marie Walewska, for allowing me to photograph and reproduce the portrait by Gérard on the cover, and his son Count Hubert d'Ornano for making it possible.

A particularly warm thank you goes to Mr Vigo and Lady Maryel de Wichfeld for their generous hospitality on the lovely island of Elba, where most of Chapter 11 was written and to Mr John Saumarez Smith for taking the trouble to read the finished manuscript and making the constructive suggestions which vastly improved it.

I wish to express my thanks also to the Director of the Archives of the Quai d'Orsay in Paris; the staff of the Bibliothèque Nationale and the Bibliothèque Thiers; the Archives Nationales; the Société Historique et Littéraire Polonaise; Dr Guy Godlewski for his advice on the Elba chapter; Princesse Jeanne Marie de Broglie; Mme Claire de Forbin; Monsieur François Heim; Professor Rottermund, the Director of the Muzeum Narodowe in Warsaw, for sending me the reproductions of the Belotto-Canaletto pictures of eighteenth-century Warsaw; Count Adam Zamoyski for his help with the proofs and genealogical details of Polish families; the Hon. Mrs Christopher James for her comments; Mr Robert Rothschild for untangling the complicated exchange rate between 1803 and 1979 franc; the staff of the London Library; the French Institute; the Polish Library in London and in particular Dr Jagodzinski; the Mansell Collection; the Courtauld Institute; and Sotheby's and Co. I am grateful to Miss Mary Young who typed the manuscript and to the staff of Weidenfeld and Nicolson: Mr Christopher Falkus; Miss Barbara Gough for her careful editing of the manuscript; and Miss Julia Brown for assembling the pictures.

Lastly I would like to thank David, my husband, whose patience and encouragement made writing this book possible.

EUROPE IN 1812

France   Satellites   Allies

Borders of France-1789
Other National Boundaries

Norway

Edinburgh

North Sea

Denmark

Bremen
The   Hanover
Hague   Amsterdam
London   Holland
Dover   Brussels
Calais   Waterloo   CONFEDER-
                                    ATION
Amiens   Belgium   OF
Reims   Frankfort   THE
St Cloud   Paris   R. Rhine   RHINE
Fontainebleau
Tours   Strasbourg
            Dijon
FRENCH EMPIRE
            Lyons   Lausanne
Bordeaux   Geneva   Milan
Grenoble   Turin   Parma
Bayonne   Marengo   Genoa
Burgos   Nice   Lucca
Portugal   Florence
Salamanca   Marseilles   Bastia
Madrid   Corsica   Elba
Kingdom of Spain   Ajaccio
Seville

CHAOS AND
MAGNIFICENCE

In the mid-eighteenth century the largest country in central Europe was the kingdom of Poland, or 'the Commonwealth of Poland' as its inhabitants called it. Its territories stretched from the Baltic south to the Black Sea, from the Oder a thousand miles east to the Dnieper.

In the west, Poland bordered Prussia, then ruled by Frederick the Great. From his splendid palace of Sans-Souci, surrounded by French works of art and a brilliant group of confidantes, the philosopher-king cast a greedy eye towards his eastern neighbour, his desire heightened as much by the vastness of the potential spoil and Poland's known internal weakness as by his need to connect East Prussia with the rest of his kingdom.

To the north lay Sweden, a traditional enemy, weak now but never to be trusted. To the south, beyond the Carpathians, Austria also watched, interested; she was ostensibly friendly but she would miss no opportunity to aggrandize her empire.

From the east, across the Dnieper, came a far greater threat, for here lay the enormous land-mass of Russia whose sovereign, Catherine II also kept a greedy eye on Poland. Having forced the weak Poles to elect her ex-lover Stanislaus Poniatowski their king, she now hoped to acquire a large portion of Polish territory and particularly the lands which had once belonged to the old principality of Kiev, where the majority of the inhabitants were of Orthodox faith.

Surrounded by such covetous neighbours, even a strong country would have found survival difficult. But Poland was not strong. Once a great power in central Europe, indisputably regarded by the world as chief representative of the Slavonic race (Russia was considered a land of mere barbarians), this proud, high-spirited nation had steadily deteriorated to an impotence difficult to believe. Here was a vast country, beautifully endowed by nature, with hundreds of thousands of acres of fertile soil producing a wide variety of crops, vast forests, immense pastures feeding fine cattle, a network of navigable rivers connected by a sophisticated canal system with the Baltic and the Black Sea; it was a country that should have been the granary of Europe. Instead, Poland was rotting away in obscurity, without ships, without trade, without gold, obliged to import even basic necessities at exorbitant prices. It was now as isolated as an island, without influence, without much contact with the intellectual and cultural life of the rest of Europe; yet it could not fail to attract covetous neighbours.

Part of the trouble was its size. In the latter part of the eighteenth century Poland's territory extended to over 32,000 square miles, an enormous area, most of it an undulating plain, connecting the lowlands of Germany with the great plains of Russia. There were no natural boundaries in the west or in the east: only the Carpathians in the south and the Baltic in the north provided some kind of a barrier.

The nucleus of the country had been the so-called 'old kingdom', central Poland, the lands within the Vistula basin. In the fourteenth century the duchy of Lithuania, the picturesque country of deep forests and rolling hills in the north-eastern corner of the Baltic, entered into a voluntary union with Poland; Prussia and Livonia became dependencies a few years later, expanding the country's territory by one-third. Wars with the Cossacks brought in the *'dzikie pola'* ('savage steppes'), the lands from Kiev to the Black Sea, the furthest edge of European civilization. This was an ancient battlefield, where for centuries

Commonwealth soldiers had fought Turks and Tartars; where in the long grass man still hunted man; where the outlaw sought refuge and robbers hid in ambush to plunder the caravans that were eastward bound. No one knows how many battles were fought there, nor how many men were killed, for no one would have witnessed it – or wanted to. It was an eerie land. Frontier guards told in lowered voices how at night the shades of those killed 'in the midst of their sins' rose from their long death-sleep howling like vampires. A practised ear could tell the difference between the howl of a vampire and that of a wolf. At midnight, ghosts on horseback raced across the steppe ahead of the wolves to overtake travellers 'wailing and pleading with them' for a sign of the Holy Cross. 'Sometimes,' said the guards, 'whole legions of ghosts appeared and came so near to the post that the sentries gave the alarm.' This was always said to be a bad omen, a portent of national disaster, such as war or plague.

Only one highway, the ancient caravan-route, connected the Wild Lands with the west. It ran from Kiev, crossed the Dnieper and the steppes and went on to the foothills of the Carpathians, through Cracow, the lovely medieval capital of the old kingdom. It then followed on west, through Prague, toward Vienna.

In the north there was only one really well-travelled route : the highway between Berlin and Warsaw. It veered north to the Baltic to connect with the so-called 'amber route' (amber was a much-valued export from the Baltic provinces of Poland) through East Prussia. Travellers proceeding east from Warsaw towards Moscow did so at their own peril. Most of them preferred to go to St Petersburg by sea and continue to Moscow from there. The remaining roads were mere tracks, impassable for at least four months of the year. There was no money in the Treasury to maintain them.

The powerful Vistula river, which crosses the country from south to north, had always been the principal artery for commerce and distribution of food. But here too only the northern part of the river was at all navigable. The wide, well-planned network of canals, which should have solved the country's distribution problems, was too badly maintained to be effective. And there was no money in the Treasury to modernize it.

These were formidable obstacles, but other countries – like Prussia in the west – had faced similar problems and survived and prospered. Geographical factors contributed to the state of the Polish nation, but anarchy was at the root of the trouble. Where a king's rule was needed, she had only irresponsible, rather mad feudal squires, who had managed to steal the government from the king and his ministers. Dominated by a handful of prima donna feudal lords, the landed gentry seemed content to accept increasing internal ruin in the name of exaggerated personal liberty.

The power of the nobility was unique in Europe: the reason for it was primarily the fact that Poland's throne was not hereditary but elective. It was the Diet (the *Sejm*), composed exclusively of landed gentry, who elected the king; as a result, he remained beholden to the particular faction which had put the crown on his head. To their original privilege of freedom from taxation and 'any other obligation except that of military service', the nobles added the right of deciding all questions of peace and war. Since they controlled both the Treasury and the armed forces, they also controlled the royal ministry. Their whim alone assigned funds to conduct war, build canals or schools, or initiate any project that today we call public expenditure. They automatically distrusted not only royal ministers but also powerful townspeople who had obtained any royal privileges, such as local autonomy. As they grew in power, they increasingly refused to share political influence with the 'plebeian burghers'. Slowly but steadily they all but eliminated the rights of the middle classes; townspeople, for example, could not own landed estates and in consequence could not participate in legitimate politics. The wretched peasant, having no one to protect him, was reduced to a state of virtual serfdom, though serfdom (which existed in contemporary Russia) was illegal in

Poland. The entire government of fifteen million people passed into the hands of 200,000 selfish, generally ignorant country squires.

The crowning absurdity of the Polish system was the infamous law, the *Liberum Veto*, which demanded total acceptance of any piece of legislation by the *Sejm* or Diet. If one deputy out of a total of about five hundred voted 'no'. he doomed any proposed bill. 'Whether from malice, stupidity or obstinacy,' a contemporary Polish writer noted, 'all our counsels and consultations come to naught. It is a disgrace to the civilized world to have a government such as ours.'

Royal attempts to abolish or even curb the veto proved futile. The Diet, composed as it was of landed gentry, always supported any nobleman, however half-witted or pretentious, bent on opposing vital reforms proposed by king or ministers. In such circumstances constitutional reform, indeed almost any vital legislation, became impossible. For almost a hundred years the Diet passed no laws and accomplished but little business. Although it continued to meet regularly, one or more members always exploded any attempt at legislation by invoking the *Liberum Veto*. The country was collectively committing suicide.

The army had virtually been abolished, because the nobles refused to pay its expenses; the diplomatic service had been eliminated for the same reason. Law courts were a scandal : venal judges and crushing legal costs meant that persons of small means could not sue the rich and powerful, no matter what the offence; in criminal cases, weak and corrupt magistrates seldom delivered verdicts, and those delivered were rarely enforced; magistrates and associated officials held insufficient authority to arrest and prosecute lawbreakers. Ironically, Polish statute books abounded with excellent laws and ordinances conducive to public welfare and security. But such statutes were meaningless, since no one could enforce them.

Other archaic and self-defeating laws tied the monarch's

hands. A seventeenth-century edict allowed the king to appoint, but not to dismiss, cabinet ministers and senior administrative officials. Various administrative branches thus degenerated into lifetime sinecures of immense personal profit to the holders, who were rarely called to account for graft or maladministration. If the Diet initiated an inquiry into a particularly flagrant abuse, a deputy, bribed by the concerned official, merely shouted 'I disagree', which ended the inquiry. So venal was the nobility that Augustus III of Saxony, one of the last kings of Poland, wrote in his Memoirs that he had 'the greatest difficulties in preventing the selling of the Ministry of Finance to the highest bidder'.

By the 1760s Poland was the laughing-stock of western Europe. But while the country was slowly sinking to a primitive level of government, individual Polish nobles enjoyed a life of magnificent feudal splendour. Altogether about 500,000 families qualified as belonging to the nobility. Basically everyone who carried arms was a noble, *szlachcic*. (The word is a derivative from the German *'schlacht'*, 'combat'.) But only about half those who owned inherited land counted for something. The remaining half, a poor, uneducated but spirited lot, divided their allegiance between the various 'chiefs of clans' – the great families of the day – in whose armies they fought and at whose individual 'Courts' they usually found sinecures and employment. The majority of landed gentry thought of themselves as westerners, in the fullest sense of the word, and would have resented being called 'oriental'. They knew some Latin and French, travelled to Paris or Vienna and, whenever they could afford it, sent their sons on a 'once in a lifetime' grand tour. Yet among the members of the Polish Diet more heads were shaved in the Turkish style than powdered and peruked in the French style, and the ornate ostentation of noblemen's lives, their love for glitter and gorgeous trappings, had an oriental flavour about it.

Land was the source and foundation of wealth. Some of the

most powerful magnates had holdings of more than half a million acres and owned several towns. They fashioned their residences after the palaces of France or Rome, employed Italian cratfsmen and hired skilful chefs, who produced some of the finest dishes in Europe. They maintained hosts of *payuks, hayduks*, lackeys, messengers, personal militia, gamekeepers, grooms, valets and many other retainers chosen from the peasantry, whom they arrayed in resplendent uniforms of Turkish and Magyar origin. Prince Karol Radziwill retained at least ten thousand such; Count Felix Potocki reputedly had fourteen thousand at his Court in Kaniow in the Ukraine. It was a point of honour not only to maintain as many parade servants as possible but to dress them splendidly. *Payuks*, like Turkish janissaries, usually wore loose grey breeches, flowing mantles with wide sleeves and towering *tschapkas*, like grenadiers' busbies, surmounted with silver aigrettes. Turkish daggers hung in silver sheaths from richly embroidered silk girdles. *Hayduks* wore tightly fitting Hungarian jackets embroidered with lace and silver and complemented with rich fur cloaks that hung rakishly from one shoulder, and small turban-shaped caps embroidered with silver thread. Hussars, a sort of personal militia, appeared even more splendid. They wore carmine uniforms surmounted by silver cuirasses and semi-visored helmets, trimmed with a generous ridge of goose feathers. When mounted, they carried long lances with gleaming sharp steel points. The Polish magnate spent vast sums in mounting these small armies, but it was a point of honour to have as splendid a retinue as one's rank and wealth allowed. He himself rode only thoroughbred Arabian chargers, his saddle encrusted with precious gems and beneath that a blanket richly embroidered in silver and gold. 'I like to feast my eyes upon gems,' replied Prince Sanguszko when asked about his eye-dazzling collection of saddles.

A great nobleman ruled his own province – which might be as vast as one of the Home Counties in England – as an independent potentate. He surrounded himself with all the pomp and ceremony of a Court, which often outshone the royal Court at Warsaw. Grand Hetman Branicki's palace at Bialystok was called 'the Polish Versailles'. Prince Czartoryski maintained an equally resplendent country mansion at Pulawy; Powazki – his other estate – was famous for a park studded with ornate pavilions, built in the classical style, each representing a symbolic theme, such as Friendship, Wedlock, Life and Death. In one pavilion, dedicated to Fame, the lord coyly inserted his own bust between those of Copernicus and da Vinci. Another famous estate included ape colonies, which lived on artificial islands in the middle of a gigantic moat.

The living conditions of peasants working on the land were for the most part dismal. 'They exist resigned to their misery,' observed a contemporary traveller from Sweden. 'They believe that God placed them on this earth with only one purpose: to till the lord's land and die under the whip of his factor.'

The lords ran their estates on the royal pattern. A treasurer looked after general household expenses. A cupbearer saw to the wine cellars, a vast item of expenditure. An equerry supervised the stables – perhaps the most expensive charge of all. A major-domo headed the establishment; like other officials he was always a nobleman. He controlled the 'gentlemen servants', youths of noble birth, mostly poor kinsmen, who had been fortunate enough to obtain a place in the lord's house and thus secure their future. They ate at the major-domo's table, wore swords, the distinguishing mark of a Polish gentleman, and were never required to perform menial service. Their principal duty, other than being amusing courtiers, was to escort their lord on horseback when he visited some other magnate. Typical attire was a grey serge frock-coat, with green satin waistcoast, a flowered silk girdle with gold tassels, a green hat trimmed with feathers and red felt boots. These handsome young men, riding ahead of the parade servants, colourfully symbolized the lord's status. The magnate's wife often had her own establishment, or small Court, where certain kinswomen, ladies of high birth but small estate, attended her around the clock. These chosen ones were often brought up with the daughters of the house, shared their tutors and amusements, received an allowance and a dowry and were eventually married off to suitable noblemen.

Here was a landed patriarchy, not without its good or at least its unique points. Strong family affections formed its base. Every nobleman's house, large or small, religiously preserved family trees that showed every branch of kinship from the earliest times – some went back to the twelfth century. Stern, unrelenting tutors taught youth of both sexes their pedigrees along with their catechisms. Such knowledge was vital for later life, for no one could get an official appointment, a Maltese cross or any other perquisite worth having, unless he could trace descent from a noble ancestor *on both sides* through at least ten generations. King Augustus III had difficulties in establishing the noble credentials of a great-grandmother, a fact carefully noted and critically commented upon by the nobility.

As in a Scottish clan, blood prevailed over wealth. A great magnate always acknowledged kinship with a poor relation; even a cousin in the fourth degree was regarded as a member of the intimate family circle. Within the narrow limits of their world these nobles were egalitarian. 'My father', writes Countess Potocka, 'always treats the poorest gentleman of ancient descent as his equal, kissing and embracing him and calling him by his Christian name whenever he sees him. But he has an aversion for people of dubious origin and will admit none of them to his presence.' Thus, whenever a powerful family chose to unite for political purposes, it usually prevailed, unless another family, equally powerful, opposed it. Such clashes often led to feuds and even to limited civil wars and further wasting of the country's resources.

Firmly rooted in the earth, these lords of old Poland derived extraordinary vitality from it. As a rule they were kind and generous to a fault; they were affectionate husbands, indulgent fathers, though usually very stern masters. They delighted in open-air sports and martial exercises. They loved the danger of a hunt far more than its mere exercise, and in the elk, bear and wild boar of their uncharted forests they found quarry to tax all their skills and courage. They regarded fox-hunting and hare-coursing as poor sport. One of the great potentates of north-eastern Poland, when invited by King Augustus III to his palace near Warsaw to follow the hounds, reportedly remarked: 'Why should I go and hunt rats and mice in Warsaw, when I can always find wild boars in my own forests?'

They were also fiercely individualistic; they submitted to no authority, least of all to their king's. They generally despised their monarch and wanted no part of the hush and punctilio of a royal Court. Their hospitality was legendary. They spared neither trouble nor expense in welcoming a guest. When, after the French Revolution, Prince Lubomirski invited Prince de Ligne with other fugitive French aristocrats to his castle, gorgeously attired *payuks* lined the road for several miles, while cannons thundered salvoes from the castle walls. Then the host appeared riding an Arab stallion, with gem-encrusted saddle and bridle of pure gold studded with rubies. A banquet for one thousand people followed. 'It is reported that the Prince had to mortgage a whole town in order to pay for the banquet,' a contemporary recorded.

Unlike many members of the Continental aristocracy of the period, the Polish *'grand seigneur'* received but scant formal education: a smattering of Latin – enough to appear fluent – some French, a limited amount of geography and European history. The average magnate wrote so poorly that no one could decipher his letters. When the lord wrote to a relation or friend in his own hand, as was demanded by protocol, he simultaneously dictated to a secretary, perched at a desk in the next room. The secretary then attached his calligraphic copy as a sort of key to the lord's own hieroglyphics and forwarded them both.

The great ladies of Poland often received a far better education than their husbands. The most famous *grande dame* of late-eighteenth century Poland, Princess Isabella Czartoryska, exercised a most civilizing influence on Polish society : she was not beautiful but unusually intelligent, witty, decisive and firm. Educated at Versailles, she married Adam-Casimir Czartoryski, the richest man in Poland and a singularly enlightened man.* With his blessing she made their house a meeting-place for French and Polish intellectuals. From their residence, the famous Blue Palace in Warsaw, French culture radiated to all parts of the country.

But such enlightenment was rare. Because of a natural earthy exuberance, which scorned 'the amusement of letters', the average Polish nobleman devoted himself to gluttonous eating and drinking, when he was not pursuing the pleasures of the field or the boudoir. In particular he regarded hard drinking as a virtue, as did his neighbours the Russians. Drinking was certainly not regarded as a vice but rather as the distinguishing mark of 'a real gentleman'. Grand Hetman Branicki, Governor of the Ukraine, advised the last king, Stanislas II, that he could not expect to become popular 'unless he could get drunk with his cronies at least twice a week'. A host welcomed his visitors with a stirrup-cup of huge dimensions. If the guest drained it at one draught, he won general approval; if he followed that feat by drinking a gallon of old Hungarian wine before dessert, he was fêted and cheered, welcomed into the very bosom of his host's family, his every wish granted without question.

Exuberant, unruly and fond of drinking as they were, these colourful gentlemen were also deeply religious. 'A man', said Count Branicki, 'can jog along happily in this life if he has enough money and good health, but he shouldn't be caught dying in the middle of his sins.' He himself scrupulously observed all Catholic prescriptives : he sang every day with his

* His correspondence in Sanskrit with Sir William Jones of the East India Company was published by Clarendon Press (Oxford 1968).

servants the Hours of the Immaculate Conception, fasted on Fridays, flogged himself every Good Friday and suffered terribly 'now and then' from qualms of conscience.

The masses of lesser nobility followed the example of the magnates as far as means permitted, particularly those sufficiently well off to live on their own estates among their tenantry. The others were mere hangers-on swelling the retinues of the great houses; they supported that 'golden liberty' which was responsible for ruinous anarchy.

We may disapprove of the Polish magnates of the day, but it is difficult to dislike them. Their excesses resulted from too much life, not too little. Irresponsible, swashbuckling, arrogant, but not wicked, if their minds were muddled, their hearts were sound. Born and bred to command, kings of their world from birth, they saw no reason why this happy state of affairs should not continue for ever, and not one among them possessed sufficient strength and vision to point out that they were hurling themselves into an abyss. Freedom – individual and collective – obsessed them, but they could not understand why its preservation should call for personal sacrifices on behalf of the whole country. They were but a small fraction of the nation, but they totally disregarded the remaining mass of their countrymen. They long lacked enlightened leadership, and when it came, it was too late to carry out the reforms. By the 1780s disaster was at the door. After the partitions of Poland, the entire force of their primitive, fearless natures concentrated on retrieving the independence they had lost.*

Ironically, the man who presided over the downfall was not

* In the first partition of 1786, Poland lost one quarter of its territory to Russia, Prussia and Austria. Contemporary observers called it 'collective rape'. In 1793 – at the second partition – Russia took all the eastern provinces – a territory of 96,000 square miles, while Prussia took over the greater part of central Poland; this time Austria abstained. Finally, in 1795, the third partition of Poland was effected by successive treaties between Prussia, Austria and Russia, and the name of Poland disappeared from the map. (King Frederick of Prussia remarked that he enjoyed dissecting Poland leaf by leaf, 'like an artichoke'.)

a powerful magnate. Stanislaus Augustus Poniatowski came from a comparatively modest provincial nobility, but one related to the illustrious and powerful Czartoryski family. Thanks to his mother's influence, he received a careful education. At the age of twenty he travelled to Paris 'where his beauty, elegance and above all his *esprit*' vividly impressed Madame Geoffrin, one of the great intellectual hostesses of eighteenth-century France. At the age of twenty-two he accompanied the British Ambassador, Sir Charles Hanbury Williams, to St Petersburg as his secretary (some said lover as well). 'The moment the Grand Duchess Catherine (later Catherine II) set her eyes on the Pole,' writes Count Leo Naryshkin, 'she declared that she wanted him for her own.' She apparently saw him first at a Court ball in honour of the Tsarina Elizabeth's birthday; she was struck by his 'fine expressive eyes and the pensive beauty of his face'.

Stanislaus appears to have had doubts. In his nursery days he had heard fearful tales of grim happenings at this notoriously corrupt Court; he saw nothing but pitfalls ahead, which kept the fear of Siberia constantly before his eyes. He also had moral qualms. 'A strict education kept me remote from crapulous commerce in my youth,' he writes in his Memoirs, 'and a natural predilection for good society preserved me in my travels . . . singular as it may sound, I was still, at twenty-two, what very few men can say they are at that age – a virgin.' But the young Grand Duchess's insistence and her 'dazzling, raven-haired beauty', combined with Naryshkin's connivance, finally won him over. He forgot about Siberia, gave in, and for much of his life remained enthralled by Catherine.

This romance had far-reaching consequences. When the former King Augustus III of Saxony and Poland died, the Polish nobility met in Warsaw to elect a new king. Catherine, now Empress of Russia, let it be known that her 'candidate' for the throne of Poland was Stanislaus Poniatowski, her former lover. This came as a complete surprise to the Poles, but with 'eight thousand Russian troops surrounding the field of election, there was little the electors could do but vote "yes".' Just before the election Stanislaus allegedly wanted to withdraw, but then changed his mind, reflecting that 'if I became king, the Empress might perhaps marry me – otherwise she would be unlikely to do so.' Alas, such a thought did not enter her head, as by then she had a new lover, the more virile Orlov. Nonetheless, she expected subservience from her newly created king.

Stanislaus modelled his Court on Versailles and filled it with prominent men of letters, painters and architects, who transformed Warsaw into a beautiful capital. He then set himself the crucial task of reforming Poland's constitution and, assisted by a group of prominent Polish thinkers and politicians, succeeded far beyond expectation. The new Constitution, promulgated on 3 May 1791, was one of the most enlightened and sensible documents of the period. The Polish Diet, now aware of the danger into which its irresponsibility had led the country, passed it unanimously. But it came too late. The Tsarina of Russia and the Prussian King Frederick were determined to complete the annihilation of Poland.

Given a long period of peace, Stanislaus could have made a good king. But neither his character nor external circumstances allowed it. The nobility had not wanted him, and his moral flabbiness and lack of those earthy qualities so appreciated in Poland immediately lost him the confidence of his subjects. With the third partition in 1795, Poland's name disappeared from the map. The King and his Court were exiled to a small town north of Warsaw. The atmosphere of the once elegant and spirited Court had changed, and only a few courtiers remained. Among them, faithful to the King until the last, was his Court Chamberlain, Anastase Colonna Walewski, soon to become the most talked-about husband in Europe.

I
THE MANOR

A poplar-lined road – blurred with dust in the summer, a muddy quagmire in the autumn – led to the white manor house of Kiernozia, a modest neo-classical structure surrounded by several acres of parkland. Beyond it, around the walls of a grey-steepled church, clustered a group of whitewashed houses, thatched with reeds. The village spilled over past the cemetery grounds and tailed off in the direction of the main road to Warsaw, some twenty-five miles away. Even now, one is struck by a mood of melancholy in this timeless place, induced by the unrelieved flatness of the land.

Around it stretched the vast Polish plain – mute and sombre – all the way to Moscow. Like some gigantic quilt it lay, strewn about with thick forests, criss-crossed by meandering rivers which emptied their waters in the Baltic.

In the first months of the year 1800, the mistress of the white manor house was a handsome, energetic young widow, who, in spite of her abounding vitality, felt that life had treated her with undue harshness. Eva Laczynska, born Zaborowska, was, like so many Polish women of her time, a victim of history. Married at eighteen to a dashing neighbouring landowner whom she adored and by whom she had had seven children, she found herself widowed in her thirties, following the heroic death of her husband in battle against the Russians. His death left her in sole charge of a large family and a run-down, debt-ridden estate.

B

The Laczynski family was an ancient one, much respected, grown eminent in the service of their native country through the ages. In 1506 Samuel Laczynski, a distinguished soldier and courtier, was in attendance at the wedding of King Sigismund I of Poland to Princess Bona Sforza of Milan in Cracow, which was then the capital of Poland. According to contemporary chronicles, this colourful knight fought a duel with a visiting Swedish envoy who had dared to make fun of some intricate figure in a traditional Polish dance. Samuel, known for his fencing skills, first engaged his opponent quite gently but, once wounded, lunged forth with such fury that he cut off the Swede's head in one stroke, causing it to 'sail forth into the air, way beyond the ramparts of the castle'. Surprisingly enough, this inhospitable act won him no reprimand from the king. On the contrary, from then on he was held in highest esteem by the Court, including the Swedish delegation to the wedding. His fame as a master fencer, whose touch was both 'neat and decisive', spread north throughout Scandinavia.

At the end of the sixteenth century another Laczynski, Jerome, won fame as a distinguished jurist, whose *Compendium Judiciorum* for the kingdom of Poland, written in Latin, the language of the educated classes, became the first legal textbook for university studies in Cracow. Records of later years mention several Laczynskis 'noted for valour' in fighting against the 'infidel Turks': one of them accompanied King John Sobieski on his expedition to rescue Vienna. There are records also of prominent citizens who held important state offices in the land. In the eighteenth century the younger branch of the family established itself in eastern Poland, while the older and more ancient branch returned to its origins in Mazovia, in central Poland. There they purchased the estates of Kiernozia, where, according to the Niesiecki Annals, they flourished.

But – as was always the pattern in Poland – family fortunes were tied inextricably to the fate of the country. During the reign of the last king, Stanislaus Poniatowski, they suffered a drastic reverse when the three partitions took place and the

Above The Manor of Kiernozia, drawn by Alexander Walewski at the age of
fourteen

Below The Castle of Walewice, family home of Anastase Walewski

A little-known portrait of Marie Walewska, attributed to Jacques-Louis David

A study of the Emperor Napoleon by Jacques-Louis David, 1808

Two views of Warsaw, c. 1785, painted by Bernardo Belotto-Canaletto, nephew of the famous Venetian painter

Above the Royal Castle
Below the Cracow Faubourg

family lands were incorporated into Prussia. Matthew Laczynski, Eva's husband, took over the estate from his older brother when the latter decided to enter Holy Orders. Matthew was well liked in the district because of his good looks, cheerful disposition and administrative talents. He was elected *starosta* (a sort of local sheriff) and was in line to become the next Lord Lieutenant of the county. In the meantime, however, Poland's internal situation went on deteriorating, as greedy neighbours began to mass troops on its frontiers for the third time in ten years. Early in 1794 Matthew joined the volunteer citizens' army of amateur soldiers, land-owners, merchants and peasants who, armed with scythes, gathered at the gates of Warsaw in a desperate attempt to stop the Russians from occupying the last remaining portion of Polish territory. He died a hero's death on the battlefield of Maciejowice, while attempting to drag a wounded friend away from the path of a Cossack charge.

Matthew's death plunged the entire province in deep mourning; it also signalled the beginning of decline for Kiernozia. Energetic, though somewhat scatterbrained, Eva was simply unable to cope on her own, in spite of much good-natured advice instantly proffered by the neighbours. So, as time went on, the decline continued at an ever-increasing pace. For years no one had properly rotated the crops or looked after the orchards and farms. Cash returns decreased, expenses mounted, debts increased. The manor house itself, in spite of its fine architecture, well-proportioned windows and massive, finely designed entrance had acquired a shabby, uncared-for appearance. Even the spacious courtyard, paved with flagstones and enclosed by a wrought-iron balustrade, was now overgrown with weeds. The interior cried out for paint, and – to make matters worse – the house was plagued by colonies of bats, which had taken residence under the eaves and used to swoop down at night the moment the candles were brought in.

Although unable to cope with the management of her once prosperous estate, Eva Laczynska insisted on bringing up her children in the traditional ways of Polish nobility. There had been seven of them to begin with, but only two sons and three daughters survived: Benedict, the eldest, Theodore, Honor, Marie and Catherine, the baby, three months old when her father was killed. Marie was the beauty of the family, and on her all her mother's plans centred. It was hoped that one day she would make a rich and spectacular marriage and assure a carefree existence for them all. But in the meantime the boys had to be educated, so, borrowing heavily from a local merchant and mortgaging the revenue of a year's harvest in advance, Eva sent Benedict to Paris to study at a military school, while the second boy, Theodore, went to a leading boys' boarding-school in Warsaw. The girls, when their time came, would attend some suitable finishing-school in the capital, where they would be taught to play the piano and a little singing, while dabbling in European history and learning some French and Italian.

Marie was born in Brodno, a little provincial town near her home, on 7 December 1786. The first partition of Poland had already taken place, and the whole nation, united for the first time in years, was still reeling under the shock. Like her brothers and her sister before her, Marie was nursed by a pink-cheeked, robust peasant woman from the village – a fixture in every country household of the period. She grew strong on a diet of yoghurt, black bread, poppy cakes and farm produce, and played games with her friends, the peasant children in the village. Life went on peacefully in the rhythmic, endless cycle of the land. Mazovia is a land of flowers: of lilacs and jasmin in the spring; of innumerable cornflowers and red poppies and fragrant lime trees in the summer; a riot of red berries and golden marigolds in the autumn. The hedges are early starred with primroses and wild pansies; the pastures are white with moondaisies, golden with buttercups, red with sorrel and campion. The great fields of corn, oats and rye sway gently in the wind, stretching far out towards the horizon. Tethered cows graze in the meadows; herons strut ponderously along the banks of the streams, looking for catch. It is a peaceful and fertile land, condemned by history to be constantly coveted by aggressive neighbours.

Marie's early childhood was happy, though she was often alone. Of her brothers, Benedict, nine years older, was away from home most of the time, while Theodore, one year her senior – who was to become her best friend and adviser in later life – was a boisterous little boy, always out hunting rabbits or climbing trees with equally exuberant companions. But it was a secure existence, its pattern unchanged for generations, punctuated by religious holidays and small local events such as the arrival of the first flight of storks in the spring (most important as the date determined the pattern of weather for the harvest), the first strawberries of the season, harvest festivals in late summer, the beginning of the shooting season in September and above all the coming of cold weather and the snow. Winter meant sleigh rides through the silent white-clad countryside and Christmas with all its attendant magic.

Marie was not yet eight when her world fell apart. The popular insurrection against the Russians, in which her father had participated, was defeated. The battle of Maciejowice had been lost, and the approach to Warsaw lay wide open. The Russian Field-Marshal Suvorov marched on the capital taking the suburb of Praga by storm, massacring over twelve thousand of the inhabitants, including women and children, till the streets were banked high with corpses. Europe re-echoed with tales of the carnage of Praga, which surpassed the worst days of the Terror in France. In Poland it was to be remembered for generations.

One rainy October day, Matthew Laczynski's body was brought back to Kiernozia to be buried with full military honours in the crypt of the family church. Eva, clad in deep black widow's weeds, surrounded by a sad little cluster of her flaxen-haired, blue-eyed children, followed the funeral cortège.

Marie never forgot that day. It was then that her hatred of the Russians and an exalted, almost mystical patriotism took root. Curiously enough, the man who helped her to crystallize her feelings and formulate her beliefs was a Frenchman, Nicholas Chopin, the father of the great composer Frederick. How did this young scholarly product of a French peasant family from Lorraine come to be teaching in a remote manor in the depths of the Polish countryside over six hundred miles from his home? One reason was the French Revolution and the shifts in human destinies it had caused. But the Chopins seem to have had a connection with Poland for some years before the Revolution. Nicholas and his parents came from the village of Marainville in Lorraine (today part of the Département des Vosges) which belonged to a Count Michel Pac, a Polish aristocrat who had emigrated to France in the service of King Stanislaus Leszczynski, father-in-law of Louis xv of France. Chopin's father was an accountant, and he seems to have advised Count Pac on matters of French *comptabilité*. Nicholas, as a very young man, made friends with Adam Weydlich, a Pole long established in France, employed as an administrator in the running of the Pac estate office.

Early in 1790, when Nicholas was barely nineteen, Weydlich had to travel to Poland on his employer's business and suggested that Nicholas should accompany him to Warsaw as his aide. They had intended to return in a few months, but by then the French Revolution was in full swing, and travel had become difficult. As time went on, it appeared that all able-bodied young Frenchmen faced conscription into the ranks of the Revolutionary Army, which was rapidly being formed to oppose the Austrian and Prussian forces ominously concentrating on France's borders.

Young Nicholas Chopin, brought up in the ways of the *ancien régime*, far away from revolutionary centres and ideas and of a rather careful and conservative turn of mind, did not particularly relish the prospect of risking his life for the Revolution. He prudently decided not to return to France 'just yet' and to try earning his living in Warsaw, which at that time was full of French *émigrés*, fleeing the horrors of home. Jobs were easy to get, as French was Poland's educated classes' second language and any household of note harboured at least one French tutor or governess – it was positively uncouth to be without a Frenchman in the house. Not surprisingly, twenty-year-old Nicholas decided to stay in Poland for the time being; he was to remain for the rest of his life. He eventually married a Polish woman, who first bore him several daughters and later, in March 1810, when he was almost forty, presented him with a son, Frederick.

But all this was still in the future. In the meantime a living had to be earned. It transpired that young Nicholas possessed a remarkable gift for languages. In no time he taught himself Polish, and soon he could also read and write German. Life must have been pleasant for him, for in 1791, in a letter to his father back in Lorraine, he talks of Poland as 'his adopted country'.

As the threat of the third partition of Poland drew nearer, patriotic fervour throughout the country rose to a feverish pitch, and the young Frenchman, who only three years before had refused to enlist under the 'tricolor', found himself joining the Polish Volunteer Army. Nicholas Chopin fought in the battle of Maciejowice, in which Matthew Laczynski fell, and was himself wounded during the capture of the capital. We do not know who introduced him to the Laczynskis, but in 1795 we find him installed at Kiernozia as teacher and part-time accountant. He remained with the family for six years.

No correspondence between Marie and Nicholas Chopin has survived, but we know from contemporary accounts that she was devoted to him. Her excellent French, her musical training – far superior to anything taught in a Warsaw finishing-school – her knowledge of geography and of French history (which used to pleasantly surprise Napoleon and later enabled her to hold the friendship of many prominent people), were all due to the excellent teaching and affectionate dedication of the studious, intense young man from Lorraine. It was that intense quality in Nicholas's nature that made him so wholeheartedly espouse the cause of the unhappy land he had adopted. During the long evenings, when the fires were banked high and candles flickered and guttered, or sitting under the willow trees on the lawn, where Eva and Marie liked to sew, they talked of the tragic events of the last years. Surrounded by family and assorted visiting neighbours, they endlessly speculated on what the future might bring.

Nicholas's son and Marie never met; Frederick Chopin was only seven when Marie died at the age of thirty-one in Paris. But they shared a feeling for Poland, so exquisitely mirrored in Chopin's music, a strain of ardent, almost exalted patriotism which was to remain with them both through their short lives.

As the eighteenth century drew to a close, news from France became the main topic of conversation throughout Poland. The name of Napoleon Bonaparte, general and then First Consul, was on everyone's lips. Italy and the Egyptian campaign stirred imaginations. Hundreds and then thousands of young men slipped secretly out of the country to enlist in Bonaparte's armies; soon an entire Polish legion of twenty thousand men was formed under the command of General Henry Dabrowski in Mantua, and no soldiers could have believed more in the expressed ideal of 'liberty, equality and fraternity'. 'God is with Napoleon and Napoleon is with us,' ran the motto of the legionnaires. Fighting in the Italian campaign, shoulder to shoulder with French troops, they won universal admiration for their courage and immense stamina. Hope springs eternal in a Polish heart, and it was not long before they persuaded themselves that it would be only a matter of time before the victorious genius of Bonaparte, having conquered the rest of Europe, as he had the Austrians in Italy, would restore Poland's independence in return for their gallantry.

> March, march, Dabrowski,
> From Italian soil on to Poland,
> Under your leadership
> We shall regain our freedom....

sang the legionnaires marching through the Lombardy plains.

The song became so popular that it was adopted as the national anthem and is being sung in Poland to this day.

Several of Marie's cousins, as well as her eldest brother Benedict, joined forces with Napoleon. Benedict's letters fanned Marie's patriotic fervour. He was now a full lieutenant in Napoleon's army and had become a hero to his family and particularly to his younger sister, who worshipped Bonaparte through him. In her childish world Napoleon – the liberator – assumed an almost religious aura, like one of those saints she had been taught to pray to on holy days. Every scrap of news about him was carefully recorded and cherished, and she covered the walls of her room with childishly scribbled poems in his honour.

We do not know how Nicholas Chopin viewed his pupil's infatuation or indeed whether he approved of Napoleon. By now plans had been made to send Marie to a boarding-school in Warsaw, and her teacher was moving on to a new post as tutor in the household of Count Skarbek, some nine miles from Kiernozia, where he would be in charge of three boys.

It is from the memoirs of one of the Skarbek boys that we have a description of Marie at that time: 'On our way to spend the winter in Torun, we often used to visit Madame Laczynska, whose husband had died so tragically in the recent uprising. She had a very beautiful teenaged daughter, Marie, with incredibly large blue eyes, blonde hair which she wore down to her waist and a particularly sweet expression on her face. She made me think of an angel or a wood-nymph.'

A few months before her fourteenth birthday, Marie departed for the Convent of Our Lady of the Assumption in Warsaw, where young ladies of good families were sent to complete their education.

Warsaw seemed a marvel, a metropolis, the first big city she had ever seen. Built partly on a plain, partly on an escarpment, it had then about eighty thousand inhabitants, later expanding to 120,000. Bisected by the Vistula, nowadays embanked between quays, then a wide, powerful stream flowing between

high craggy banks, the town had expanded rapidly since Sigis-
mond III made it the capital of the country and transferred the
Court there from Cracow. Since time immemorial, Warsaw had
been a key post for trade between Russia, Scandinavia and
central and southern Europe, a stopping-post for caravans heading west. It was a city of contrasts: of hot summers and savage
winters with winds blowing mercilessly across the vast plains
all the way from Siberia, of fine Baroque palaces, brand-new
patrician town-houses with neo-classical façades, sumptuous
churches and long stretches of rickety wooden structures with
wares scattered all over the place, bazaar-fashion. The people
who crowded the streets had blonde hair and fair complexions,
the men in high leather boots, women in wide, heavy cotton
rainbow-striped skirts, red or green kerchiefs tied beneath their
chins. Flocks of birds could be seen disappearing beneath church
steeples or alighting on the tall poplar trees that seemed to grow
everywhere.

Warsaw was not the glamorous capital it had been at the time
of King Stanislaus II and was to become again with the arrival of
the French troops in three years' time. But it was alive, humming with people, crowded with vehicles of every description,
from peasant carts and the shabby barouches of small merchants to the carriages of the great noble families, with plumed
horses and splendidly attired out-riders. Houses were large,
sometimes with rows of outbuildings, well heated with porcelain stoves and huge open fireplaces – wood was the cheapest
commodity available. Families were also huge, and guests were
always welcome, for there was never any shortage of food or
drink.

In the city's centre, above the Vistula escarpment, rose the
walls of the royal palace, the Zamek, a Renaissance structure
built by King Sigismund III. Below it, halfway down to the
river, was a smaller palace, with a tin roof, the residence of
Warsaw's most glamorous bachelor, Prince Joseph Poniatowski,
nephew of the last king of Poland.

Marie's school was down a winding street, a stone's throw

from the castle. It overlooked the Vistula and had a large, well-kept garden, which was probably just as well, because the nuns, strict disciplinarians that they were, did not allow much personal freedom to their charges. Staid walks along the river banks, occasional chaperoned visits to the theatre and a Sunday afternoon *thé dansant* in the Baroque mansion of the Lady Canonesses – a hallowed Warsaw tradition for young ladies – were the range of permissible distractions.

Marie enjoyed the change from Kiernozia. Though solitary by nature, she found pleasure in the big city and in the company of girls of her own age. Her companions, of whom there were about thirty-five, were all daughters of other landed families, of aristocracy and rich merchants. With one of them she formed a particularly close friendship which was to last through her life. Elizabeth Grabowska, who later married a distinguished politician, Frank Sobolewski, was the daughter of Eliza Grabowska, the very beautiful morganatic wife of the last king of Poland, Stanislaus Poniatowski. A few years older than Marie, with a willowy figure and small, sensitive face, she was very intelligent and was to prove a steadfast and unusually loyal friend. Like Marie, she was a dreamer. Jean Jacques Rousseau's works had just made their appearance in Poland, and the two girls, stirred by the new romantic spirit rising in the wake of the French Revolution, fancied themselves, like the ladies in the *Nouvelle Héloïse*, pacing the woods alone in white muslin dresses, meditating . . .

But above all they dreamed about Bonaparte, the very epitome of romance, the knight errant, who was going to restore Poland's independence at one stroke. Marie's preoccupation with her hero grew daily as he made his triumphant progress through Europe. Ecstasy and hero-worship claimed her mind.

In the early summer of 1803 Marie, now aged sixteen and a half, returned home, her formal education completed. 'Marie is intelligent and studious, with a sweetness of character that made her generally loved here,' wrote the headmistress to

Madame Laczynska at the close of Marie's school term. 'She may be a little too introspective for her own good; though shy and reserved by nature, she has strong, even passionate feelings, particularly in matters concerning religion and the tragic present state of affairs in our country.'

Marie had also become a great beauty. Small, exquisitely proportioned, the little head poised proudly on the slender neck crowned with a mass of blonde, curly hair, and skin of a whiteness rare even in Poland. The chin was too rounded perhaps, but it was redeemed by a charming mouth and perfect teeth. Her most arresting feature was her eyes, which were huge, of a beautiful cornflower blue, framed by dark, curly eyelashes. They could sparkle with vivacity, could be melancholy or tender in turn, never losing their sweet expression. With her perfect body and peach-like complexion, she looked like a picture by Fragonard.

'When I returned home from school,' writes Marie in her Memoirs, 'my mother, busy as always with the affairs of the estate, hardly had time to examine me properly. Her first impression, though, must have been favourable, for she patted me under the chin and said: "Marie has grown very pretty. God help her to find a husband soon; it would be a big help for all of us." '

Eva may sound to us like a cold, scheming mother, but she was merely following the fashion of the day. In continental Europe of that period the interests of a noble family as a whole always took precedence over those of a separate member. The individual was expected, indeed often compelled, to make sacrifices in order that the family might benefit. And there was only one channel through which wealth and honour might come to a girl and through her to the family, a rich marriage to a well-born man. Not surprisingly, as she surveyed the years of toil and anxiety since Matthew's death, Eva Laczynska cast a searching eye over the province for a rich suitor for the daughter who had, so fortuitously for them all, blossomed into a beauty. A suitor was indeed about to appear on the scene. His name was Anastase Colonna Walewski, Chamberlain to the last king of Poland, owner of the castle of Walewice and the biggest land-owner in the province.

2
ANASTASE

Anastase Colonna Walewski lived less than an hour's drive by carriage from Kiernozia – a pleasant enough journey in the summer on the sandy road. Ornate and massive, with pedimented porticos, spreading balustraded wings and a colonnaded entrance-hall, Walewice was an imposing mansion, a mixture of eighteenth-century French and American Southern plantation style. It was designed by a Polish architect who had fought in the American War of Independence. Built of local yellowish limestone, it dominated its landscape with magnificent self-assurance. The front hall, its high stone walls covered with hunting-trophies of successive generations of Walewskis, the wide staircase, the banquet hall, which could accommodate a hundred guests, its saloons hung with imported French silks – all told of long-established prominence and wealth.

The owner of this splendid domain, then sixty-eight years of age, had been married twice: first at the age of twenty-three, then at thirty. He had been a widower for ten years, and one of his grandchildren, a girl, had just become engaged to be married. Of medium height, but still slender, slightly bow-legged (this defect was looked on kindly in Poland, as denoting one who had spent much time in the saddle), he had noble, straight features – which showed to particular advantage under his French-style peruke – small hands and finely set blueish eyes. He walked with a brisk, springy gait, and his complexion, for some time of a yellowish cast, had recently resumed the rosy colour of its youth. It was rumoured in Warsaw that the esteemed Chamberlain had undergone a mysterious rejuvenating cure 'in the hands of a special masseur, while in Paris'. His clothes fitted him to perfection. He generally wore a variation of a French courtier's dress: silk stockings and low patent-leather shoes with diamond buckles. 'No one', said Prince Joseph Poniatowski, the well-known dandy and the most handsome man in Warsaw, 'ever has clothes that *happen* to fit better than Anastase's. How does he keep his figure at his age?'

Walewski's tastes, unlike those of most of the Polish aristocracy, were essentially urban. After the death of Stanislaus Poniatowski, the last king of Poland, whose friendship he had enjoyed for so long, and in view of the tragic political situation in the country, he had deemed it 'essential and proper' (as he explained to his friends) to retire to his rural seat to cogitate. His retirement was made agreeable by the castle's well-stocked library, which was rare among Polish houses of that period. Its polished mahogany round tables were carelessly piled with the latest editions of French classics and books by Polish writers in Latin, and volumes by Voltaire and Rousseau's much-talked-about treatise *Considérations sur la Pologne* occupied a prominent place on Anastase's own writing-table near the window. This annoyed his elderly sister, who disapproved of Rousseau and 'all those ladies in transparent white muslin dresses he invented'.

But Anastase was restless. Pleasant as it was to lounge about Walewice's spacious rooms, to stroll along well-tended paths under avenues of lime trees, to supervise the construction of an orangery or a new pavilion in the park, it was nevertheless more exciting to attend a fashionable city reception or watch a French play at the small Kameralny Theatre in Warsaw, followed by a discreet little supper in the company of a few friends. He still fancied himself as something of a Casanova and a sometime patron of arts, and was fond of reminiscing about his past conquests, who reputedly included well-known actresses both in Rome and in Warsaw – and 'even in Paris', he added with a smug expression on his face. An exception among his fellow nobles, Anastase detested sport; he considered it 'a crashing bore', fit only for those 'provincial, hard-drinking nit-wits who had never read a book in their lives'. So, whenever the mood moved him to make an appearance in the capital, Walew-ski summoned his butler, ordered the carriage be made ready and, aided by a valet, carefully patted his powdered peruke in place, pulled on silk stockings and proceeded to Warsaw, where he owned a small but elegant mansion in the most fashionable part of town. Here was a pleasant enough life-style for a retired nobleman, and Walewski seemed to be thriving on it.

'Has it not struck you lately, my dear Ania,' wrote Princess Jablonowska to her cousin, 'that our dear Anastase is looking particularly well these days? I would be tempted to say, without undue modesty on my part, that my dear uncle is probably the youngest sexagenarian in Warsaw. A third wife would not find him lacking in any of the manly virtues, I dare say. . . . He may still spring a surprise on us all.'

Princess Jablonowska's words proved to be prophetic, but at the time they were written, Anastase had no desire to change his agreeable existence. He rarely missed a social function in Warsaw and was often seen about with his former Court friends, drinking and gambling in town. But suddenly, in the summer of 1803, he departed radically from this pattern, spend-ing more and more time in the country. The reason soon became known.

One afternoon, shortly after Marie's return from her school, Anastase drove out to Kiernozia to advise her mother on some business. He had of course known the Laczynskis for years and, like the rest of the county, had been saddened by Matthew's premature death. As a neighbour he felt duty-bound to keep an eye on the widow and counsel her whenever some new tax regulation was imposed by the Prussian commissioner of the district. He liked Eva, though he considered her 'too bossy for his taste'.

Anastase had last seen Marie as a child, shy and silent, her hair drawn severely back in two plaits, bent over an exercise-book. She had curtsied, and he remembered having waved to her briefly on the way to tea with her mother. He was quite unprepared for the sight which greeted him on that late summer evening in the shabby sitting-room of Kiernozia. 'By God!' he exclaimed to himself. 'She has suddenly become a woman – and what a beauty!' He who had spent many years pursuing beautiful women about the capitals of Europe knew beauty when he saw it. This sweet, virginal girl, demurely concentrating on her embroidery, was a rare gem. But to shine she needed a setting worthy of her matchless looks and grace. He would provide it. He would take her to Paris, to Rome, summon the best of craftsmen to adorn her, and wherever they went, he, Walewski, would be the envy of all men . . .

He left the house in a state of great agitation, only to reappear again in a few days bearing gifts of fruit and rare flowers from his hot-house. He announced that he was giving a ball at the castle 'in honour of his beautiful neighbour's coming of age'.

Though by now an accomplished dancer as a result of her *séjour* in Warsaw, Marie had never yet been to a ball; naturally the prospect filled her with excitement. Naïve and modest, it never occurred to her that her elderly admirer might have some ulterior motive. But her mother soon realized what was afoot, and the prospect filled her with delight. This was the solution to her troubles: a brilliant match for her daughter, a rich, well-connected man to advise her and perhaps even bail her out of her financial plight. It was an answer to her prayers. She was shrewd enough, however, not to mention her hopes to Marie. It was too early, and she might easily be frightened; after all, the prospective suitor was more than fifty-two years older than her daughter; even his youngest grandchild was six years her senior.

Next Sunday they all lunched at Walewice after church. 'The food was splendid, but the company very dull,' recorded Marie in her sketchy Memoirs. 'We went home laden with cornets of sweets, nougats and bunches of flowers, having promised to return next Sunday to discuss details of the ball. On the way back in the carriage Mother was in very good humour.'

Over 150 people, mostly neighbours, attended the ball. Anastase, resplendent in his uniform of Grand Chamberlain (to the late King Stanislas), knee-breeches, patent-leather shoes, silk stockings, but no peruke, received his guests in the stately hall of the castle. 'As our carriage drove up to the entrance,' noted Marie, 'our host handed me a gigantic bouquet of sweetheart roses. They were lovely, but somehow I felt sad, because the pink buds looked incongruous next to his old wrinkled face and bald head. . . . He offered his arm to my mother and led us into the main drawing-room, where we were introduced to the guests.'

The ball opened with a stately polonaise led by Anastase and Madame Laczynska and continued through the night. Young and old alike danced and drank merrily to the strains of the local gypsy orchestra. As always in the provinces, Polish country dances prevailed – the mazurka, with much clinking of spurs and flouncing of skirts, and *kuyaviak*, the dance of the region, a fast waltz with gentlemen dropping on one knee to kiss their ladies' hands, as they tripped in a circle around them.

Marie was much in demand and was enjoying herself. Of the several attractive young men who had danced with her, she thought one particularly outstanding by his aristocratic good looks, fine figure and charming manner. He had an exceptionally nice voice. She didn't catch his name in the introductions; he was obviously a foreigner, though he spoke French perfectly. Saxon or Swedish, she thought. Soon they were chatting away as if they had known each other all their lives. 'He was protective and gentle,' she recalled. 'I felt I could talk to him about everything. Though quite young, I noticed he had a whole row of decorations on his chest, and I thought he must be very brave.' He told her he had been travelling from London to Warsaw when the axle of his carriage had broken on the road near the castle, and Walewski had invited him to stay while it was being repaired. The breakdown was indeed fortuitous.

Marie was enchanted with him. It was the first time her heart had stirred for a man, and she sensed that he felt the same about her. We have to rely on Marie's description of how she learned the identity of her admirer and the effect his name had on her.

As they prepared to leave for home, Anastase, always gallant, congratulated Marie on her conquest. 'Count Suvorov is one of the most eligible men in Europe,' he said. 'Not only is he most charming but also immensely rich, and in spite of his name being of the same family as the dreaded Field Marshal, he loves and understands our country and deplores the brutal Russian campaign of nine years ago.'

It was said in contemporary accounts that young Suvorov visited the family several times in the next week or ten days. He had fallen in love with Marie and felt that she too – however unwillingly – liked him. Indeed, he had almost made up his mind to marry her.

It was not unusual, even at a time when patriotic feelings ran high, for a Polish upper-class woman to marry into Russian, Austrian or Prussian aristocracy. Friendships and social inter-course between prominent families went on regardless of wars, occupations and shifting frontiers. But to Marie the name of Suvorov spelled horror. Never, no matter how attractive the man, would she contemplate an attachment to a Russian and particularly to one of that name, which brought back all the memories of her father. It was out of the question – she never wanted to see that young man again.

What would have been the outcome of the romance had the young people been left to themselves? Would Marie have relented, her heart defeating her exalted patriotism? Would this worldly young man, used to feminine admiration, have been patient enough to withstand what to him must have seemed a long, undeserved ordeal? The answer will never be known, for the discussions were suddenly interrupted by the arrival of Marie's elder brother, Benedict, home on leave from Napoleon's army. There was no doubt in Benedict's mind what to do. His sister could not possibly marry a Russian, let alone a Suvorov.

If she was to be married off – and Benedict, who was now head of the family, agreed with his mother that it would be to everyone's advantage if she was – why not to the esteemed and prominent neighbour who seemed to have developed such a passion for her?

Soon after that the young Russian went away. He rejoined a Guards regiment in St Petersburg and had a distinguished career in the army. The stage was now set for Walewski, who openly pressed his courtship with the help of Benedict and Madame Laczynska.

Marie now entered a period of her life to which she later referred as a nightmare. The shock of young Suvorov's departure, the prospect of marrying an old man who was physically repugnant to her, the stern persuasions of her brother – whom she both feared and revered because he was fighting with Napoleon – the unrelenting pressure from her mother, worried lest another suitor might be lost, all combined to bring about a deep depression in her. She was not yet seventeen, and this would have been a harsh awakening for any girl, let alone one as sensitive as Marie.

Whether from anguish or because of a chill she had contracted, or both, she fell ill with what we today would probably call a virus pneumonia. When, after several weeks, she was pronounced 'out of danger', she found, sitting at the foot of her bed, her old suitor, looking at her with concern. By now she was resigned to her fate and determined to do her duty by her family. After all, he was old and kind . . . at least he would not make any demands on her.

According to a book published in France in 1934 by one of her Ornano descendants, *The Life and Loves of Marie Walewska*, Marie wrote to Elizabeth Sobolewska, who was then married and living in Paris, about her fear of her mother and her brother's bullying tactics. She described how 'she locked her door and refused to go downstairs' during one of Anastase Walewski's visits. The same book quotes a letter from Elizabeth, supposedly sent a few weeks before Marie's projected marriage to Anastase, begging her to reconsider the idea, arguing that a loveless marriage never works and depicting the dangers she would find herself in 'once she discovered the attractions of physical love, outside marriage'. The letters are couched in romantic nineteenth-century language and would be interesting to quote if it were not for the fact that there is some doubt as to their authenticity. D'Ornano's book was written in the form of historical fiction.

There is also some uncertainty about the exact date of Marie's marriage to Anastase. The distinguished Polish historian Mauersberger puts it at 17 June 1803, which would have made Marie sixteen and a half years of age. But this date has been challenged ever since a suspicion arose that, at the time of Marie's divorce in 1812, the relevant document might have been altered in transcript and the date put back a year, in order to make the coercion argument more convincing. One is inclined to share this view. Indeed, the most likely guess is that they were married on 17 June 1804 and not 1803; at that time Marie would have been seventeen and a half years of age.

But, whatever the exact date, the wedding could not have been a particularly happy occasion. The melancholy little bride, bereft of feeling, and the old gentleman, beaming with self-satisfaction, were united in a quiet family ceremony at the local church of Kiernozia. Following the established tradition of Polish gentry, the Walewskis remained on their country estates throughout the summer; they left for a protracted honeymoon abroad in early autumn, as soon as the harvest was in. Heading south, via Cracow, they proceeded by way of Vienna to Bad Gastein, where Anastase regularly took the waters, then continued to Italy through the Brenner Pass, sufficiently early in the year to avoid the hardships of travel across the Alps in the winter. Their final destination was Rome. It was thought to be beneficial for Marie's health to spend the rest of the winter in the sunshine, and Anastase hoped to be granted an audience with the Pope. He was eager to take his wife to the Colonna Palace in Rome to see some portraits of his ancestors, relatives of Pope Martin v, who had emigrated to Poland at the end of the sixteenth century.

Travel to Italy in the early nineteenth century was still considered an adventure, particularly when crossing the Alps through the Brenner Pass from the Austrian Tyrol. The guides were unreliable and tracks could suddenly be erased by early snow, storms and avalanches. Travelling Englishmen would stop in suitable places and fire pistols at the mountains in order to disturb the still air and cause the snow to slide down from the peaks; this was deemed an effective device to forestall an avalanche. To help individual travellers, hospices were built by religious orders along the main passes; the monks kept stores of food and wood for the fireplaces, good beds, warm blankets, brandy and sturdy dogs who could sniff out a live body under the snow. The Walewskis undoubtedly carried a full complement of kitchen equipment and bed-linen, as beds were rare in Italy in those days, and local inns – the *osterie* – as bad and comfortless as in centuries past.

In spite of every inconvenience visitors to Italy never stopped coming: some as pilgrims, lured by the hope of eternal salvation, but most drawn by the sun, the landscape and the wealth of celebrated monuments. For travellers from northern Europe, a winter in Italy was the substance of a dream come true.

Travelling by slow stages and visiting Verona, Bologna, Florence and Lucca on the way, the Walewskis arrived in Rome in late January 1805. They remained throughout Easter, and Marie wrote contentedly to Elizabeth, describing the Holy Week ceremonies in the Sistine Chapel, the Mass composed by Mozart, the beauty, the warmth and the general delight of being in Rome. 'He is kind,' she wrote of Anastase. 'He paid all of my mother's farm debts. . . . I must be a good wife to him. . . . Does one ever get *all* one wants in this life ?. . .' Though she did not mention it in her letter, Marie was by then expecting a baby, which may account for her tone of half-resignation, half-contentment.

A Walewski family tradition maintains that Marie and

Anastase met the famous French writer, Germaine de Staël, in Rome that Easter. It is possible. Madame de Staël was a friend of the family of Henriette de Vauban, leader of Warsaw society, who would certainly have given her friend Anastase letters to her. Circumstances might have brought them together, for that autumn, when Marie and Anastase were starting on their honeymoon, Madame de Staël fled from the master of France across the Alps to an Italian interlude of great literary adulation and romantic voluptuousness. It was the beginning of her romance with the handsome, aristocratic Pedro de Souza, whom she met at a reception given in her honour by the Academy of the Arcadians in Rome. Having exhausted the delights of Naples, they returned to Rome for Easter, and it is then that they might have met the Walewskis. The character of Corinne, the heroine of her current book, was just beginning to take shape in Madame de Staël's mind. It is not known whether Marie contributed anything to it by her presence in Rome.

Soon after Easter Count and Countess Walewski returned to their Walewice estates, and it was there that on 13 June 1805 their son Anthony Basil Rudolph was born. He was a puny, delicate and sickly child, who was immediately swept away from his mother by a crowd of elderly female relatives.

3

THE FRENCH ARE
COMING

On 27 October 1806, to the sound of drums and martial music, the Emperor Napoleon, followed by regiments of the Imperial Guard in scarlet tunics and bearskin busbies, entered Berlin through the Brandenburgh Gate. Mounted on a grey Arab horse, dressed in the simple green uniform of the Lancers and the famous *tricorne*, the Grand Cordon of the Légion d'Honneur across his chest, he rode slowly, alone, ten paces ahead of his troops. Behind him followed a galaxy of stars – a brilliant array of marshals, generals, *aides de camp*, staff officers, resplendent with gold, caracoling in full feather and rainbow plumes, glittering with jewels. It was a beautiful late autumn day, with a slight nip in the air. The trees on Unter den Linden had turned red; the sky was blue; immense crowds lined the pavements. They were obviously enjoying the magnificent spectacle, for, as the Emperor rode by, they cheered, much to the surprise of the victors. 'The Berliners seem very much at ease with us,' remarked Barrès, one of the generals, 'they are pleased we gave a good hiding to their king. . . .'

As they approached the huge equestrian statue of Frederick the Great, the Emperor rode forward at a gallop, circled the statue, took off his hat and saluted Frederick with his sword. The entire retinue followed suit.

Already, three days earlier, he had taken up residence at Potsdam in Frederick's palace of Sans-Souci. Much as Napoleon despised the present ruler of Prussia, the sad, vacillating Frederick William, whom he had just defeated at Jena (he called him 'that booby William'), he had always admired Frederick. 'He was a genius, and he loved France . . . had he lived, this war would never have taken place. . . .'

He visited the king's apartments, tried on his field-glasses, sat at his desk, fingered his books. Exercising the privilege of the victor, he took away the sword of the great Frederick and his military belt. He also took his alarm clock, a heavy solid silver object, which he used constantly in later years and carried away with him to St Helena.

That autumn in Berlin Napoleon was approaching the apogee of his power. France, Italy, Holland and Germany, as far as the Oder, united under his arms. Immense quantities of men, money and material were at his disposal. It is little wonder that he felt supremely confident. 'On the Elbe and the Oder we have won our India, our Spanish colonies and Cape of Good Hope,' he dictated to Ménéval, his secretary. The previous year, by his victory at Austerlitz, he had broken the power of the Habsburgs and had forced the young Russian Tsar Alexander into a humiliating retreat. Three times, since taking command of an army in 1796, he had taken the field against Austria, and three times he had won, forcing her to ever greater territorial concessions. As a result, Austria's lands in Italy, now renamed 'the kingdom of Italy', with himself as its king, became a state within the French Empire; Austria's other Adriatic possessions, Istria and Dalmatia, were simply annexed to France; the Austrian Tyrol went to Bavaria, a new ally. As a buffer against Russia, partly to fill the vacuum left after Poland disappeared from the map, he created the Confederation of the Rhine; sixteen German states were grouped into a single entity, a vassal state ruled by France. The Empire of Charlemagne was thus brought to an end and the Napoleonic legend and force of arms had fashioned a new empire. The dream of a united Europe had been with Napoleon for a long time, and at last he could begin to discern its living outlines taking shape.

In all Europe only two bulwarks remained against the tide of the conqueror's progress: England and Russia. Powerless against England at sea since the disastrous battle of Trafalgar, he nonetheless correctly diagnosed her Achilles heel: her necessity to trade with the Continent, to import wheat from the Baltic provinces in exchange for British manufactured goods, for coffee and spices from the Antilles. It was in Berlin that Napoleon issued his famous decree closing all Continental harbours to British ships. All merchandise, parcels, post, any person travelling to or from England, was to be held up; every Englishman on the Continent was to become a prisoner of war. If Napoleon could not reach the island with his sword, he was confident that he could isolate it and gradually bring the English to their knees.

Like many a blockade since then, this proved hard to enforce, though it effectively deprived German, Italian, Dutch and Swiss men of their favourite steel razor-blades from Birmingham. Their families missed not only the coffee, sugar and spices they had become used to but also a great variety of inexpensive English goods, such as the woollens, cottons, scissors and cutlery which the French factories of the day were unable to provide. The blockade was resented in conquered Europe's households, and the popular discontent it created helped to bring about Napoleon's eventual defeat.

There remained Russia: her armies were still in front of him, though at a great distance, encamped along the line of the Vistula river in Poland. They had been there since October, as allies of the once great armies of Prussia, now defeated. Tsar Alexander had refused to join in the peace negotiations after the Prussians met with disaster at Jena, and had vainly tried to revive the Coalition by urging Frederick William to continue fighting and by trying to draw Austria back into the conflict. Unsuccessful in both attempts, he now seemed determined to continue the war alone with the help of his single remaining ally, Sweden.

At this critical stage of his wars Napoleon was thirty-seven years old. He was no longer the slender, intense, youthful general of the days of Rivoli and Mantua, 'burning eyes in a worn-out uniform', the passionate lover, penning ardent letters to Josephine, his unfaithful bride of a few weeks. 'Rome had now replaced Sparta', as Victor Hugo was to write years later, and the young prodigy of the Italian campaigns had become the Emperor, the law-giver, the new Caesar. Though he now had most of Europe at his feet, he was still contemplating new conquests. His powerful imagination – that *'goût de l'impossible'* as he called it – roamed all over the world.

Physically he was at his peak. His powerful, broad-chested body exuded energy. He was always standing, walking, or riding, but rarely seated, and his capacity for work was prodigious. The pale olive complexion was clear and smooth, the brow wide and high, the blue-grey eyes penetrating and unflinching. He had to watch his weight when in Paris but was always extremely fit on campaign. Though only five feet seven inches tall – the average height for a Frenchman in those days – he emanated dynamic self-assurance. Masséna used to say that 'he seemed at least two feet higher, when he put on his general's hat.'

Yet, despite the long string of military victories, despite grandiose strategic plans, despite the adoration of his troops, Napoleon frequently gave the impression of a man essentially lonely. 'In Berlin,' writes Constant Wairy in his Memoirs, 'the Emperor was very much alone and absorbed in his thoughts. He used to pace the floor in King Frederick's study, hands clasped behind his back, stooping slightly, muttering to himself. . . . I saw him pause in front of the picture of Voltaire, which had been left untouched, and look at it inquiringly. . . .'

Unlike his generals, he did not trouble himself about women. Since Cairo days he had not had a mistress while on campaign. But Josephine's spell was on the wane. Years before, she had deceived and hurt him. Though it would be four more years before he could bring himself to break with her and in a way would continue to love her to the end, she had lost that magic enchantment she had once exercised over him. In ten years of marriage she had failed to give him the child he so much wanted. Worse, she managed to instil a cruel doubt: could it be that it was his fault? After all, she had two children of her own. The ever-present, searing question rarely left him: was he capable of giving life, of siring a dynasty?

There had, of course, been many women in his life: passing affairs, some of whom held the stage for a time, others playing small parts; still others flitting across the scene, alluded to in contemporary records by name or sometimes merely by initials. So far none of them had had any political influence. Long ago Napoleon had sworn never to let himself be dominated by a woman.

We know from contemporary memoirs that at this particular stage of his life Napoleon's attitude to the fair sex was one of cynicism and contempt. 'Women', he would say to his associates, 'they belong to the highest bidder. Power is what they like – it is the greatest of all aphrodisiacs, they are fascinated by it. . . . I take them and forget them. . . .'

Though basically a family man he did not seem to expect love any more. At this stage, more pressing matters would have crowded out such thoughts. For there in Berlin couriers brought news of the sudden advance of Russian armies westward into East Prussia and Poland. It was clear that war with Russia would now have to begin in earnest. Orders went to Marshals Murat and Davout to march into Poland, all the way to Warsaw, but to go in not as conquerors but as liberators. Poland's help in the coming offensive was essential.

The Poles awaited Napoleon as a messiah. No sooner had his advance corps moved east from Berlin than he was besieged with deputations and petitions urging him to reconstitute the Polish monarchy 'under a French general if possible'. He, the champion of human freedom, must liberate Poland. Napoleon undoubtedly respected Polish sincerity and France's debt to the sadly oppressed land. Since 1796, the start of the Italian campaign, twenty thousand Polish volunteers had filled his ranks.

Of the six thousand Poles who had sailed with Leclerc to San Domingo (Haiti) to quell the insurrection of the natives against France, only eight hundred returned; the rest were victims of malaria and Toussaint l'Ouverture's troops. Volunteers made up the dreadful loss. At Rivoli, Marengo, Mantua, Ulm and Austerlitz, and in the present campaign, Poles fought and died for the glory of the Napoleonic eagles.

But when it came to Polish freedom, Napoleon moved with a caution which, as time went on, dissolved into outright dissembling. It was a difficult situation. The Emperor was well aware that no matter what differences might exist between Russia, Austria and the defeated Prussian state on any other subject, all three would be unanimous in opposing the reconstitution of an independent Poland, for it would mean the loss of the territories they had taken. The partitions could not be undone, they claimed.

Prussia's feelings in its present abased condition Napoleon could afford to disregard, but he was reluctant to annoy Austria, whose neutrality would be important in the coming conflict. Nor did he want to irritate Russia prematurely, by inciting the Poles to insurrection. Still, he needed Polish recruits, horses, provisions of food and accommodation for his enormous army of over 300,000 men.

To the Polish deputations which approached him in Berlin he seemed to promise a new day : 'France has never recognized the partitions of Poland,' he told them. 'Shall I set up the throne of Poland anew and thus restore a great nation to life? God alone, who has the fashioning of all things, can help me in it.'

While sending these words of Delphic cunning throughout the old kingdom [noted Baron de Comeau, a diplomat on Talleyrand's staff], he also used to say to us, 'Poland, so much the worse for them. They allowed themselves to be partitioned. They are no longer a nation, they have no public spirit. The nobles are too much, the people too little. I will first take their recruits and make soldiers out of them. Then we will see. I shall take Prussia's portion, Posen and Warsaw, but I will not touch Austrian Cracow or even Russian

Vilna. . . . So much the worse for their dreams. I don't care what becomes of them in the end. . . .'

On 3 November 1806, shortly before resuming his march east, Napoleon issued a proclamation. To the people who had been fighting in his ranks for the last ten years he announced: 'I cannot proclaim your independence until you have shown that you are ready to defend your rights with arms . . . not until you have an army of forty thousand men will you be worthy of the name of a nation.' In addition he demanded that Poland supply all food, horses, fodder and material for his troops. When Polish statesmen asked for some guarantees in return, he accused them of being 'unpatriotic and selfish'.

But no matter the severity of Napoleon's demands, the vagueness of his promises, the majority of the Poles believed him, and his words plunged the country into a frenzy of joy. Pathetically optimistic and trusting, it opened its arms to the apostle of freedom and to his marching armies.

On 27 November 1806, a Thursday, a day of light rain and scattered fog, the inhabitants of Wola, a Warsaw suburb, heard the distant clatter of a cavalry troop. Loud cries at once rose into the air: 'The French are coming, the French are coming. . . .' Windows flew open, crowds jammed narrow streets. The news was quickly carried to Warsaw, which almost exploded with excitement, as splendidly-turned-out hussars, one of Murat's reconnaissance patrols, entered the city. The main body of the army was to arrive the next morning.

To understand what we felt at the sight of this first handful of warriors, one must have lost everything and hope for everything like ourselves [Countess Potocka wrote in her diary]. They suddenly seemed to us like the guarantors of the independence we had been expecting from the hands of the great man, whom nothing could resist. Popular intoxication was at its height; the whole town was lit up as if by magic. There was no need to allot quarters to the new arrivals; people fought for them, carried them off, vied with each other in treating them best. . . . Those of the citizens who knew no French borrowed the language of the dumb and by signs of delight and bursts of glee made their guests comprehend that they freely offered them all that their house contained, cellar included.... Tables were laid out in the streets and squares; Napoleon was toasted; there was general embracing and, as the weather was chilly and damp, an inordinate amount of drinking....

Only a week before, a few marauding Russian detachments had made an unexpected appearance in Warsaw but withdrawn rapidly when faced with the hostility of the inhabitants. Two days later, the ubiquitous General Koehler, the Prussian Military Governor of Warsaw, who had ruled the province in the name of King Frederick William II, packed his bags and was seen leaving Warsaw in the direction of East Prussia, where his defeated king had taken refuge. With him went the remaining detachments of Prussian troops, ignominiously pursued by bands of jeering schoolboys, who threw stones after them. As they left, the Prussians set fire to the wooden bridge on the Vistula, cutting Warsaw off from its eastern suburb of Praga.

Excitement spread in the city like wildfire. Jubilant crowds filled the streets, and the whole of Warsaw society spent that evening at the Teatr Francuski (French Theatre) in the Radziwill Palace, watching a performance of Corneille's *Cid*. 'It was close to midnight when we finally left the theatre after a very splendid performance,' recalled Frederick Skarbek in his engaging Memoirs. 'The bridge was still burning ... we drove home under a crimson sky, there was no need for torchlights....'

Next day Warsaw was free, ready to welcome the legendary French. A Citizens' Council, composed of Warsaw's most prominent men, was formed to take over the government of the city. They prepared to greet Prince Joachim Murat and hand over the keys to the capital.

As it happened, Marie had already met with French troops at Walewice two weeks earlier and had formed an unexpected friendship which was to lead to dramatic developments in her life.

On the march towards Warsaw, when Marshal Davout's

troops occupied the town of Lowicz, the nearby castle of Walewice became the headquarters of the Guards Brigade staff. The
Walewskis, who since September had been spending most of
their time in Warsaw, much to Marie's satisfaction, had come
down a few weeks before to be with Benedict, Marie's brother,
who was quietly recruiting volunteers in the province for
service in Napoleon's army. When Davout's staff arrived, the
Walewskis moved to the estate manager's office down the road
to make room for the military.

It had been raining for days. The hitherto beautiful autumn
had turned into the wettest winter on record, and the road in
front of the house had become a torrent of mud. Standing in
front of her temporary residence one morning, surveying the
slushy quagmire at her feet, Marie noticed coming towards her
a young cavalry officer of 'well-bred looks and charming expression' who smilingly offered to carry her across the road to the
flagstone-paved terrace in the castle's courtyard. As he deposited her gently on dry land, this dashing French Sir Walter
Raleigh introduced himself as Lieutenant Charles de Flahaut of
the Imperial General Staff; he was on his way to Warsaw,
where 'the Emperor was expected shortly'. In the few days that
followed, he saw the Walewskis several times and on leaving
asked permission to call on them in the capital. The blonde girl
with the enormous melancholy blue eyes struck him as a vision
of beauty amid the rain and the mud of the countryside.

Charles de Flahaut, who was then twenty-two years of age,
was one of those romantically attractive personalities who
peopled the Napoleonic stage. Son of the great statesman
Talleyrand and Adelaide de Flahaut, lover of Queen Hortense
and reputedly father of the Duke of Morny, he was to marry
Margaret Mercer Elphinstone, the daughter of Lord Keith, and
to play a prominent, though intermittent, role in the political
life of France after the Restoration. His mother, the beautiful
and clever Countess Adelaide de Flahaut, was later known as
the novelist, Madame de Souza. She had met Talleyrand, then
bishop of Autun, at the Court of Louis XVI during the early days

of the Revolution. She was seventeen, married to a man in his fifties. Adelaide and the unconventional bishop started living openly together, and soon the young countess produced a son, whom she called Charles after her lover. Her husband, the Count de Flahaut, seems not to have been particularly disturbed by the mysterious appearance of an heir, and the pair continued to go about together. Though his affair with Adelaide petered out after a few years, Talleyrand always took great care to keep in touch with his son and saw to it that in the current campaign young Charles was attached to the staff of the Emperor.

Talleyrand himself was in Berlin at that time, reluctantly contemplating the prospect of travelling to Warsaw over Poland's terrible roads. He was soon to be reunited with his son, and Marie would be presented to him. The consequences of that meeting were to change her life.

Back in the capital, Marie, the shy, introverted young woman, became a dynamo of feverish activity, working with the ladies of Warsaw, organizing hospitals, nursing units and first-aid courses. They prepared homes for the marshals and generals, restoring the royal castle to some of its former splendour in preparation for the imminent arrival of the Emperor. This was no mean task as the place had stood empty since the last king's departure over ten years before.

But while Marie was busy, her husband was growing increasingly frustrated, and the reason was hurt vanity. Those 'arrogant young men on the Citizens' Council', as he called them, were not paying nearly enough attention to his freely proffered advice on how to conduct negotiations with Napoleon. They seemed to forget that he had served as Chamberlain to the last king of Poland for twelve years – that he was unquestionably Warsaw's foremost expert on Court etiquette and good manners. Why did they not listen to him now?

Why indeed? We can only assume that the 'young men' who formed the provisional government of the city, considered Walewski a pompous bore. Never brilliant, though very well educated, his arrogance and conceit had already antagonized

47

many people, just as his marriage to a child-bride had made him a laughing-stock in Warsaw society.

Walewski was now seventy-one. He had aged considerably since his marriage, and he was not physically particularly well. Though suffering from gout and insomnia, he continued to drink and eat to excess. Yet he rarely missed a social function in Warsaw, where he invariably escorted his beautiful wife to a sofa full of aunts and cousins, then contentedly joined his old friends for vast amounts of food and wine.

Poor Marie would have enjoyed these gatherings but for the fear of inciting Anastase's jealousy. She need only smile at a young politician or dance the mazurka twice over with the same partner to be instantly rebuked by an indignant look on the old, wrinkled face. Biting remarks then followed in the carriage on the way home.

Marie, who was approaching her twentieth birthday, was no longer the blushing provincial girl from an impoverished country estate. In Vienna and Rome, where they stayed on their wedding-trip, she had learned how to dress and how to please. She now knew how to walk gracefully, and whenever she overcame her natural shyness and Anastase's ill humour permitted, she shone as an exquisite dancer. She knew she was beautiful – she could see it reflected in the eyes of the men when she entered a drawing-room. But her diary notes of the time abound in such sad little remarks as: 'I looked nice the other evening, but what of it? . . . Anastase sulked all the way home. . . .' She was far too conservative and too timid to strike back. Before the arrival of the French, she tended to be gloomy and depressed; her mother noted 'a sort of suppressed lament in her that betrayed a hidden strain of melancholia'. This tendency to gloom is a characteristic of the Slavs and usually increases with age. Marie, finely tuned as she was, might have fallen prey to depression had she not become caught up in events that abruptly took her out of herself.

Now that the French army was in Warsaw, her naturally cheerful disposition rapidly bubbled up to the surface. No work was too much, no assignment too onerous. She was happy. After the semi-torpor of her life at Walewice, the excitement inspired by the arrival of the liberators had brought her back to life with a jolt, setting her intense patriotism afire. Napoleon had left Berlin, his destination Posen. He could arrive at Warsaw any day. She was certain that it would be only a matter of months before he defeated the Russians and reconstituted a free Poland.

All Warsaw turned out to welcome Prince Joachim Murat and his troops. Despite cold, rainy weather, it was a city *en fête*. Church bells rang, crowds were everywhere, flags flew from windows, balconies, even chimneys. Deputations of merchants and tradesmen in the colourful medieval costumes of their respective guilds and carrying elaborately carved standards pressed forward in the narrow streets. A Jewish delegation sallied conspicuously forward, brandishing a huge black and silver canopy with the Ten Commandments embroidered on it in gold thread. Thousands of cheering schoolchildren lined the pavements.

At the head of the distinguished citizens who formed the welcoming delegation rode Prince Joseph Poniatowski, nephew of the last king of Poland, future Marshal of France, a man who was to go down in history as one of Poland's greatest heroes. In years to come, Napoleon was to refer to him as 'the natural king of Poland – the person who summed up all the qualities and all the faults of his nation'. Prince 'Pepi', as he was popularly known, was of the stuff of legends. Now forty, fearless and chivalrous, of handsome dark looks and a magnificent physique, he was generally popular in the country and much loved by the ladies. Since the partitions of Poland, which he had fought to prevent, he had been living quietly in Warsaw in the small eighteenth-century palace left to him by the late king, his uncle, and trying to keep out of politics; that was not always easy for one with such a historic name, a popular following in the country and close family connections with the Courts of the three occupying powers.

Poniatowski's mother was Austrian, a Princess Kinsky. He had spent most of his childhood in Vienna, had been commissioned in the Austrian army and spoke German long before he learned Polish. Through his father he was related to the powerful Czartoryski family, whose pro-Russian sympathies were well-known. The King of Prussia, a Hohenzollern relation, addressed him as '*mon cousin*' and considered him a member of the family. It was at King Frederick William's request that he had been asked to take over the administration of the capital after the Prussian commander withdrew. 'He seems to have a foot in every camp,' said Napoleon, before he got to know him in Warsaw, forgetting that in his family connections Poniatowski was no different from the rest of the central European aristocracy. There was no question, however, as to where Prince Joseph's loyalties lay: he was a great patriot, prepared to fight and die for Poland if that would serve the cause of her independence.

Surprisingly for one endowed with so many worldly blessings, Poniatowski had never married. As a very young man, when visiting Brussels at the time of the French Revolution, he had met Henriette de Vauban, a French *émigrée* several years older than himself. She became his companion in Warsaw, ran his house and eventually brought her husband over from France. The three of them lived together, in perfect harmony, in the Prince's palace, 'Pod Blacha' ('the palace with the tin roof'), next to the old royal castle on the river. The 'arrangement' was not generally known, and to thousands of Polish young ladies Prince 'Pepi' continued to personify the bachelor of their dreams.

'At about three in the afternoon,' notes a contemporary account, 'we heard distant strains of a spirited cavalry march, as the excitement of the crowd reached feverish proportions. . . .' It was a grey, late-November day. From the city gates Prince Joseph and his troops watched a glittering if slightly theatrical troop gallop at full speed towards them. The foremost figure, a tall man in his mid-thirties, rode a magnificent white Spanish stallion, its elaborate tack encrusted with silver and jewels. He wore a green velvet cloak lined with sable, white leather breeches with red boots and solid gold spurs; from beneath a green velvet hat topped with white ostrich plumes, black curly hair spilled on to his shoulders. Riding in the French fashion, legs thrust forward, he galloped towards Prince Joseph, jewels, gold, lace, feathers fluttering and glistening. Prince Joachim Murat, Grand Duke of Berg and Cleves, Marshal of France, victor of Auerstadt and, not least, brother-in-law of the Emperor Napoleon, had arrived.

In flawless French Prince Joseph welcomed him to Warsaw. Murat bowed and was preparing to ride on when one of the delegates, representing the Association of Merchants, raised his arms, fell to his knees and thundered a special greeting: 'Salve Rex Poloniae.' Beaming with delight, Murat dismounted from his horse, shook merchant Kilinski's hand and embraced him. By then the crowd had taken up the words, and Murat rode into the city cheered as if he had already been elected king. This was a very real ambition of his, forever frustrated by Napoleon.

The Marshal moved into apartments in the palace of Count Stanislaus Potocki, who gallantly yielded the entire first floor, crowding himself and his family in the upper rooms.

The Prince called on my mother the next day [Anna Potocka wrote in her Memoirs]. Not knowing much of his background, we were a little disappointed. His face is without nobility and entirely devoid of expression. He has the majestic air of actors who play at being kings. It is easily seen that his manners are sham . . . he did not talk badly, but he had to watch himself carefully, which produced an unnatural effect. His Gascon accent and various soldier-like phrases belied the Prince a little . . . he did not converse, he talked and one had to listen with a respectful deference.

Anna Potocka had further reason to be annoyed with Murat. Preparing for bed one night, she investigated a noise outside her boudoir only to discover His Imperial Highness 'with a lighted *flambeau* in his hand, creeping along the walls to her bedroom'. When she abruptly refused his attentions – she threatened to report the incident to her father – the great Marshal studied her unbelievingly and whispered, 'But don't you care for princes, Madame?'

Murat had brought with him a substantial number of troops: six cavalry regiments, eight dragoon regiments, horse artillery and a multitude of cannons – a force shortly followed by Davout's infantry corps, Augereau's hussars, the Imperial Guard, King Jerome's (Napoleon's youngest brother) mounted troops and others. Altogether close to eighty thousand troops were billeted in or near Warsaw, taxing facilities to the limit.

The city loved it. Everyone seemed determined to entertain the French. Even the poorest family insisted on bringing a French soldier to their home. Men came from the neighbouring countryside to hand the keys of their houses to passing French officers. The Poles are generous by nature and, until the time when the army's abuses cooled general enthusiasm a little, their hospitality knew no bounds.

The city of Warsaw gave a reception in the newly refurbished castle to honour Prince Murat. It was a memorable and colourful night: next to the blue and red uniforms of the French army shone the greens and golds of Polish legionnaires; jewelled ladies wore both the sumptuous traditional dresses of the Polish nobility and French-style Court dresses; men with clean-shaven heads in the Turkish fashion mixed with those who wore powdered perukes, in contrast to the stern, whiskered faces of French officers. 'The French', a contemporary account noted, 'were thrilled at the sight of so many pretty women. . . .'

Dancing was even attempted, but this led to certain confusion. The Polish ladies were adept at the mazurka, the polonaise and other national dances, retained despite the general francophilia of the Polish nobility, but only a handful of Paris-educated ladies knew the French *contre-danse* with its intricate figures and changing steps. This was the sort of crisis in which

Henriette de Vauban excelled. Why not ask the French guests to teach them? Both Murat and Prince Camillo Borghese, Napoleon's brother-in-law, proved to be excellent dancing-masters.

Anastase and Marie attended the reception for Murat. A Polish newspaper account of the entertainment noted that Marie danced the *contre-danse* with Charles de Flahaut and also 'talked to Talleyrand after supper'. Talleyrand must have just arrived. As Napoleon left Berlin, he commanded his Foreign Minister to follow him, and the old diplomat had no choice but to comply, which he did with the greatest annoyance and much discomfort, cursing the broken and muddy roads, proceeding with extreme caution lest his carriage overturn. He was slightly mollified, however, when on arrival he was given as his residence the newly modernized palace of a rich Baltic merchant named Tepper, on Miodowa (Honey) Street. It was the best dwelling in town, like staying with the Rothschild of the day.

According to the usually reliable memoirs of the Countess von Kielmansegge, when Talleyrand and his son discussed Warsaw society, Charles de Flahaut mentioned the beautiful châtelaine of Walewice. Father and son both agreed that 'there was at least one compensation for the terrible climate of this otherwise dismal country – the number of attractive women about, who in their education and manner resembled the best of the French.' Countess Kielmansegge also notes that Marie and Anastase dined with Talleyrand and Flahaut (who by now had formed a close friendship with Countess Potocka) a few days after the Foreign Minister's arrival, and that Talleyrand appeared to have been 'much struck with Marie's beauty and also her intelligence'. This man, who was such an excellent judge of good taste in all its forms, was to remember Marie throughout the ever-changing panorama of events which crowded his lifetime. Affection would be too strong a word, but he liked her and was to give her valuable counsel. He used frequently to remark that 'with her fresh, innocent looks Madame Walewska should have been painted by Greuze'.

Talleyrand had always been a strong partisan of an independent Poland, and he deeply deplored the partitions. He was convinced that a strong Poland was essential to the peace of Europe and to the equilibrium of the Continent, as a northern barrier and buffer state between Russia and the West. He was right, of course, but it took another hundred years for his ideas to be realized. In the meantime, in spite of endless memoranda on the subject, he never managed to persuade Napoleon of the necessity for such an arrangement. To his Foreign Minister's closely reasoned arguments, as to the petitions of the Polish patriots, Napoleon gave vaguely encouraging answers but not much more. Would it be more likely that Napoleon, who on this question had shown himself so immune to logic and reason, might perhaps be more susceptible to appeals coming from a beautiful, intensely patriotic woman?

There is no certainty as to whether Marie's appearance on the scene touched off some Machiavellian scheme in Talleyrand's mind at that particular time, but he made quite certain that Walewski and his young wife were included in the invitations to the forthcoming festivities connected with the Emperor's arrival. He also went out of his way to be particularly pleasant to Anastase, even to the extent of pretending to remember meeting him at Versailles some twenty-one years before – an attention that pleased the vain Walewski immensely.

Exciting as the arrival of Murat's and his troops must have been, it was nothing compared with the emotion generated by the imminent arrival of the Emperor himself. This was to be a majestic affair, with Napoleon parading through two enormous triumphal arches, beautifully decorated and lit, right in the city centre, and inscribed:

> Long live Napoleon, the Saviour of Poland,
> He was sent to us straight from Heaven.

Torch parades moved across town; bonfires were lit round the castle; hand-made Napoleonic golden eagles adorned houses and shops, and the two principal theatres, the National and the Francuski, held open performances for the public.

All these preparations were, however, frustrated by Napoleon's unexpected arrival late in the night of 18 December. As the main road to Warsaw was virtually impassable because of accumulated mud and raging floods, he arrived on horseback, after a twenty-eight-mile dash from Lowicz, stopping only once to change mounts. Accompanied only by a small cavalry escort and Berthier, Prince of Neuchâtel, the Chief of Staff, he rode straight to the castle, stopped in the courtyard for a drink of water, woke up the wardens and ordered supper. He then went straight off to bed.

Next morning Warsaw was all astir, but Napoleon refused to see delegations or be seen. He had plenty of work to do. For the war was just about to begin in earnest.

Only a short distance from Warsaw, in the northern triangle formed by the rivers Narew and Wkra, Benningsen's Russian armies, reinforced by the remnants of Prussian troops, were waiting, combat-ready for the arrival of the French, whose military columns marched through the festive streets of Warsaw on their way to the front. The Emperor, escorted by his Guard of Honour, reviewed the troops every day but appeared to be totally unaware of the cheering crowds and welcoming arches; his attention was concentrated on the army, their supplies and equipment.

Gradually the festive spirit subsided, and an atmosphere of nervous tension gripped the capital. 'It began to feel more like the eve of a battle than a welcome to the Liberator,' noted the *Gazeta Warszawska* (*Warsaw Journal*). Four days later Napoleon left Warsaw for the front as unexpectedly as he had arrived. On 22 December he drove east towards Pultusk, escorted by the Imperial Guard and a regiment of Polish Lancers. 'Next day,' notes the *Gazeta Warszawska*, 'a strong cannon fire could be heard in the city . . . from the east.'

Between Christmas and New Year the French armies fought

three consecutive battles in appalling weather conditions. Napoleon's advantage over his military opponents had always been his armies' ability to move fast and to confuse the enemy by unexpectedly changing their direction of attack. In this particular campaign, however, the water-logged ground immobilized both the artillery and the horses. 'My men are unable to stand straight in this hurricane wind and pelting rain,' reported Marshal Lannes from the front.

We had to tie our shoes to our waist with cords [wrote Coignet, one of the officers], otherwise we would have lost them in the mud. If a cord broke, the shoes disappeared in the quagmire... sometimes we had to seize the whole leg and scrape it off like a carrot and carry it forward with both hands, then turn around and do the same with the other leg, all this while weighted down with guns and ammunition.... No... I will never be able to describe accurately what we suffered....

At one point even the Emperor's carriage became stuck in the mud and started sinking; then the axle broke. Finally a horse had to be brought to the door; the Emperor slid from the seat onto the saddle and galloped off.

No wonder the morale of the army began to show signs of strain. They were fighting a difficult campaign six hundred miles from home in a horrible climate, with sparse provisions. 'No more wine, hardly any beer, and what there is is exceedingly bad,' wrote Marbot, one of the generals. 'Muddy water, no bread anywhere and quarters which we have to share with pigs and cows.'

Even veteran soldiers complained. It was during these difficult days that the nickname 'grognard' from 'grogner' was coined. 'Chleba' ('bread'), they called to the Emperor. 'Chleba niema' ('no bread'), he had to shout back. 'Take us home, we want peace,' mumbled others.

'Give me four more days,' Napoleon announced at the end of December. 'After that we go into winter quarters.'

And indeed, after the inconclusive battle of Pultusk, when the

Russian armies withdrew and the French became bogged down in their pursuit, orders went to the army to retire into winter quarters. 'It's all over for this year,' Napoleon wrote to Josephine on 31 December 1806. 'I am returning to Warsaw.'

Marie was in Warsaw all through Christmas, tending the wounded in the hospitals. More and more of them came in every day, cold, hungry, covered with mud, taxing the slender facilities of the local volunteer units. All the available public buildings and many private palaces were converted into hospitals; boarding-schools were closed so that beds could be offered to French soldiers, 'those heroes fighting for our independence'. Women gathered together to sew hospital linen, turn sheets into bandages, stockpile medicines. Families vied with each other in offering food and hospitality to the wounded.

It was in this hectic half war, half hospital atmosphere that Marie spent the last week of the year. In spite of Anastase's objections that she was overtaxing her strength, she worked long hours, driving off in her carriage in the morning, returning home only in late afternoon in time to see her young son before he was whisked off to bed by her aunts. Baby Anthony, now one and a half years old, was still the same puny, over-protected child, fussed over by a crowd of elderly female Walewski relatives. Only with great difficulty had Marie obtained their permission to bring him up to Warsaw for Christmas, as the air of the capital was considered unhealthy for small children. Now that Christmas was over, he was to be taken back to Walewice, smothered under a mass of satin coverlets and fur bonnets.

Marie acutely resented this appropriation of her natural rights. Naturally warm-hearted, her resentment was brought on by maternal affection rather than pride, and she suffered from the separation. But as time went on, she resigned herself to what seemed inevitable – at least for the present. 'I will have him back to myself when he grows older,' she confided to her friend Elizabeth Grabowska, who had been commiserating with her. 'And I will bring him up as a great patriot. . . .'

Elizabeth Grabowska, Marie's companion from the convent, was now married to a much-respected politician, Frank Sobolewski, a future Minister of Justice in 'post-Congress of Vienna' Poland. Warm, spontaneously affectionate, generous to a fault, she was universally adored, and her salon in Warsaw was one of the most popular meeting-places in the capital. Barely a few years older than Marie, she was nevertheless more sophisticated and practical and often worried about what she called her friend's 'patriotic exaltation'. Elizabeth's attitude to the French was much tougher, tempered by her husband's commonsense. She hoped that Poland's continuous sacrifices would 'shame' Napoleon into doing something 'tangible' for the country. So far he did not even have the time to meet any of the delegations; all he did was to issue requisition orders for immense quantities of foodstuffs for the armies. Marie assured her friend that things were 'bound to be different' when the Emperor returned from the front.

One late afternoon in December, on their way back from the hospital, Elizabeth and Marie stopped the carriage in front of the Zamek. Workers were putting finishing touches to the gilt-work in the great assembly-room on the first floor, where it was hoped Napoleon would attend a reception. 'We walked up to the huge empty ballroom,' Marie recalled in her Memoirs. 'I was stunned by the thought that quite soon I might see him in this very room, in the flesh. An inexplicable fear seized me. I called for my carriage and went home.'

Napoleon returned to Warsaw on 1 January 1807, in the late evening, and announced that he planned to remain for the rest of the month. The army had gone into winter quarters. 'Your mud has saved the Russian army for the time being,' he said. It was carnival time – they might as well enjoy themselves.

Wednesday 7 January was set as the day on which a reception was to be held at the castle by the Emperor to meet Warsaw society; eagerly-sought invitations were delivered by uniformed footmen to each name on a list, compiled by Talleyrand with the help of Countess Tyszkievicz, Prince Joseph

Poniatowski's sister. At Napoleon's request it was a fairly extensive and representative list: not only the nobility and the clergy
but writers, poets and prominent Warsaw merchants were
included.

As the day of the presentation drew near, Marie's intense
exaltation gave way to shyness. Left to her own devices, she
would gladly have returned to the country and continued to
dream, rather than face meeting her idol in the flesh. Having
him in the same city, living just a few streets away from her
own home, seemed enough. It was hard to think of him as a
person – he was more like a supreme being. How could she ever
bring herself to talk to him? She had lived with a dream for so
many years now, hugging it to herself, guarding it from outside
interference, that she was loath to have it disturbed.

She suggested to Anastase that they decline the invitation.
But she met with an indignant refusal. Walewski was not going
to be deprived of his meeting with the Emperor, and that was
that. And anyway, what was the matter with Marie – she who
for years had talked of nothing but Napoleon? It must be her
nerves. She had better pull herself together at once and order a
suitable dress for the reception; no expense was to be spared. He
also gave orders that the family diamond and sapphire necklace,
which suited Marie so well, be brought up from the country to
Warsaw at once. And Henriette de Vauban, Anastase's old
friend and adviser, was asked to call on Marie to instruct her in
matters of imperial etiquette.

On Wednesday 7 January Warsaw lay silent under a deep
blanket of snow. As night came over the city, swallowing the
frost-covered domes of the churches, a glittering procession of
carriages made its way to the royal palace set high over the
Vistula escarpment. The river was a curving band of darkness,
but the eighteenth-century façades glowed softly in the light of
innumerable torches.

In the old palace of Polish kings the brilliantly lit drawing-
rooms formed the background against which Poland displayed
the flower of her society; everyone had come to meet the Con-

queror of the West. This was the evening of evenings, not to be missed for anything in the world. Everyone's vanity and curiosity were stretched to the limit. It was as if the fate of the nation depended on the success of the presentation.

We can only guess at Marie's feelings as, flanked by her two sisters-in-law and preceded by Anastase, wearing his full uniform of the Court Chamberlain with the blue ribbon of the order of the White Eagle across his chest, she crossed the long gallery between two rows of soldiers of the Imperial Guard dressed in crimson.

Prince Joseph Poniatowski, ablaze with gold and colour, more handsome than ever in his tight white leather breeches, greeted them at the entrance to the main drawing-room, where the presentation of the ladies would take place. The main drawing-room was *a giorno* lit by hundreds of candles in the splendid chandeliers made for the last king of Poland by Murano craftsmen in Venice. Portraits of Polish kings, spanning eight centuries (beginning with Mieshko I, the pagan chieftain who, converted to Christianity in 966, brought Poland into the embrace of the Catholic Church), looked down upon the glittering assembly from walls covered in yellow damask.

Most of the hundred or so women in the room wore narrow, high-waisted dresses embroidered with silver and gold thread. The younger ones, following the fashion of the day, bared their shoulders, framing them in antique lace collars, which produced a neo-classical, Medici-like effect. Henriette de Vauban, in spite of her mature years, had the lowest *décolleté* in the crowd. Anna Potocka, Alexander Potocki's lovely, artistic wife, who was expecting a baby at the time, wore a black velvet dress *à la* Van Dyck and the family diamonds in her hair.

Marie's entrance drew many admiring looks. Her narrow blue velvet dress was the same colour as her eyes, and it matched her sapphire and diamond necklace; a twisted silvery cord circled her narrow waist, Grecian fashion. Her blonde hair, coiled at the neck, escaped in unruly curls framing her charming Botticelli-like face. She took her place next to her sister-in-law and waited, eyes fixed on the big mahogany doors at the far end of the room.

'We waited for quite a long time,' records Anna Potocka in her Memoirs, 'and I must confess that we were all a little afraid.' Napoleon could be unpredictable. It was said that he had been working very hard, and he might easily be in a bad humour, in which case the presentation would be a failure. Stories of his strange behaviour with the ladies abounded. He could be gauche, absent-minded or downright rude. Had he not recently reduced a well-known Saxon lady to tears by asking why her husband was so unfaithful to her? Had he not told a venerable, aristocratic lady that she was too old to wear a *décolleté* dress and asked an eighteen-year-old girl how many husbands she had had? One never quite knew what to expect. The atmosphere was tense.

Suddenly the room stirred. Two footmen flung open the doors, and Napoleon appeared in the doorway with Talleyrand and Marshal Duroc behind him. He paused in the doorway for a moment – as if contemplating some inner, far-away vision. Was he thinking of Paris, where he would have wanted to be in this New Year? The vision receded, and he moved forward at a brisk pace.

The Emperor came into the room, as if this was a review field-fast and with a slightly bored expression [writes another chronicler, Anna Nakwaska]. But as he looked around, his face gradually softened, the powerful brow relaxed ... as he surveyed us with evident approval. '*Ah, qu'il y a de jolies femmes à Varsovie*', I heard him say as he stopped in front of Madame Walewska, the young wife of the old Chamberlain Anastase, who happened to be standing next to me....

It can be easily believed that, as the chronicler says, 'Napoleon's face softened into a smile', for here in front of him, pink with emotion, stood an enchanting child-woman — blonde, white-skinned, with an exquisite figure and the most extraordinarily beautiful eyes. There was something infinitely sweet about her – it was not the gaily challenging face of a coquette he knew well or the face of a sophisticated society woman, secure in the knowledge of her charm; melancholy and inno-cence and goodness and great tenderness, all mingled in her expression and must have appealed to the Emperor.

On rising from her curtsey Marie met the full force of the famous 'infinitely powerful gaze'. No word was exchanged between them. He lingered for an imperceptible moment, then moved on.

Later, after the introductions were over, Napoleon was seen standing aside in a deep window-recess, talking to Talleyrand and pointing to the old Chamberlain and his wife. 'Who is she?' he asked. 'She is the daughter of a noble house, married to a man almost fifty years older than herself. Her name is Marie Walewska.'

4
THE COURTSHIP

Marie went home that evening unaware of the impression she had made; her mind was in a turmoil. It did not seem quite real that, after years of worshipping at Napoleon's shrine, admiring his portraits, poring over his writings, dissecting the legends about him, she had actually seen her idol in the flesh. She had been much too overwhelmed with emotion to take in the details of his face, yet, like all those who came into contact with Napoleon, she had felt the magnetic power of his personality upon her. Stendhal used to call Napoleon's gaze 'astonishing' – '*ce regard fixe et profond à la fois*'. She admitted that it had frightened her in the first instant, but then 'his stern expression changed, his eyes softened'. He was gone before she recovered from her trance.

Though it did not occur to Marie that the Emperor had singled her out for attention, most people in the distinguished assembly were certain that his words, '*Ah, qu'il y a de jolies femmes à Varsovie*,' proudly spread around the room by one of the Polish ADCs, were directed at the lovely Madame Walewska. A discreet buzz went around. Why Marie, the shy and retiring young bride from the provinces, when there were so many beautiful and worldly women in that very room? It was all quite unexpected, but it remained to be seen whether the Emperor's interest would last until Talleyrand's ball a few days later.

The Foreign Minister's ball, which the Emperor had promised to attend, was to be the opening of Warsaw's carnival season and the most brilliant function the devastated capital had seen since the days of the last king of Poland. As most of Warsaw's great houses were occupied by foreign dignitaries or French army marshals, and the Emperor himself was at the royal castle with his staff, it seemed the best of solutions when Talleyrand suggested his large, comfortable town-house for the ball. He went about the preparations with gusto. Couriers brought wines, flowers and assorted delicacies all the way from opulent Dresden; Napoleon's own *chef d'orchestre*, Kappelmeister Paer, was summoned and arrived in a fast sledge from Berlin, accompanied by his wife, a well-known singer. It promised to be the outstanding ball of the year.

On 17 January 1807 a brief paragraph appeared in the official journal, the *Gazeta Warszawska*: 'His Majesty the Emperor attended a ball at the house of the Minister of Foreign Affairs, the Prince of Benevento, during which he chose the wife of Chamberlain Anastase Walewski as a partner in a *contre-danse*.'

'It was one of the most interesting functions I have ever attended,' wrote the gossipy Anna Potocka in her Memoirs. 'The Emperor danced with Madame Walewska and talked to her for some time. . . . I saw him squeeze her hand at the end of the dance, which surely must have meant something.'

Marie and Anastase were late getting to Talleyrand's ball, because for the second time in a week Marie had been overwhelmed by shyness. The exhilarating prospect of finding herself again in the presence of the Emperor – thrilling as it appeared to others – filled her with apprehension. She could not explain how she felt, but she would have given anything not to go to the ball. Faint rumours had reached her. People said that the Emperor had found her attractive; the rumours were nothing but whispers, but enough to make Anastase preen himself like a peacock. At last she was doing justice to his name. He insisted she appear in a magnificent toilette, but she chose a simple white satin dress with a faint gold and pink lining and a wreath of laurel leaves for her head, as was the fashion of the day. She dressed particularly slowly that evening; Anastase, his eyes on the clock, angrily urged her to hurry, afraid they would miss the Emperor's arrival at the party. Wrapped in a fur-lined blue cloak, Marie watched from the window of her carriage as the crowds lined the way to Talleyrand's house, hoping to catch a glimpse of the Emperor. Barrels filled with burning tar lit the narrow, winding streets of the Old Town. In the eighteenth-century courtyard of Talleyrand's residence the Emperor's Guard of Honour stood motionless at attention, bayonets fixed.

The dancing was already in full swing, which meant that the Emperor had arrived. As they entered the first drawing-room, young Louis de Périgord, aide-de-camp to Berthier, the Chief of Staff, rushed forward: the Emperor had ordered him to find Marie and invite her to be his partner in a *contre-danse*. Even Anastase was bewildered by his wife's meteoric rise to pro-minence – he did not expect it to be quite so fast. But there was nothing Marie could do but comply.

It was a distinguished quadrille: the Emperor, with General Berthier and his two brothers-in-law Murat and Camillo Borg-hese, formed the men's foursome; Marie, facing the Emperor on the floor, had Elizabeth Sobolewska with her and two other beautiful ladies, one of whom most likely was Countess Potocka. It did not take long for the sharp-eyed Warsaw ladies to conclude that the Emperor was an atrociously clumsy dancer; he paid hardly any attention to the music, mixed up all his figures and seemed to treat the whole idea of dancing as a joke. He was obviously much more at home on the battlefield than on the dance-floor.

'Would you say, Countess, that I am a good dancer?' he asked Anna Potocka, after a particularly clumsy performance. 'Sir,' answered the worldly young woman, 'for a great man you dance perfectly.' Everyone laughed, and only Prince Camillo Borghese, who took his dancing very seriously (it was the only thing he could do well), looked somewhat pained.

It soon became clear that Napoleon was enchanted with

Marie, her exquisite grace, wide blue eyes, blonde curly hair and youthful fire; he found beguiling the mixture of innocence and melancholy she conveyed. He stayed unusually late at the ball, and it was noticed that he observed her from a distance. To her dismay she became the centre of attention, of much whispering behind the fans, the target of countless monocles and lorgnettes, jealous looks from the women and admiring glances from the men. The valiant General Bertrand and handsome Louis de Périgord, scion of a great family, paid her particularly assiduous court – a mistake on their part which they duly repented. Years later Napoleon himself recounted the incident in his Memoirs, dictated to Montholon on St Helena.

Bertrand and Périgord must have been quite obtuse that evening: not realizing that I was interested in Madame Walewska, they danced attendance on her and were constantly under foot, dazzled by her beautiful eyes, no doubt. Bertrand should have been the wiser of the two, but I saw him during supper lean over Madame Walewska's chair so closely that his epaulettes almost touched her naked white back. By then I had had enough of those two: I summoned Bertrand and ordered him to rejoin Prince Jerome's army on the Baltic forthwith. He never knew what hit him. . . . As for de Périgord – I told Berthier to send him off to East Prussia. . . .

Anastase, bursting with self-importance, escorted Marie home. At noon the next day a carriage drew up in front of the Walewski's house in Bednarska Street. Out came Marshal Duroc, Chief of the Imperial Household, carrying a gigantic bouquet of flowers and a heavy parchment letter with imperial green seals; he was there to deliver a message to Marie from his master. The contents of the letter shook the young woman to the core: 'I saw no one but you, I admired only you; I want no one but you; I beg you to reply promptly to calm my ardour and my impatience.' The letter was signed: 'NAPOLEON'.

Marie sent word to the Marshal that there would be no reply. Undaunted, Duroc returned the same evening with another bouquet of flowers and another letter. This time the tone was different: gone was the imperial summons, the churlish impatience; the words were those of a man in love, a reader of romantic fiction such as *Paul and Virginie* and *Corinne*: 'Did I displease you, Madame? Your interest in me seems to have waned, while mine is growing every moment.... You have destroyed my peace.... I beg you to give a little joy to my poor heart, so ready to adore you. Is it so difficult to send a reply? You owe me two.' The scratchy signature with an impatient flourish said: 'NAPOLE'. But this too remained unanswered.

Poor Marie. For a woman of her sensitivity and pride, this abrupt transformation of her legendary hero into an ordinary mortal, inflamed with desire, unashamedly suggesting a lover's meeting, must have been a brutal shock. How could the great Emperor have misunderstood so completely the noble feelings she held for him? He demanded sacrifices from her country. Like most of her compatriots she was prepared to give him anything – her possessions, money, jewels, even her life if need be – all except this one thing he so obviously wanted from her.

How was she to be expected to cope with this situation? After all, it was barely three years since, urged by her family, she had entered into a loveless marriage with an old man, and it had taken her all this time to come to terms with her new life. She had suffered acutely at first, but slowly resignation took over, and with it came peace. Marriage vows, once contracted, could never be dissolved, so she must learn how to live with the situation. She remained faithful to Anastase; all the intensity of her nature was now channelled into service for the cause of the liberation of Poland. It had become her life-force.

The Emperor's love letters, beguiling as they seem to us, offended Marie deeply. Who did he take her for? On what grounds did he and the distinguished Marshal, his envoy, assume that she would be willing to gratify his wishes – she, a married woman of a prominent family, and a mother? She must have felt insulted and infinitely disappointed in her hero.

But if Marie was disturbed, so was Napoleon according to the testimony of Constant Wairy, his faithful valet and a meticulous diarist.

The day after the ball [writes Constant], the Emperor was in a state of unusual agitation. I was amazed to find him so restless. He could not remain still for a moment ... he got up, paced the floor, sat down, got up again, it was hell ... no matter how I tried, it was impossible to dress him ... [I] thought his toilette would never be finished. ... The moment breakfast was over, he summoned a high dignitary of the Count (I had better not mention his name) and dispatched him to pay his respects to Madame Walewska and convey the Emperor's wishes to her. I understand that Madame Walewska proudly rejected the proposal. Perhaps it was too sudden – it might have offended a lady of her class – or perhaps she did it out of coquetry, as is usual amongst women. All I know is that the dignitary returned highly embarrassed and surprised at the lack of success of his mission. Next morning the Emperor woke up even more obsessed by the lady. He did not say a word to me, though he usually chatted amiably while dressing ... he still had not had an answer to his letters and he simply could not understand it; he considered himself irresistible to women, and I really believe that his *amour-propre* had been hurt. ...

That evening, 19 January, Napoleon was giving a dinner and concert at the castle, at which he asked Countess Tyszkievicz, sister of Prince Joseph Poniatowski and Talleyrand's close friend, to be his hostess. The Walewskis were also invited, as had long ago been Talleyrand's plan. Though upset and infinitely reluctant to attend, Marie could not fail to appear short of creating a scandal. At dinner she found herself seated next to the charming, well-mannered Duroc, with the Emperor directly across the table from her. According to chroniclers' accounts, which vary somewhat in their reports of the evening, the Emperor, while conducting general conversation on current political subjects with Polish statesmen, 'never stopped looking at Marie during the meal'. Now and then he communicated in a kind of sign language with Duroc, at which both men seemed to be very adept, and which Marie found oddly childish. Apparently, at one point during the meal, the Emperor, 'never taking his eyes off Marie', put his left hand on his heart; at the sign Duroc promptly turned to Marie, asking why she was not wearing the flowers sent to her earlier that day. Rather spiritedly she answered that she had given them to her young son.

'The Emperor left directly after dinner and never attended the concert,' wrote Madame Nakwaska in her Memoirs. 'But just before his departure he was seen going up to Madame Walewska and talking to her with an almost tender expression on his face. . . .' Soon after – it is not quite clear whether it was late the same evening or early next morning – another letter was delivered to Marie by the long-suffering Master of the Imperial Household.

There are moments in life when to be in an elevated position constitutes a real burden, and I feel it now most acutely. How can a heart, so very much in love, be satisfied? All it wants is to throw itself at your feet; but it is being restrained . . . my deepest longings are paralysed. . . . Oh, if only *you* wanted it! You and you alone can remove the obstacles that separate us. My friend Duroc will tell you what to do. Oh come, come . . . all your desires will be granted. *Your country will be so much dearer to me* if you take pity on my poor heart.

The signature this time was just an 'N'.

Whoever suggested the key phrase, 'Your country will be so much dearer to me if you come', was astute, for the wording gave another dimension to the Emperor's love-letter and made it harder to ignore. Even Marie could see it.

By now Marshal Duroc's pilgrimages to Bednarska Street had attracted widespread attention, and numerous people came forth to offer advice to Marie. Benedict, the model soldier, follower of Bonaparte for ten years, his eye set firmly on his career in the army, talked to her 'not as a brother but as a Polish patriot'. She, his sister, had been honoured by fate; she had been chosen to help Poland. He, the head of the Laczynski family, gave her his blessing . . .

Anastase, to whom the letters were finally shown, inclined his head, beamed inwardly, looked pious and pronounced '*Placet*'.

The events had naturally been causing great excitement among the female contingent gathered around Prince Joseph Poniatowski at the Blacha. Henriette de Vauban saw it as a development in the best tradition of the Court of Versailles, where a reigning favourite was *de rigueur*. She beckoned to her friend and unofficial lady-in-waiting, the comely Emily Cichocka, to follow her and ordered that the carriage be made ready. The two ladies hurriedly drove off to the Walewski mansion to extend their felicitations to Marie. Emily Cichocka, who, together with Marie's brother Benedict was to have a decisive influence in persuading her to go to Napoleon, was one of the celebrated beauties of the Blacha, the seraglio of adoring females (the '*cour d'amour*', as the Warsaw wits had nicknamed it), gathered around the dashing Prince Joseph, under the watchful eye of Madame de Vauban. This slightly theatrical character, now somewhat faded ('*sèche de corps et d'esprit, mais encore vaporeuse*'), filled the palace with attractive youngish women, not always of the best reputation, to whom Prince Joseph, in his rather desultory way, paid court whenever the mood moved him. Emily was one of the stars of the Blacha: tall, supple, with melting black eyes and an alluringly generous mouth. She had a sultry, gipsy-like look about her and was reputed to be 'very hot-blooded'. She had already jettisoned two husbands and was shortly to become the wife of a young army officer twenty years younger than herself. Marie had met her in Warsaw through Madame de Vauban, and an unlikely friendship had sprung up between these two totally different young women. Emily had a reputation for fast living, but she too was a great patriot – a trait which added to her vivacity and good humour, and must have endeared her to Marie.

While Henriette de Vauban congratulated Anastase and fanned his ego, Emily went to work on Marie. How could she even consider turning down the Emperor's plea to visit him – particularly as he had specifically mentioned the cause of Poland? Would she ever forgive herself if, annoyed by her refusal, he became hostile to the Cause? She was being given the supreme opportunity to play a role in the destiny of her beloved country. She ought to be grateful for it.

Contemporary accounts suggest that Emily and Madame de Vauban went so far as to imply to Marie that not only Prince Joseph but other prominent Polish statesmen were urging her to go to the castle. 'It would be of immense benefit to Poland,' they were supposed to have told Emily, 'to have a Polish woman installed at the castle, as an official favourite and channel for communications with the Emperor.' It has since become part of popular legend that Prince Joseph and assorted high-ranking notables drew up a state memorandum which they presented to Marie, formally requesting her to become Napoleon's mistress, 'in the best interests of her country', and quoting the biblical Esther as a worthy example to follow.

It is hard to believe that distinguished 'high-ranking Poles' would have talked about an 'official favourite' at the castle. The position of a favourite – a *maîtresse en titre* – was never part of a Polish tradition. There had never been the equivalent of a Pompadour, a du Barry or, for that matter, a Potemkin at a Warsaw Court. The king's mistress, if there was one, was regarded as his own private affair with no right to political patronage; she would have lived quietly, pretending to be sharing a house with her husband, and she would have been received in society according to her husband's rank. Adultery on the part of a woman (standards were different for men) had always been frowned upon. The beautiful Madame Grabowska (Elizabeth Sobolewska's mother), a long-time mistress and eventually the morganatic wife of the last king of Poland, whose children by the king were all brought up at the castle, was – even after a passage of years – still officially regarded as the wife of the good General Grabowski, and all the king's children by her bore the name of her husband. It was the Polish way of doing things, and it is very unlikely that such an argument would ever have been used. Nevertheless the pressure on Marie continued, and finally she agreed to go.

The society chronicler Françoise Trembicka, who was in Warsaw at the time, tells us that Emily finally won Marie over when she said, 'Go to the Emperor, talk to him about Poland, *nothing need happen.*' After all, it was up to her : indeed, nothing *need* happen at all ... Clutching at this compromise as if it were a life-raft, Marie put herself in God's hands and agreed to go to the castle that evening. Emily and Madame de Vauban lost no time in sending a message to Duroc. And to make certain there would be no change of heart they remained at the Walewski mansion until darkness, when the imperial carriage drew up at a discreet distance from the house. Wearing a large round hat and a cloak, Marshal Duroc settled the trembling and heavily veiled fragile figure on the seat next to him and drove off to the hidden, riverside entrance of the castle, which must have seen many such arrivals through the ages. He then led her up one short flight of stairs to a study, faintly lit by two candelabra and wall-sconces. Marie found herself alone with the Emperor.

We have to rely on Constant Wairy's account of what happened at that first interview :

Madame W. finally agreed to see the Emperor between 10 and 11 pm that night. The same distinguished Court official I mentioned previously was sent to escort her to the castle. While waiting, the Emperor kept pacing the floor furiously, displaying excitement and impatience quite unusual for him : he constantly kept asking me what the time was. ... At last Madame W. arrived, but in a terrible state. ... Pale, trembling, her eyes full of tears ... she could hardly walk unaided and kept clinging on to her escort's arm. ... Later, while she was with the Emperor, I heard her sobbing ... my heart ached for her. I don't think the Emperor got any satisfaction out of her during the first interview ... they just talked. ... About 2 am I was rung for, and I saw Madame W. still crying and dabbing her eyes with a handkerchief. The same dignitary took her home. I was sure she would never return. . . . But she did, a day or two later at the same hour. . . . She still looked pale but she was not crying any more. . . . Her lovely face showed deep emotion. . . . The visits continued until the Emperor left Warsaw. . . .

As Constant says, the Emperor got nothing from her during that first interview. She cried most of the time and looked scared. Emily, who presumably had heard it direct from Marie and repeated it to Madame Trembicka, said that Marie returned home that night much calmer and greatly reassured. She had been spared. Napoleon had been kind and solicitous – he had asked her about herself and her family and particularly about her marriage; he wondered why she had married Anastase. She talked to him of the need to restore Poland's independence. He called her '*ma douce colombe*' ('my sweet dove') and gently urged her to return again to see him, until she promised she would.

One would have every reason to suppose that Napoleon might have been put off by the tears, the trembling, the exalted patriotic speeches. There he was, the conqueror of Europe, the object of universal feminine admiration. Only a few weeks before, in Berlin, renowned beauties from the Austrian and Prussian aristocracy had clustered around his Court, awaiting the Emperor's pleasure. And here was an unsophisticated young woman of a noble, but not princely, background, whom he had singled out for his attention, who kept putting up such a tiresome resistance. What was the matter with her? She was not a coquette; her reluctance was perfectly genuine. Then what was it?

But there was obviously something in Marie's innocence, the way that his ardour genuinely frightened her, and in her unfeigned devotion to the cause of her country, that appealed to the protective side of Napoleon's nature and, strangely enough, moved him. Also, Napoleon could never resist feminine tears, as Josephine had learned long ago. 'They tug at my heart-strings,' he used to say. He determined to woo Marie Walewska and win her over.

Next morning, as the much happier Marie was attending to her *toilette*, came one more letter, accompanied by a large red leather box with the name of Dresden's most famous jeweller on it.

Marie, my sweet Marie – my first thought is for you – my first desire of the day is to see you again. You will return, won't you? If not the eagle will fly to the dove. . . . I will be seeing you at dinner tonight – I am told. Please accept this bouquet, as a secret link between us among the surrounding crowd. Whenever my hand touches my heart, you will know what I mean, and I want you to reciprocate the gesture at once. Love me, my sweet Marie, and don't let your hand ever leave your heart.

N

The romantic letter, duly reflecting the spirit of the age, was delightful, but the gift of a magnificent diamond brooch in the shape of a flower-arrangement infuriated Marie. Why did he have to keep offending her so? Did he not understand that she could not accept such a gift? She refused to wear the sumptuous jewel at the dinner given for the Emperor by a member of the Polish Provisional Government that night – one more occasion in the chain of festivities by which Warsaw paid homage to the Liberator.

Napoleon, more and more obsessed by Marie, or perhaps challenged by her resistance, 'frowned and looked thundery' when he noticed that she was not wearing the brooch. Frightened, she quickly raised her left hand to her heart and 'noticed with immense relief that the look of extreme annoyance disappeared from his face'. Soon after, Duroc passed on a discreet message: the Emperor wished to see her at the castle at about eleven that night. By now she was too much afraid of him to hesitate, so she went, hoping in her supreme innocence that perhaps this time too she would be reprieved.

But it did not work out that way. We shall never know the exact truth of what happened during that second meeting, but in memoirs written years later for the benefit of her three sons,

Marie implied that she became 'the unwilling victim of his passion'. Some historians suggest that Napoleon simply raped her. Who is to know? The truth must be somewhere in between. It is likely that, encouraged by her first visit, imbued with a burning sense of mission, Marie envisioned a platonic, 'Paul and Virginie' sort of meeting of minds, during which she would put forth some tremendously convincing arguments which would force Napoleon to consider the immediate restoration of Poland. In spite of the earthy passion of his letters, Napoleon was still a sort of 'supernatural' person to her – it was like being with a god from Olympus.

Of course it was asking too much of fate. At some point during that nocturnal *tête-à-tête* either the Emperor tired of hearing about Poland or his passion reached a crescendo. Marie might have wished it had not happened that way, but her subsequent behaviour was certainly not that of an injured, hostile woman who had been abused against her will.

As Constant meticulously recorded: 'After that night she came to see him every day.' In fact, for the rest of Napoleon's stay in Warsaw, she divided her time between her own house, where her husband and brother Benedict treated her with mounting respect, and an apartment at the castle, adjoining Napoleon's own quarters.

The imperial romance was conducted against the background of a complex political situation. Though popular enthusiasm for the Emperor continued unabated, the general euphoria surrounding the presence of French troops in the province was evaporating fast, due to widespread abuses by the army and the heavy demands it imposed on the greatly impoverished countryside. Not only were the Poles expected to raise an army of forty thousand men and to provide all the material and supplies for French units, but it all had to be done instantly. Marshal Davout, the French Military Governor of the province, a man not particularly friendly to the Poles (he considered them 'unreliable'), daily seemed to come up with new, equally onerous demands. There was a general scarcity of food, and when a shortage of bread occurred in the army distinguished Polish generals were ordered to sally forth in the rain to visit the mills in person and make sure that deliveries of flour would reach the French quartermaster's warehouses by next morning. 'We did not get home until midnight,' wrote Joseph Wybicki, the famous general. 'We were exhausted and furious.'

To maintain the *Grand Armée* in its winter quarters in northern Poland was indeed a formidable task, as it was a region where peasants could barely feed themselves. Even when supplies had been collected in the rear, lack of wagons and the state of the roads prevented their reaching the troops. Napoleon's armies were used to living off the land ('like a plague of locusts', a Prussian general complained after Jena). They had marched across the lush German countryside leaving empty byres and pillaged towns in their wake; but here, in the denuded Polish plain, in the midst of a severe winter, there was nothing to requisition or to plunder. Assembling provisions for men and fodder for the thousands of horses became a quartermaster's nightmare.

To make matters worse, French soldiers stood in urgent need of refitting. Their clothing, already worn out by the long Prussian campaign, was inadequate for the rigours of a Polish winter. And here again the warehouses of Warsaw, Posen or Polish Torun were expected to rapidly supplement the stocks of overcoats, shoes, fur hats and other winter clothing ordered from countless depots throughout Germany and desperately slow in reaching the front line. It was a monumental shopping-list, made even more impossible by the fact that Marshal Davout demanded that all items be supplied 'right away'. Friction was bound to arise.

Napoleon, who had studied Rulhière's famous work, *Histoire de l'anarchie en Pologne*, was thoroughly briefed on the situation within Poland. He was aware of the prevailing dissensions among the Polish leaders of the day. Not everyone, it seemed, was a Napoleonic enthusiast. Prominent families with estates in

Russian-occupied eastern Poland, led by the powerful Czartoryski family, had everything to lose by taking arms against the Tsar. Not only would their lands be confiscated but hopes of restoring a Polish kingdom with a member of the Romanov family at its head – an idea Alexander I had been toying with since his accession to the throne – would certainly be doomed.

'What did His Imperial Majesty offer us in return for our sacrifices?' asked Prince Joseph Poniatowski during his first conversation with Napoleon in Warsaw. His words made the Emperor very angry. Was the Prince demanding guarantees? How unpatriotic of him. The Poles must first earn their freedom by wholesale sacrifices for the French cause. There must be no hesitation.

It had been a bizarre interview. There was Prince Joseph, the magnificently handsome nephew of the last king of Poland, representative of the old aristocratic order, standing in the long gallery of the Warsaw castle, which had been his home since childhood and to which he had always returned in the last twenty years after fighting for the freedom of Poland, being accused of lack of patriotism by a foreign, self-appointed Emperor. In return for total unconditional support from Poland Napoleon promised nothing. It was an inauspicious beginning.

Gradually, however, the relationship between the two men improved. Napoleon's own sound judgment of people, Talleyrand's diplomatic persuasion and Murat's energetic championship of Prince Joseph made Napoleon appreciate and admire Poniatowski. Four years later the Prince became a marshal of France. But it was Marshal Murat, above all, who smoothed the choppy waters in Warsaw, for he had personal considerations at stake.

From the beginning of the Polish campaign, Murat had looked on Poland as his future kingdom. Jerome, Napoleon's youngest brother, had the same ambition, but Murat did not know that. In the old days Polish nobles had frequently chosen as their elected king a brilliant soldier. For a nation of horsemen, what better candidate for the crown could there be than Murat, the famous cavalier who had proved himself on so many battle-fields, and whose accession would make Napoleon's sister queen of Poland? From the moment he crossed the border, Murat had been preparing for the part he hoped to play. Instead of a French marshal's uniform, he adopted a gorgeous costume of his own invention, intended to make him appear like a Polish 'magnifico'. That was how he rode into Warsaw on 28 November at the head of the First Chasseurs and his brigade of dragoons.

Once arrived, he had every reason to expect that his dream would be realized. Pro-French Polish nobles formed a brilliant circle at his receptions and spoke freely of their hope of seeing the kingdom restored under a prince of the imperial family. He became a personal friend of Prince Joseph, whose integrity and magnificent horsemanship Murat was the first to appreciate. Prince Joseph, in his generous way, assured the Marshal that he himself never thought of aspiring to the crown of his ancestors; he even presented Murat with a national heirloom, the sword of the valiant sixteenth-century Polish King Stephen Batory. The gift delighted Murat, for, as he confided in a letter to his wife, 'it seemed like an assurance that the sceptre itself could not be far away.'

But Napoleon refused to commit himself to a decision. He played with the idea and continued to toy with it until it was too late. Had he adhered to it firmly and insisted after his victory at Friedland on the creation of a free Polish state under an independent monarch, he would have secured as an ally a whole nation, whose support would have proved invaluable to him in later years. But even when, on 14 January 1807, he finally decided to form a Provincial Polish Government (with Prince Joseph as Minister for War), he refused to give any assurance to Murat or indeed to discuss his future plans with Polish statesmen.

In the meantime, however, the Warsaw carnival season, en-livened by the presence of the French, was in full swing. The days were filled with rounds of dinners, card-parties, supper-parties, theatre and various other distractions of the day. One need only glance at the social notes in contemporary newspapers to pick up the tempo of Warsaw life in January 1807.

17 January: a ball given by His Excellency Prince de Talleyrand-Périgord, Prince of Benevento; 18 January: His Majesty the Emperor honours with his presence a performance of *Perseus and Andromeda* at the National Theatre; 20 January: a concert at the castle; 22 January: a dance at Marshal Murat's house; 24 January: a dinner-dance at Prince Camillo Borghese's house. And so it went on.

I entertained many Frenchmen in my house [writes Anna Potocka in her Memoirs]. We played cards, but most of the time we talked. . . . Prince Borghese, the Emperor's brother-in-law, often came to see us. He was mad on dancing, and whenever the conversation veered to a more serious subject, he would immediately get up, fetch a few chairs, arrange them in pairs in the middle of the room, as if they were couples, and, singing some fashionable air, would dance all around, practising the figures in the *contredanse*. . . . General Exelmans came, and so did charming Louis de Périgord, Alfred de Noailles, the handsome Lagrange and of course the most attractive of all, Charles de Flahaut. . . .

Anne Potocka had an understandable preference for the more refined type of Frenchman. For her, as for other young women in Warsaw's sophisticated society, 'Glory was not quite enough.' Napoleon's marshals, though eager for amorous adventures, were, by and large, pretty rough characters. There was Lefèbvre, the future victor of Danzig, an ex-army sergeant, a big gruff man of the people, with a long chin and thick Alsatian accent; Oudinot, the brewer's son from Bar-le-Duc, wounded thirty-four times, whose favourite occupation was shooting candles with pistols after dinner; Ney, a red-haired, tobacco-chewing hero, and of course Murat, the popular pretender to the throne of Poland, with his outrageous Gascon accent and his predilection for theatrical clothes and brothels. It was difficult sometimes to predict the dashing marshals' behaviour at polite dinner-parties.

79

D

Napoleon's other brother-in-law, Camillo Borghese, scion of an old Roman family, the husband of beautiful Pauline Bonaparte, was of course a man of the world, but unfortunately he did not have a brain in his head.

But there were other notables to please the ladies, for the attractions of the carnival and the imperial presence in Warsaw brought a host of distinguished visitors. Indeed the entire international élite of subjugated Europe was making its way to the Conqueror's headquarters. In January alone the chroniclers noted the presence in Warsaw of two German kings (Bavaria and Württemberg), several German princelings and many representatives of the old Roman and Austrian aristocracy. Warsaw's young vied with each other in learning to distinguish the various foreign uniforms in the streets: Italian generals, Austrian envoys, staff officers from Bavaria and Württemberg, Swedish and Dutch Court officials. The most sensational of all were the exotic, bearded figures of the Turkish and Persian envoys in their splendid oriental attire. The Emperor's daily review of the troops at the parade-ground near the castle attracted crowds of spectators. He generally arrived at about 11 am accompanied by Talleyrand and Maret, the Minister of State, and surrounded by a brilliant retinue of his marshals – 'the heroes of the century', as they were reverently referred to. The Emperor's stark greyish-green uniform and his dark *tricorne* contrasted dramatically with the feathers and the plumes, the gold and the jewels, the red velvet and the sable-lined capes of his entourage. Thousands of Polish eyes, adoring and full of hope, watched the Emperor intently every morning, trying to guess from his face what he had in store for their country. But the face remained inscrutable.

That was Napoleon's public face. In private His Majesty was in love. 'You were so beautiful yesterday, that for long in the night I could still see you in my mind. . . . I reproached myself for having insisted you come to the parade . . . it was so cold. . . . I look forward with happy anticipation to seeing you at the dance

Prince Joseph Poniatowski, Commander-in-Chief of the Polish Forces,
by Marcello Bacciarelli

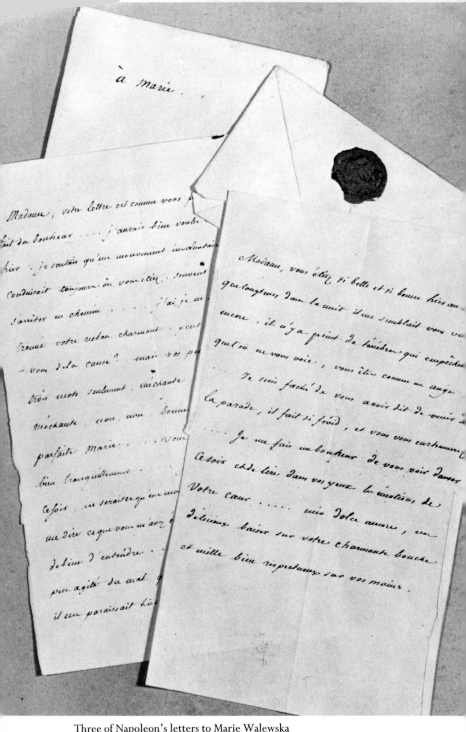

Three of Napoleon's letters to Marie Walewska

Madame, je reçois votre charmante
lettre . vous avez eu un vilain temps
vous êtes bien fatiguée et mauvais chemins
mais vous vous portez bien, c'est le
principal . Je compte sur votre
promesse . vous savez tout le plaisir
que j'ai à vous voir . mille choses
aimables partout, et un tendre baiser
sur votre charmante bouche, Marie!
ce jeudi 23 avril .

Napole

à Marie

tonight. *Mio dolce amore*. . . . I kiss your charming mouth and your hands. . . .' And again, a few days later, another letter, written on a small scrap of paper at six o'clock in the morning:

I long for you to reassure me that you are not feeling too tired. . . . I long to know how you spent the rest of the night . . . all through the night you were in the same place in my thoughts . . . the memory of last night will never leave me. Marie, remember that I love you, that you have done me the favour of sharing my feelings. Will you promise to remain constant?

Napole.

Marie's letters to Napoleon have not survived, but she must have written and responded to his tender missives for there exists another letter from Napoleon, written at approximately the same time, also without a date but marked six o'clock in the morning:

Your letter is like yourself – perfect. It made me immensely happy. I wanted to talk to you at the Assembly last night. . . . I felt propelled in your direction; instead I was forced to stop on my way several times to talk to people. I don't know why, but I found your ribbon delightful. . . . Can you guess the reason? I noticed an expression of sweet melancholy in your eyes. I cover them with kisses.

Napole.

As the news of the Emperor's infatuation spread around, Marie found it painfully difficult to escape from being the centre of attention at the innumerable social functions in the town, at which Napoleon always wanted her to be present. 'We played whist last night after supper,' notes Anna Potocka. 'I was bidden to the Emperor's table. . . . Madame Walewska does not play cards, but the Emperor always wants her in the room, within his sight.'

Even on a quiet afternoon at home, she was besieged by admiring visitors. 'I recall', noted the old gossip Madame Nakwaska, in her diary, 'paying a call on Madame Walewska recently and finding the King of Bavaria in her sitting-room, together with an assortment of young Guards officers and two

Polish noblemen from Lowicz. The husband of our reigning beauty was in an adjoining room, talking business with two bearded Jewish merchants.' Ludvig Charles Augustus Wittels- bach of Bavaria was indeed one of Marie's admirers. But not for long. When told of the competition facing him, he packed his bags and left Warsaw, judging it more important to keep in Napoleon's good graces than to win favours from a lady, no matter how beautiful.

Marie's life now revolved around two axes: her home and her daily visits to the castle, to which she went with the full knowledge of her husband, a silent smile on the part of her mother and the excited encouragement of her brother Benedict. It was odd that, out of the entire family, Marie was the only one who felt guilty about breaking her marriage vows.

She daily grew more fascinated by Napoleon. She was not afraid of him any more: he was so human. 'It amazed me', she later told Elizabeth Sobolewska, 'how interested the Emperor was in personal gossip.' He interrogated her at length about Polish personalities of the day, their private lives, animosities, love affairs. Like many other leaders before and since then, he found it a useful device to assess the human and political picture of the country he was in. For her part, Marie insisted on reminding him of his promises to Poland. But all she ever got from him was: 'Be patient. Because of you your country is very dear to me now.' All Napoleon's future plans depended on the outcome of the approaching battle with the Russians.

At the end of January Benningsen's Russian armies, composed chiefly of peasants inured to the misery of the weather, launched a winter offensive in East Prussia against the left flank of the French over-extended line of winter quarters. The Emperor, convinced that he must enter on a fresh campaign, left Warsaw on the night of 30 January for Willemburg in East Prussia. His last two hours at the castle were spent alone with Marie; he would do everything in his power to be with her again very soon, he assured her.

At Eylau, amid deep birchwood forests, the Russian armies

halted to offer battle in defence of the fortress of Königsberg. On 8 February, a day of terrifying, smothering blizzard, Napoleon launched an attack. The result was a stalemate; neither army had won; the casualties were calamitous. Over fifteen thousand Frenchmen lay dead or wounded in the snow. When the Russians fell back towards Königsberg, Napoleon was unable to follow them. It was the first time that the *Grande Armée*'s progress had been halted. In temperatures now averaging twenty-two degrees of frost, the snow continued to fall, a silent terror enfolding the marching armies. On 17 February the Emperor began to retreat to his new winter quarters at Osterode in East Prussia. 'Don't be alarmed at the news,' he wrote to Marie, who was in Warsaw with her mother. 'I will soon take on the Russians again. But long before that you will be able to come and see me.'

5
THE IDYLL

Spring must have seemed a long way off to Marie on that snowy April morning in Warsaw when, wrapped in a voluminous fur pelisse and escorted by her brother Benedict, she took her place in the carriage and set off for Napoleon's headquarters in East Prussia.

She travelled in a commodious, well-equipped *berline* (complete with cooking-stove and chamber-pots), dressed in a fur-lined travelling suit, lynx-lined cloak – as was the fashion in Poland – hat and muff, with fluffy rugs round her feet. Their destination was a country of myriad lakes and oak forests on the Baltic which in the last three months had become the theatre of a war of attrition between the Russian commander Benningsen and Napoleon.

For Marie, the decision to rejoin Napoleon at Finkenstein must have been an act of supreme courage. The risk involved was enormous. In Warsaw the 'affair' could still be contained as long as appearances were kept up. She was protected by the solidarity of her class and the universal patriotic fervour for the French. In this exhilarating atmosphere sacrifices for 'the Cause' had a flexible interpretation. Added to it was the open connivance of her husband, determined to overlook the affair. It could all still have been explained as a temporary lapse. After a few quiet months in the country everything could have reverted to normal. Marie's prestige in society would have been enhanced; the diarists would have enjoyed commenting on the scandal; and life would have reverted to normal.

But this journey was something quite different, for from here there was no going back. It signalled the final break with her past, leaving not only her husband, to whom she was tied by religious marriage vows she respected, but also abandoning her son – perhaps for ever. For even the old Chamberlain, who in his ridiculous vanity had been delighted to overlook Marie's infidelity as long as an Emperor was involved, would have blanched at the enormity of the scandal which was bound to engulf them all if Marie's presence at Napoleon's military head-quarters became publicly known. This was no place for a woman of Marie's social rank, and certainly no place for the mother of his son.

What could have made her disregard the fundamental rule of behaviour of her class? The best-meant patriotic intentions ceased to be relevant at this point. Did Marie realize the serious-ness of the step she was about to take? True, the Emperor had given her a firm promise that absolute secrecy would shroud her visit. No one – with the exception of Constant Wairy, his trusted valet, and Méneval, the secretary – would know of her presence at the castle. She would arrive after dark, be escorted by her brother to her own, separate, specially prepared apart-ment, where she would find Napoleon waiting. 'Trust me – *ma douce colombe*,' he had written. 'You will be safe with me here . . . come . . . hurry. . . .'

Did she already, at this early stage of their relationship, trust him so utterly that she was prepared to put her entire future in his hands? Or did she, as her brother was to claim many years later, regard this journey as another patriotic mission, another occasion to plead the cause of Poland? Or was it simply the impulse of a woman in love, rushing into the arms of a man, who, besides being her lover, was also holding the key to the destiny of her country? We shall never know the real answer, but patriotism and a certain sense of mission certainly played a role. The war was at a critical juncture: the French armies had now been in Poland for five months, exacting a heavy toll from the population. Napoleon's promises continued vague; so far no Polish statesman had been able to pin him down to specifics. Why should not Marie take on the role of an unofficial ambassador to his Court, particularly as he had summoned her, even begged her to come to his side?

This was the line of reasoning adopted by Benedict and the feminine circle at the Blacha. It might even have had the tacit approval of some of the members of the Polish Provisional Government. But, exalted patriot as she was, and a devout Catholic to whom adultery was a cardinal sin – even if it was construed as a means to save Poland – Marie was first of all a woman, a young woman whose senses had just been awakened. She could not have forgotten those January nights at the castle in Warsaw when, after the dreadful initial trauma of surrender, she lay in the arms of that extraordinary man. He was awe-inspiring and frightening perhaps, but also a tender and passionate lover – a man who, unlike her husband, was still young and well formed, and the hero of her childhood. The high-sounding patriotic motives marshalled in her diary for the benefit of future historians undoubtedly played their part in the venture, but Marie, though not yet fully in love – this happened during her stay in East Prussia – must have embarked on the journey not solely with misgivings but also with very considerable excitement.

Leaving these reflections aside, one returns to the elegant *berline*, lumbering over the frozen roads of northern Poland. Contemporary accounts of the weather, abstracted from Napoleon's correspondence and military records of the time, lay stress on the exceptionally late spring that year. It had been freezing hard on 6 April, snowing on the seventeenth, 'January weather on the twenty-first'. Only on 16 May does there appear a more cheerful note: 'leaves coming out at last'.

They had about ninety-three miles to cover, and Benedict

must have worried about the state of the roads further north, once they came to the clay soil of East Prussia. The log roads, over which one bumped so painfully in dry weather, became treacherous when covered with thick, slimy red mud, causing innumerable accidents from overturned carriages or broken axles. Travelling was much easier in conditions of snow and ice, when the clumsy coaches could be exchanged for swiftly-moving sledges.

They lodged the first night at Pultusk, the ancient seat of the archbishops of Plock and the scene of much of the recent fighting. Napoleon and his staff had spent the last days of the year there in a small peasant house (which still stands), poring over campaign plans. It must have been a grim stay. 'We have water coming up to our stomachs,' Napoleon wrote to his brother Joseph from Pultusk on 31 December 1806.

Benedict and Marie luckily missed the worst of the rains. Travelling about ten hours a day, stopping just long enough to exchange horses and for the midday meal, they came to the lake country of East Prussia. They passed medieval fortified castles built by the Teutonic Knights, who for over three centuries had held sway over this part of the world. The Knights were a semi-military, semi-religious organization originating with the Crusades, dedicated to the spreading of Christianity among unbelievers. They had always been a thorn in Poland's flesh, ever since the early years of the thirteenth century when a Polish Duke Conrad of Mazovia invited the Teutonic Order to protect his territories against the incursions of pagan Prussian tribes. Duke Conrad has ever since been blamed for introducing this dangerous element into Poland, for although the Knights managed to overcome the unruly tribes in less than fifty-three years – a task the Poles had been unable to accomplish in four centuries of warfare – their rule proved to be so tyrannical that the unhappy population begged the Polish kings to take them under their protection and make them part of the Polish realm. The result was an endless succession of battles between the Poles and the Order until the Knights were finally subjugated and reduced to a tiny enclave in East Prussia, which later became the nucleus of the powerful Prussian state. The picture of the Teutonic Knight, hooded, clad in black, a huge cross round his neck and a sword in his hand, burning and pillaging in the name of Christianity, had been a familiar motif in Polish folk ballads through the ages.

Now this was all French-occupied territory, patrolled by detachments of Murat's cavalry. It was the furthest point in Napoleon's European Empire, its lines of communication stretching more than six hundred miles from Paris.

As the journey progressed, Marie and her brother were frequently stopped by pickets and mounted patrols on the look-out for signs of a Russian advance. Benedict's travel orders must have had a magical effect, for at all control-points they were respectfully bidden to proceed. Osterode, where they arrived in early evening, enchanted Marie with its charming houses painted pink and pastel blue. It was a small Hanseatic town, tidy and cheerful, in the midst of so-called 'Copernicus country', for a short distance from there, in the thirteenth-century town of Frauenburg, Nicholas Copernicus had lived and carried out his astronomer's observations in the tower of the local cathedral.

Osterode, where the General Staff had been staying only a week previously, was full of bivouacking soldiers, commandeered peasant carts and army wagons. A courier was waiting for Marie with a letter signed in Napoleon's illegible hand: 'You have had bad weather, and I fear you must be tired after this interminable journey.... I pray your health has not suffered. You know how I rejoice at the thought of seeing you ... do you remember your promises? ... A most tender kiss on your beautiful mouth, Marie....' It was signed 'Napole'.

The castle of Finkenstein, which was burned by Russian troops at the close of World War II, was then an imposing feudal residence, built in the eighteenth century for a Graf von

Dohna, an official at the Court of Frederick the Great. The classical main building and the two vast wings contained at least a hundred rooms, a vast library and oak-panelled saloons, hung with the von Dohna hunting-trophies. Most rooms had huge, log-burning fireplaces, a fact which pleased the Emperor. 'We are in a fine castle with many fireplaces,' he wrote to Talleyrand shortly after moving to Finkenstein. 'I like to get up in the night and sit in front of an open fire.'

Soon after, he wrote to Marie: 'I would like to see you. . . . It's up to you. . . . Never doubt my feelings for you. . . .' Then on 5 April: 'Would you really be willing to brave the discomfort of the journey? I will see you with the greatest delight, as you can well imagine. . . . I kiss your beautiful hands and your charming mouth. Napole.'

At least a hundred staff officers lived in the main body of the castle; others camped in the extensive grounds.

I found everybody there [wrote young Anatole de Montesquiou, newly arrived at Finkenstein from Berlin with dispatches], Caulaincourt, Duroc, Lannes and Berthier – Murat strutting about in a *uniforme de fantaisie* – half of it is meant to be Polish, half Lord knows what. . . . Talleyrand is expected any moment. Louis de Périgord and Flahaut looked bored and glad to see me. They were anxious to hear the latest news of the Paris season – for it was the first time ever that they had missed it. . . . We shot duck on the two lakes in the park, and much gambling went on. . . . There was also some talk about a mysterious beauty, *'une candide beauté'*, who – rumour had it – had arrived one night *'dans une grosse berline'* and was installed in the Emperor's apartments . . . but no one knew for certain. . . .

The passing rumour died down, for no one ever managed to catch a glimpse of 'the beauty'.

Marie arrived with Benedict from Osterode just before midnight in a downpour, when no one except the posted guards was about. Benedict must have been well briefed, for he carried out his plans with military precision. As they drove to the specially designated entrance at the rear of the castle, Constant appeared in the doorway, a lighted *flambeau* in his hand, to greet Marie in the name of the Emperor.

Marie's room at Finkenstein can be reconstructed in detail, for most of the furnishings were preserved intact until 1945, when the castle was burned. We know it contained a fine canopied bed with red damask curtains, a thick carpet and a huge tiled porcelain stove, built into the thickness of the wall. Opposite the bed was a wood-burning fireplace, its cheerful glow lending gaiety to the otherwise sombre surroundings. It was kept in constant use by the Emperor himself, whose room immediately adjoined hers. Next door was a small sitting-room from which a secret door led to Napoleon's study.

In these cosy surroundings Marie spent the happiest six weeks of her life. With the exception of Constant Wairy, the valet, and Méneval, Napoleon's secretary, she saw no one, not even her brother. Nor did she have any desire to. All through the last weeks of April and rainy May she remained cloistered in her room, working on her embroidery, reading or just dreamily contemplating the fire. Her bedroom overlooked the lakes and the parade-ground. Now and then. carefully hidden behind a curtain, she watched the military bustle going on, a lonely, discreet spectator unnoticed by the world outside.

Napoleon spent every free moment with her. They breakfasted together in bed, a habit he had never acquired with Josephine, who liked to sleep late. Their meals were served to them by Constant on a small map-table by the fire; and he liked to dictate his letters to Méneval in her presence.

From his distant castle on the Baltic, six hundred miles away from the Tuileries, Napoleon governed his far-flung empire of seventy million people by letter, law and decree. He was always as much at home in his study with parchment and ink as he was on the battlefield. As he himself used to say, 'I am fitted for both : active and sedentary service.' He could deal with complex legal problems, issue administrative decrees and promulgate new laws while sitting on a camp-chair by a bivouac fire on the eve of a battle. For in addition to current campaign plans, army musters and quartermasters' reports, the whole mass of infinite details relating to the vast administrative structure of his lands had also to be attended to. Endless couriers, half-asleep from exhaustion, changing horses at least thirty times since leaving France, dashed incessantly between Paris and the army's headquarters carrying the famous cabinet-boxes. These were leather briefcases with the words 'Dépêche de l'Empereur' engraved on them. Carefully packed and locked by Lavalette, Napoleon's secretary in Paris, they were handed rapidly from man to man until they reached the headquarters. Méneval had the other key. On arrival the briefcase was rushed to the Emperor, wherever he happened to be at the time: even in the midst of a battle he was known to tear open the box and avidly read its contents.

It was the same at Finkenstein. Every day couriers left for Paris, Rome, Amsterdam, Milan or distant Naples, carrying letters, orders, decrees on the widest variety of subjects. Elderly state officials from the Council of State in Paris were asked to undertake the terrifying journey from one end of Europe to the other, in the very depths of the winter, to report to the Emperor on the functioning of their ministries.

According to the records of his correspondence, in the spring of 1807 Napoleon wrote over three hundred letters, and most of them were sent out from Finkenstein.

4 April: Napoleon to his brother Louis, King of Holland: 'You govern your nation like a docile, timorous monk.... A king issues orders and does not beg.... You had better apply those paternalistic, effeminate traits you display in governing your country to your domestic life and use the inflexibility for which you are known in your marriage in the affairs of the state....' And again to Louis a few days later: '... A prince of whom they say: "he is a jolly good fellow" is lost as a king....'

19 April: Napoleon to Regnault, Minister of the Interior, in Paris: 'Something is missing in a well-run state if a diligent

young man is unable to obtain advice on what he is best fit to study and is forced to waste months, or even years, on false starts. The *Collège de France* has been set up; it is functioning well; it now ought to be enlarged and some kind of career advisory service established. . . .' There followed observations on a new project: the possible establishment of two new chairs in literature and history, at the Collège de France.

20 April: Napoleon to Regnault, Minister of the Interior, in Paris: 'I am writing to the Minister of Police [Fouché] on the subject of that foolish woman Madame de Staël. . . . She is to remain in Geneva and must be forbidden to travel abroad, where she can only cause mischief.'

6 May: to Napoleon Joseph, King of Naples: 'My brother: when you start issuing new money, please make sure that it is of the same value as the French currency. I have already sent orders to this effect to my Italian kingdom and the Confederation of the Rhine. . . . I want the whole of Europe to have one currency: it will make trading much easier. . . .'

16 May: Napoleon to his brother Jerome, who was suffering from piles: 'The best way to make them disappear is to apply leeches . . . three or four will do. I myself applied this remedy ten years ago and have not been bothered since. . . .'

16 May: note on a new school for the daughters of the recipients of the Légion d'Honneur:

What will the young ladies at Ecouen be learning? You must start with religion; I want them to be brought up as believers and not as philosophers. They then ought to learn arithmetic, and read and write of course, good spelling is very important . . . they ought to know something of geography and a smattering of history, but make sure they are not taught any Latin and no foreign languages, please. . . . But above all they must learn domestic crafts: sewing, embroidery, cooking of course. . . . It is necessary for them to learn how to dance – for it is also good for their health. . . . I also recommend the teaching of music. . . .

The letters went on and on, on the widest diversity of subjects.

The room where he worked had deeply-recessed windows framed by red-velvet curtains. A log fire burned in the ornate fireplace, casting flickering shadows on the high ceiling. While Napoleon dictated, often restlessly pacing the floor, occasionally helping himself to pinches of snuff from his little gold box, Marie sat in a corner bent over her embroidery, quietly listening.

Marie was twenty years old and had not, until now, known the meaning of love. Whatever romantic stirrings she might have felt for young Suvorov must have gradually been erased by her three years of marriage to an old man. In Warsaw she had suffered from shock, when her long-idolized hero was suddenly transformed into an aggressive lover. Though her newly awakened body had instinctively responded to him, it nevertheless took a long time for her mind to catch up. There was also the feeling of guilt towards her son and her husband, and the knowledge that she had sinned in the eyes of her Church. It was all very confusing.

But here, in the peace and seclusion of her room at the castle, cut off from the rest of the world by a barrier of absolute secrecy, she found herself living in the closest intimacy with the most remarkable man of the age, the man she had hero-worshipped since childhood, who had come and claimed her for his own and whose passion she now fully returned. No wonder Marie abandoned her struggle; this time her surrender was complete. 'I really felt I was married to him,' she later told Elizabeth Sobolewska, her friend. The very fact that her lover happened to be the all-powerful Emperor on whose word the future of her country depended added an even deeper dimension to her feelings and helped to erase the vestiges of guilt that remained.

Loving Napoleon as she did, selflessly (all she wanted was freedom for Poland), Marie came to understand the one, curiously immature side of his nature: his need for reassurance in the sexual sphere. Coming from the great conqueror, she found it touching; it appealed to her tenderness, and, being the kind of woman she was, it made her love him even more. She was able to reassure him, and this alone set her apart from all other women in his life.

Napoleon's fear of, even obsession with, impotence, went back a long way. Though inordinately proud of his smooth skin, silky hair and finely shaped small hands and feet, he had always worried about what he called his 'feebleness in the game of love' ('*la faiblesse dans le déduit d'amour*'). Walter Henry, the British army surgeon, who, together with Antommarchi, Napoleon's doctor, assisted at the post-mortem examination of Napoleon's body at St Helena, wrote in his report: 'The private parts were seen to be remarkably small, like a boy's.' It was a condition connected with a deficiency of the pituitary gland.

Napoleon's physical shortcomings were well known in the army. On campaigns he bathed outside his tent in full sight of the troops and his physique was commented on in bawdy language by his generals and his soldiers, but it did not seem to detract from his stature. Caulaincourt in his Memoirs quotes an often-repeated joke circulating among the soldiers, to the effect that the Emperor carried his '*amours*' in his head.

At the beginning of their marriage Josephine had wounded him deeply by circulating the cruel quip, 'Bonaparte – *bon à rien*'; and her well-publicized affair with Captain Charles drove him to protracted philandering. To the conqueror of men, virility was of supreme importance, as was the founding of a dynasty. As years went by and no children appeared, and his affaires became more and more superficial, Napoleon became convinced not only that he was sterile but that he could not even give proper physical satisfaction to a woman. His approach coarsened, as women came to him because of the benefits they hoped to derive from the association. He gradually became immune to the sniggering and rumours behind his back. It did not matter; he paid them, and that was enough. One of those fleeting affaires was with Eléonore Denuelle, a promiscuous young woman, lady-in-waiting to Caroline Murat, his sister. A child was born at the time of that brief liaison, a boy, allegedly fathered by Napoleon. In the normal course of events he would have been elated but, unfortunately, rumour had it that Eléonore used to confer her favours on Murat at about the same time as on the Emperor; so the cruel doubt remained.

Marie was too innocent to rate the physical performance of her lover, but even had she been more experienced, it would not have mattered to her. She loved the man, and she worshipped the Emperor as the future liberator of her country. Her surrender to him was complete, unlike that of any other woman in his life. His hidden anxieties – once she sensed them – only deepened her love and released immense tenderness. Her reassurance, and later the child that she bore him, helped to remove the fear that had plagued him for years. It set him on a dynastic quest which changed the history of the Empire and of Europe.

For Napoleon, the idyll amid the lakes and forests of East Prussia was also a unique experience. What in Warsaw had been a burst of sheer carnal desire, fuelled by Marie's reticence, underwent a profound change at Finkenstein and, as he later said in his Memoirs, became his one 'real *affaire du cœur*'.

Here at last was the woman he had long been searching for. Years earlier, as a very young man, when courting Eugénie Clary, later known as Désirée, he had written *Clisson and Eugénie*, a romantic novel in which he alluded to his 'unusual nature' and hoped it might be changed 'by the love of a woman, a warm-hearted companion, who would love him for himself and bear him children'. Marie fitted that image perfectly. And in addition she was beautiful, graceful in everything she did and said, a good, intelligent listener, and – not the least in Napoleon's scale of values – she came from an old aristocratic family. 'She is an angel,' he wrote to his brother Lucien from Finkenstein. 'Her soul is as beautiful as her features.' And to his earthy brother Joseph he boasted: 'My health has never been better. . . . I have become a very good lover . . . these days.'

He jealously guarded their privacy. One morning, Berthier, the Chief of Staff, came into the Emperor's bedroom and, seeing two cups of chocolate on a tray, permitted himself a bawdy remark. Napoleon was outraged and dismissed him with a curt, 'Marshal, it is none of your business. Get out.' It taught Berthier to be careful in using his privileged right of entry to the Emperor's private sanctum.

As always at imperial headquarters, the castle was a beehive of activity, of endless comings and goings; foreign envoys, French and German dignitaries, Polish officers and notables – some of whom were personal friends of the Walewskis – kept arriving all through Marie's stay. And of course there was brother Benedict, who, though sworn to strict secrecy, could not always be trusted to keep from boasting, particularly when he had several vodkas inside him.

Marie imposed a rigorous discipline on herself. Throughout the whole of her stay she never once left her rooms; she did not even dare to look out of the window, except through gaps in the shutters. Her bedroom overlooked the parade-ground, and from her hiding-place she liked to watch Napoleon reviewing the troops in the morning. But that was about her only distraction. And yet, as she later recounted to her friends, 'I was supremely happy all that time.'

Corvisart, Napoleon's doctor, tells us something about the Emperor's daily routine, which varied, of course, according to where he happened to be. So it is possible to reconstruct some features of Napoleon's day at Finkenstein from his own correspondence, Constant's Memoirs and Corvisart's routine observations.

Napoleon liked to get up early, for, as he said, 'At dawn the brain is keenest.' He would sit in front of the fire, drink a cup of orange-water and look at the latest reports before getting into a very hot bath, where he remained for at least an hour. He adored hot baths and log fires: 'A bath is worth four hours' sleep,' he often said.

After his bath, Napoleon put on a flannel vest and trousers and began to shave. While Constant held the looking-glass, Napoleon lathered his face with soap scented with herbs and orange and, using a Birmingham razor with a mother-of-pearl handle, shaved his face meticulously. When he had finished he asked Constant whether it was all right. After shaving he washed his hands with almond paste, and his face, neck and ears with a sponge and soap; he brushed his teeth with toothpaste, then with finely powdered coral – his teeth were beautiful and always in excellent condition. Finally he rinsed his mouth with a mixture of water and brandy and scraped his tongue with a silver scraper. The *toilette* ended with the Emperor stripping to the waist and Constant pouring eau-de-Cologne all over him and 'frictioning his chest and arms with a hard-bristled brush'. Like his mother, Napoleon had a fetish about personal cleanliness and demanded it from others. Doctor Corvisart recalled how super-sensitive the Emperor was to bad smells: he claimed to be able to detect an odour even if it came from a distant cellar, and sewers were a constant source of irritation to him.

In the meantime Marie dressed slowly without the usual assistance of her maid. It was the first time in her adult life that she had travelled anywhere unattended. Her morning was spent according to Napoleon's programme for that day; if he held a parade outside, she watched it from a secret vantage-point. They lunched at about eleven at a small mahogany map-table; dinner was at about seven; now and then Napoleon left her after dinner for a game of *vingt-et-un* with his generals, at which the Emperor, as was his habit, invariably cheated. On some nights he dictated to Méneval until late, but more usually he called for bed by eleven, and the candles were blown out.

Constant, who was closest to them in those weeks, wrote about Napoleon's growing admiration for Marie: 'Her noble character, her serenity and her amazing lack of self-interest enchanted the Emperor. . . . Each day he became more and more attached to her.'

When the envoy of the Shah of Persia arrived at the castle with gifts of priceless cashmere shawls for the Emperor's household – a treasured item in the feminine wardrobe of the time, comparable with a sable coat in our day – Napoleon asked

Marie to choose several. Sensing that they were meant for the Empress, she refused, but finally after much persuasion she accepted a pale blue one, the least valuable of them all, 'because she would like to offer it as a present to a friend, who liked blue.'

Such lack of self-interest impressed Napoleon. 'Your men are brave and faithful allies,' he told her, 'and the women are beautiful and disinterested. It makes for a fine nation. I promise to do my best to restore your independence.' But when she, greatly moved, thanked him warmly, he rapidly became non-committal: 'Ah, ah, *this* particular present you would have accepted without hesitation ... but wait, Marie, you must be *patient*. . . . Politics is a slow business, it is not as easy as winning a battle. . . . You must give me more time.'

How much more time, she wondered.

Out of her bedroom window Marie watched the skeleton tree-tops beginning to fill out: they acquired a pinkish tinge, which gradually changed to golden green. Daffodils appeared in the grass; the geese on the pond in the grounds had gone back to their northern breeding-grounds. With the advent of spring the hostilities were once more resumed. It was time to leave Finkenstein.

She left as she had arrived – in the night, in a closed carriage, escorted by brother Benedict, who accompanied her all the way before rejoining his regiment at the front. She had decided not to go back to Warsaw, but to return to Kiernozia, her childhood home, and await developments there. Napoleon had asked her to 'promise she would join him in Paris in the winter'.

6

A VISIT TO PARIS

Napoleon's Polish campaign ended in triumph. On 14 June, at Friedland, as the high summer sun slowly sank in the Baltic, the Russian armies suffered a devastating defeat. With over thirty thousand men killed and taken prisoner – twenty-five generals among them – and famous guards regiments crushed or annihilated, Tsar Alexander's proud army virtually ceased to exist. He sued for peace.

Napoleon was exultant. General Marbot describes how, in his joy, the Emperor galloped at full speed towards the Niemen, the fast-flowing river which formed the boundary between Russia and the West. He reined in his horse on the high bank and stood there gazing eastwards, his silhouette outlined against the silvery beeches of the forest. His soldiers feared that he might want to pursue the enemy into Russia.

But Napoleon realized that Russia was only temporarily defeated, not conquered; it might be wiser to turn her into an ally, for he needed her help in the struggle with England, the one adversary he so far had been unable to cripple. By joining his Continental blockade, Russia – as a sea power – could effectively stifle English commerce on the seas. When Prince Lobanov, the Tsar's peace-emissary, arrived, Napoleon proposed that a personal meeting between the sovereigns should take place.

On Thursday, 25 June, a cloudy, thundery day, the two

Emperors met at Tilsit on a raft constructed by French engineers and moored on the river in midstream. It bore a magnificently decorated pavilion worthy of the memorable scene which was to take place inside it. Setting off from opposite banks, the two Emperors reached the raft simultaneously. They embraced. Alexander, the thirty-year-old blonde giant, in a black uniform with red lapels, white breeches, and a hat decorated with white plumes, towered over Napoleon in his simple grey-green field-tunic. They conferred for over two hours, while the unfortunate Frederick William, King of Prussia, waited on the river bank in the rain. He had been contemptuously left out while the victorious Emperor of the West and the vanquished Emperor of the East discoursed on how to carve up the lands between the Baltic and the Bosphorus.

The first two meetings went well, and soon the raft was dismantled, and the village of Tilsit declared neutral. Alexander and his suite moved into a row of wooden houses near the river. For over a week the Tsar and the French Emperor talked, dined together and went riding into the countryside. It was soon evident that the men had fallen under each other's spell. 'If Alexander were a woman,' Napoleon wrote to Josephine after their first meeting, 'I would make him my mistress.' An odd assessment. Did he foresee the betrayal that was to follow the courtship? 'Here I am, spending my days with Bonaparte,' reported Alexander to his mother, 'hours and hours at a time; it is like something out of a dream.' Neither the Tsar's mother nor the majority of the people of Russia shared their ruler's enthusiasm.

In Poland, the news of the unexpected Franco-Russian honeymoon, coming so rapidly after the resounding victory at Friedland, was greeted with utter dismay. After such a courtship, the terms of the peace treaty with Russia were bound to be generous – which would be a disaster for Poland.

They were a disaster. The only territorial possessions the Tsar was asked to renounce were his recent gains in Dalmatia and the Ionian Sea. He lost none of the Polish territories in the west that

Catherine II had annexed fifteen years previously. On the contrary, he was given the formerly Polish Bialystok, thus adding a prosperous town province to his lands. He had to agree, however, to the creation of a small, semi-independent new state, the Grand Duchy of Warsaw, put together from lands formerly held by Prussia. The new Grand Duchy was 1,860 square miles in area (about nine hundred square miles were added to it in 1809 from the formerly Austrian-held lands) and it had about two and a half million inhabitants. Napoleon's friend and ally, Frederick Augustus, King of Saxony was to be its ruler. It would have its own Polish administration and French laws but retain Prussian currency – all in all a strange, hybrid political creation. It was, of course, a compromise in order to keep Tsar Alexander happy but a dismally feeble response to the expectations of the thousands of Polish soldiers who had perished fighting for the glory of Napoleon. It mattered little to the Poles that the Emperor had managed to wrest some far-flung Mediterranean islands for France and that the Tsar had promised to join the blockade against England. The loss of the rich district of Bialystok to the Russians hurt the Polish land-owners in that province and terrified the families of the soldiers who, only six months previously, had answered Napoleon's stirring appeal to arms. Now their men were going to hang and their women be deported or thrown into prison. Indeed, after only a couple of months – notwithstanding the provisions of the Tilsit agreement – the Tsar's police moved in and retribution began.

Spirits sank throughout Poland. The bubbling enthusiasm of the winter gave way to widespread disappointment. The truncated Grand Duchy was hardly the independent Poland Napoleon had promised to restore. Had all the sacrifices been in vain? All through Tilsit the Polish Provisional Government had been kept ignorant of the details of the negotiations. When Stanislaus Potocki, relying on his personal friendship with Talleyrand, travelled to Tilsit to discover what was going on, he found the Foreign Minister 'silently non-committal, more sarcastic than ever, and vaguely embarrassed.'

When the truth became known, the population was indignant. Warsaw, fed on rumours emanating from the General Army Headquarters, was in such a turmoil that the Provisional Government had to issue a proclamation. It begged people not to believe in 'fables spread by our enemies'. It exhorted them to put their faith in the Emperor 'for he is the only hope we have left', a pathetic admission on the part of much-tried politicians. In July Vincent, the French Minister in Warsaw, writing to Talleyrand, who by then had returned to Paris, expressed his mounting concern:

There is still much unrest here, displeasure, mixed with bewilderment.... Every day brings in news which causes further distress.... The loss of Bialystok is deeply resented, as is the cession of the lower Vistula lands to the defeated Prussians.... I urge you to speed up the negotiations that are still going on in Dresden, so the Grand Duchy could formally come into being.

For Poland the glorious Napoleonic legend had temporarily lost its glamour, but not for long. The irrepressible optimism of the Poles reasserted itself the moment the Grand Duchy of Warsaw became a functioning unit and its frontiers were stabilized. Of course it was not what everyone had hoped for. It was hardly the ideal solution, still it was the first step on the road back to independence. There was no other choice – Napoleon *was* the only hope. Having hitched the destiny of the country to his star, it was now too late to alter course.

Marie was at Kiernozia, her childhood home, where she patiently awaited the expected summons from her lover. She was confident that it would come. Napoleon's letters, delivered through the French Minister's office in Warsaw, were characteristically brief and dealt mostly with current affairs. He wrote to her from Danzig, after the Baltic fortress finally surrendered to Lefèbvre, and on the morning after the victory of Friedland in mid-June, the same day as he wrote to the Empress Josephine. From Tilsit he headed directly for Dresden, where the constitution of the Duchy of Warsaw was to be signed and the new state, under its Saxon Grand Duke, formally ushered into being. For a while Marie hoped that she might be summoned to Dresden. Like the majority of her compatriots, she had been bitterly disappointed by the result of the Tilsit peace treaty and badly wanted some word of reassurance from the Emperor to pass on to her friends. But Dresden was to be only a very brief stop for the Emperor – barely three or four days – and the entire Polish Provisional Government would be there to discuss the final points of the constitution. Napoleon let it be known that it would be better for the Countess Walewska to stay away.

She rightly sensed that Napoleon's attention was now totally directed towards France; he had been absent from Paris for ten months and was in a great hurry to get back. Knowing him as she did, she understood his impatience, but how was she to cope with the constant yearning for his presence?

On 27 July 1807 the boom of cannon from the Invalides announced to the citizens of Paris that their victorious master had returned from the wars. Calmly triumphant, he had returned to rule France. The people around him were struck by his resemblance to the Roman emperors, as depicted on old coins. He was now ready to lay down the sword of the Commander-in-Chief in favour of the mantle of the Prime Minister. He wished to govern. 'As a despot,' whispered some of his enemies.

'It is not necessary to compare me with God,' he lightly tossed aside to Decrès, one of his ministers, in reply to a particularly fulsome tribute. Within twenty-four hours of his arrival at the Tuileries, Napoleon had resumed his usual working routine: audiences started at eight; work went on long into the night.

On 29 July he found time to write to Marie. Her nameday, the day of her patron saint, the Virgin Mary, fell on 15 August. This was also the day of his thirty-eighth birthday. He wrote a tender and affectionate letter, telling her how much she was being missed and that he would 'soon' ask her to join him in Paris. With the letter he sent a diamond and sapphire bracelet and – an even more precious present – a medallion with his portrait on it. Marie deposited the bracelet in a drawer but pinned the medallion on her dress, where she would be conscious of it all the time. Her confidence was restored; she now knew that it was only a question of time before she would be summoned to Paris.

She continued to live at Kiernozia with her mother, her two-year-old son Anthony and her young sister. Theodore, her second brother, was living on one of the adjoining farms. There had been no formal separation from Anastase, though she had fully expected him to divorce her when she returned from Finkenstein in late May. Instead he had announced that he was leaving for Austria to take a cure at Bad Gastein and would then proceed to Italy, where – according to Princess Jablonowska, his niece – he planned to remain all winter. All three of the old Chamberlain's nieces were in fact urging Marie to return to Walewice and resume her place in the big house. They were secretly proud of what they referred to as her 'historic mission for Poland'. Princess Jablonowska in particular, gay, worldly and fond of men, rather bored with her country existence, looked forward to having Marie back at the castle. But Marie was not going to expose her innermost feelings to the prurient appetites of Anastase's frivolous relations. She expected to be summoned to Paris at any moment and, in the meantime, the less explaining the better.

She remained at Kiernozia with her mother, spending hours at the harpsichord, reading plays by Corneille because Napoleon so admired them, and helping her mother in the daily round of housekeeping and general entertaining. Eva, the over-ambitious mother, had at first been perplexed by the dizzying heights of success scaled by her notoriously shy daughter. She had been somewhat embarrassed by the obliquely worded congratulations of her neighbours and some caustic remarks from her friends. It seemed that only one person, the notorious Henriette de Vauban, regarded Marie's stay at Finkenstein as an honour for the family and the country. Eva was also quite fond of

Anastase, who had always been very pleasant to her, had paid all the farm's debts and before leaving Walewice had made careful provisions for Marie. She hoped that, in spite of everything that had happened, her daughter's marriage would continue, and she did not want Anastase ridiculed. More realistic than Marie, she expected the great romance to dissolve after Napoleon's departure from Poland.

But the Emperor's thoughtful attention on the occasion of Marie's nameday pointed in a different direction. Eva saw that, after an interval of doubt on Marie's part, he had again taken possession of her daughter's mind. Eva Laczynska, sensible woman that she was, decided to leave the future to fate. Europe was in a turmoil; violent changes were everywhere taking place; and all of them would affect Poland. What else was there to do but to wait and in the meantime see to it that children were well looked after, fields tended, farm accounts supervised and friendships kept in repair?

Through the golden month of September and the rainy autumn that followed, Marie remained at Kiernozia – waiting. Thanks to her elder brother Benedict, now attached to Berthier's staff and temporarily stationed in Paris, she was kept informed of the movements of her imperial lover. She knew he had gone to Italy in November; she had heard of the pressure he had been exerting on the Pope to join his blockade against England. This worried her. A conflict between Napoleon and the Holy See would test her loyalties to the limit.

In December 1807, as he was about to cross the Mount Cenis Pass on his way from Italy back to Paris, Napoleon sent a courier to Warsaw with despatches which included a letter to Marie. With his best wishes for the New Year was an invitation to join him in Paris shortly after the beginning of the year.

A traveller crossing the continent of Europe in the early months of the year 1808 remained on French-controlled territory all the way from the Russian border on the Niemen through the near thousand miles to Paris. Imperial eagles could be seen everywhere: they flew from military depots in Poland and East Prussia, as far north as faraway Lithuania; they accompanied the flags of the separate German states, now united in a French-protected Confederation of the Rhine; they were seen throughout Belgium and in King Louis Bonaparte's Holland. Troop-transports clogged the main highways; *estafettes* – the mounted couriers who carried imperial orders and dispatches – streaked by to their far-away destinations.

To Marie, travelling with her maid, the journey must have been immensely exciting. Heading west from Kiernozia they stopped at Dresden, where Frederick Augustus of Saxony, Poland's new Chief of State, held his sumptuous baroque court. Then they went on to Leipzig, Erfurt, Weimar, crossing the Rhine at Mayence. When, after ten days of travel, their coach pulled up in front of an inn at Mayence, Marie realized for the first time that they were actually in France.

Around them lay the vast, rich countryside peopled by thirty-seven million Frenchmen, whose sacrifices had sustained the most prodigious military adventure of the age. The security of their homes, the happiness of their hearths, the temper of the countryside, even the atmosphere of the Paris salons – all remained at the mercy of the Emperor. Every *Te Deum* at Notre Dame, every victory salvo at the Invalides, exacted its own bitter price. The cost of glory determined the price of everyday bread, and the Paris Stock Exchange fluctuated according to the bulletins of the *Grand Armée*. The *tricorne* cast its shadow over the wall of every inhabited house in the land. In that winter of 1808 peace was every Frenchman's fervent dream.

From Mayence Marie proceeded on the well-travelled highway to the capital. Police records, which would undoubtedly have registered the date of her arrival in Paris that February, were destroyed in the fire at the time of the Paris Commune, but there is a note in the Archives de la Seine that a house at 2, rue de la Houssaye was taken for her by Duroc in early February of that year. Benedict was then living on the Quay Voltaire and was shortly to depart for Spain with his regiment; but it would have been quite natural if Napoleon had wanted Marie to have her own establishment in Paris, away from brotherly super-vision and Polish gossip.

Benedict and Duroc met her at the last relay before Paris. Marie had not seen her brother for some months. He had greatly annoyed her at Finkenstein, when – over-confident of his 'inside line' to Napoleon – he took part in a political intrigue to remove Prince Joseph Poniatowski from his post in command of the Polish forces. The plot was frustrated by Murat, who personally intervened with the Emperor. It was lucky that Marie happened to be with Napoleon at the time the 'cabale' was exposed, for she might easily have been implicated in her brother's machina-tions. Napoleon, who detested intrigues, was annoyed at this further example of inter-faction quarrelling among Poles, of which Rulhière's book had warned him. He did not immediately cancel Benedict's assignment to Berthier's staff, but on 1 November of the same year the over-zealous colonel found him-self in command of the third regiment of Polish lancers, destined for fighting in Spain, far removed from the centre of power, Court and military intrigues. From then on he served in line regiments; his role as Marie's escort and adviser was taken up by Theodore, the younger brother.

It would have been reassuring for Marie to see Marshal Duroc, the gentle, beautifully mannered Master of the Imperial Household and Napoleon's intimate friend, who had been such a tactful go-between in the early days of her romance in Warsaw. Slim and dark, and what would have been considered 'tall and elegant' in those days, Géraud Duroc was three years older than Napoleon. He came from an old family in Lorraine and had been with Napoleon since his first Italian campaign. After Napoleon became Emperor no one outside his family was allowed to address him in the familiar *tu* form – even in private – except Lannes and Duroc; his devotion to the Emperor was centred on Napoleon more as an individual than as a monarch. As Grand Marshal of the Palace, Duroc supervised every detail of the Emperor's safety, his food, amusements and social life, often to the annoyance of Josephine, who felt herself excluded. In the Tuileries he had a small bedroom next to the Emperor's and used to accompany him on his incognito walks through Paris. They understood each other perfectly: Marie well remembered the private sign-language between the Emperor and Duroc, which had struck her as so extraordinarily schoolboyish in Warsaw. She liked the Grand Marshal and felt comfortable in his presence. He in turn would have found her refreshingly different from the usual galaxy of females striving for the favours of the Sovereign.

Duroc escorted Marie to her temporary residence at 2, rue de la Houssaye. This is now rue Taitbout but the house itself does not exist any more. It was a small eighteenth-century townhouse in the then fashionable quarter of Notre Dame de Lorette. At the time of purchase it was somewhat erratically furnished but provided with a full staff of servants. It was only two and a half years later, when she returned to Paris from Poland after the birth of her son, that Marie had the time to organize it as her permanent residence. She lived there until 1814, when she moved to the rue de la Victoire. All we know of the rue de la Houssaye residence is that the bedroom walls were covered with blue linen material (it must have been *toile de Jouy*) and that there were two very fine Boucaut armchairs in the drawing-room and a splendid Coromandel screen in red lacquer – all probably sent by Napoleon.

There are no letters from or to Marie from that period: she was not a natural writer and, unlike the romantic heroines of some twenty-five years later, had no overwhelming urge to confide her feelings to paper. Still, it is not difficult to imagine what effect the Paris of that day – the effervescent capital of an empire in the full flowering of its power – must have had on the young, unsophisticated Polish woman, arriving there for the first time in her life. And she had not arrived as a tourist, or even as a distinguished visitor: she came at the invitation of her lover, the Emperor in whom all power and all splendour were vested.

It would have been customary for a lady of Countess Walewska's rank to have been presented at Court when in Paris, and Napoleon undoubtedly suggested it. But Marie wisely decided to remain in the background. One factor was the briefness of her stay in the capital. She arrived in early February and – according to Polish contemporary diarists – was back in Warsaw by 28 March, 'attending an evening reception'. But probably more important was her natural reluctance to confront Josephine. Marie had none of the brashness of an Eleonore Denuelle, Caroline Murat's lady-in-waiting, or the worldly self-assurance of the famous Mademoiselle George, the actress, who had publicly flaunted her liaison with the Emperor. She knew that Josephine had been told of her husband's idyll in Poland and – though Duroc assured her that she would be 'most graciously received by the Empress' (Josephine had indeed expressed curiosity about her) – Marie decided to remain tactfully in the background. Three years later the two women were to become close friends. The repudiated Empress, pursuing her solitary existence at Malmaison, came to appreciate and respect the soft-spoken, sensitive Polish Countess and her disinterested love for her ex-husband, who by then had betrayed both of them for the sake of his dynastic ambitions.

But all this was still in the future. In the meantime she needed to accustom herself to this new cosmopolitan environment and to organize her house so as to be available at short notice whenever the Emperor wished to see her. After all, this was what she had been living for all those months.

She also needed to acquire some fashionable new clothes. Napoleon attached great importance to the way women dressed. The chronicles of the Empire period abound with agonizing reminiscences of various ladies at the Courts of Tuileries and St Cloud who had suffered from his withering criticism if for some reason their costume displeased him. His remarks could be wounding – and sometimes downright rude, particularly if he happened to be in bad humour. With Marie – as she once confided to her sister-in-law – he invariably noticed what she wore the moment she came through the door. Could there be any better reason for her to visit Monsieur Leroy, the most fashionable couturier of the day?

Following the upheavals of the Revolution, *la mode* in France underwent an equally drastic reversal. Parisians who had fled from Robespierre's terror, and who were returning to France in the first year or two of the century, were amazed at the extraordinary spectacle the once-familiar streets now presented to them. Who were all these nymph-like creatures, who called themselves *les Merveilleuses*? They wore transparent muslin dresses, tied with silken cords under the bosom, revealing their heavily rouged nipples. With bare feet shod in Greek-style cothurni, they could be seen gingerly side-stepping the filth of those same old Paris streets, unchanged for two centuries and still, by the early 1800s, mostly without pavements. And all those dandified men, the *Incroyables*, with their affected looks of untidy old age, their spectacles, unkempt hair, baggy trousers, necks swaddled in high collars and flowing cravats – 'Who are they?' the *émigrés* asked themselves. 'This extravagantly baroque crowd, speaking in totally incomprehensible accents, seemed to us, returnees from the *ancien régime*, like a mass of visitors from the moon who had landed on our planet just in time for the carnival,' wrote the diarist, Victorine de Chastenay.

With the establishment of the Empire, the *mascarade gallante* – as the Parisian public called it – underwent a gradual transformation. The new master desired that women of his entourage set an example of conservative good taste. The beautiful Thérèse Tallien found herself publicly reprimanded for appearing at the Opera dressed as the goddess Diana – in other words, half-naked. One evening at the Luxembourg, while still First Consul, it suddenly struck Napoleon that Josephine's ladies were very scantily clad. He started heaping logs on the fire. *Ces dames*, he declared, 'must be freezing.' The hint was obvious to all, and changes were rapidly made.

By the time of Napoleon's coronation, the metamorphosis was complete, and what later became known as the Empire fashion had found its final outline: the waist remained very high, the sleeves were always short and puffed up, the skirt straight but revealing the figure. Hair was worn in ringlets, adorned with ribbons and precious stones. With this went thin-soled Greek sandals, their ribbons crossed and held above the calf by a gold acorn. It was a hard fashion for some women: there were no corsets, nothing to support an ample *poitrine*, no way to add inches to one's stature. 'No way to cheat nature, any more,' complained the Duchesse d'Abrantès. 'These days a plain woman tends to look even plainer, and a woman with a bad figure is lost. It is only the slender ones with a mass of hair and a small bosom who triumph. A very deplorable fashion.' For the majority of the French population, of course, it did not exist, but for the few, for whom throughout history fashion has always primarily been designed, it became a way of life which lasted for over ten years.

All fashion demands occasion to provide a foil to its wearers, and in the years of the Empire it found it around the Court of the new Caesar, for Napoleon decreed that his entourage should be as dazzling as the courtiers of the old European monarchies.

Luckily for Josephine, and for the women around her, a designer came forth of a talent equal to that of the famous Rose Bertin who had dressed the last queen and the ladies of Versailles. His name was Antoine Leroy, and he was a talented, though exceedingly temperamental man. From his establishment at 89, rue de la Loi, at the corner of the rue Ménars (his house is now a bookshop), came the most splendid creations, all in the same Empire style but different in textures, embroideries, colours and mood. He was a master at capturing each woman's individual type. The Empress Josephine adored him and thought nothing of spending as much as three thousand francs on a dress

E

– an enormous sum in those days. It was essential to wear Leroy's clothes if one aspired to being at all fashionable.

He dressed them all: the three sisters of the Emperor – Caroline Murat, the future Queen of Naples, Elisa Bacciochi, the ruler of Tuscany, and the lovely Pauline, Princess Camillo Borghese – and Hortense de Beauharnais, Josephine's daughter, married to King Louis of Holland. He even dressed Madame Mère, whose *toilette* as portrayed in David's painting of the coronation had been universally admired. Leroy's messengers, carrying huge cardboard boxes, drove their fast-moving cabriolets across Europe's frontiers, delivering festive *toilettes* to Courts at Cassel, Naples, Madrid, Lucca, the Hague, even as far away as Dresden. When Napoleon had returned to Paris from Tilsit, he sent Tsar Alexander a present of a Sèvres dinner-service and enclosed a carton of Leroy's dresses for the Tsar's mistress, Elizabeth Antonovna. 'I chose them myself,' he informed the Russian ambassador. 'You know I have a good understanding of fashion.'

Leroy amassed a large fortune and retired in splendid opulence when the Empire collapsed. He was a capricious and irascible man and a gambler, who often spent half the night in the gambling casinos of the Palais Royal. He had violent likes and dislikes and did not hesitate to send a client away if her behaviour displeased him. The unfortunate Madame Lannes, wife of the Marshal, found she had been 'dismissed' when she complained that she had been kept waiting for a fitting. Not even Empress Josephine's intervention managed to restore her to Leroy's grace. He relented only when, as Duchess of Montebello, she became lady-in-waiting to the Empress Marie Louise. As for the earthy Madame Lefèbvre, the 'Madame Sans-Gêne' of Empire society, Leroy, with outrageous insolence, let it be known that she was simply 'too common and too fat to do justice to his clothes'.

This 'Napoleon of fashion' took a great liking to Marie. There was only enough time to acquire one outfit and two *negligées* while she was in Paris on this first visit, but visiting Leroy's salon was like attending an academy of fashion and deportment. The master-couturier combined the talents of a designer with those of a hairdresser and make-up artist, and one emerged from his salon with one's looks greatly enhanced. Under his guidance Marie's beauty became more refined, her skin, after she learned light make-up, more dazzling, and her blonde hair more lustrous. As her self-assurance increased, her impact on people heightened. It must have amused Napoleon to watch his 'little Polish patriot' turning into a sophisticated Parisienne.

Though she loved being in Napoleon's Paris, Marie often missed the cloistered existence of her days at Finkenstein. Here the Emperor could give her only tiny snatches of his time – in between audiences or late at night. It was Duroc who accompanied her to the Opera and to the Théâtre Français, where the great actor Talma reigned supreme. That particular winter, in fact, Talma starred in a play with a Polish theme, called *Waclaw*, featuring a romantic Polish nobleman and his down-to-earth, supremely capable French bride. It was the hit of the season. Marie much enjoyed the lavishly staged production, the splendid costumes and the meticulous care with which the atmosphere of Warsaw was portrayed in the play.

At the Opera Duroc's box was across the stage from that of the Emperor. Napoleon rarely occupied it, but the graceful figure of Josephine, wearing one of Leroy's latest creations, lent it infinite elegance.

From time to time Duroc and Marie were joined at the theatre by Marie's Polish friends, officers stationed at nearby Chantilly. They belonged to the famous Polish Lancers, three élite volunteer regiments formed from the country's 'golden youth', equipped at their own expense. They were all enthusiastic and spirited, prepared to fight for Napoleon and for Poland 'anywhere on the surface of the globe'. Their first assignment was Spain – Napoleon's most disastrous venture.

In the winter of 1808, when the balance-sheet of the Empire, with its huge assets of people and territories and military manpower, looked so immensely impressive, the one dark cloud on an otherwise clear horizon was Spain.

Napoleon invaded the Iberian peninsula – first Portugal and then Spain – in late autumn 1807, as part of his continuous war against England. He intended to put an end to the presence of British warships on the Tagus, outside Lisbon, and along the Portuguese coastline, and eventually to capture Gibraltar. Spain was an inefficient ally and would probably have been better used as a base, but there was no real need to occupy it. No wonder Talleyrand was vehemently opposed to the venture, but by the autumn of 1807 he had ceased to be Foreign Minister. The Emperor, as it transpired, totally misjudged the strength of national feeling in Spain and the powerful influence of the clergy, whom he thought (as Rousseau's writings had taught him) inefficient and weak. He found instead that they had become powerful leaders, who rallied the country to arms.

Alas for the miscalculation. The French armies were drawn into a quagmire. 'I should never have started this adventure,' Napoleon later recalled on St Helena. By March 1808 it had become painfully obvious that the Emperor's presence was urgently required at the front.

As soon as Napoleon decided to leave for the Spanish front, Marie made preparations for her return journey to Poland. She must have reached Warsaw by the last week in March, for the meticulous Madame Nakwaska noted her presence at a Lenten reception in the capital 'looking radiant and fashionably dressed'.

She left the warm early spring sunshine of Paris, the discreet and solicitous servants of her rue de la Houssaye town-house, to return to the frozen plains of the north, where the countryside was still blanketed by snow. It had been a short visit considering the distance to travel, and one wonders why she did not remain in Paris after Napoleon had departed for Bayonne in early April. He must have encouraged her to stay on. One suspects that at this stage of her life, in spite of Leroy's worldly schooling, Marie was still too romantic and too shy to enjoy being in Paris on her own. In the absence of the man she adored, the city and its attractions might have lost their meaning for her. As Napoleon was bound to be away for some months, it was better to return home.

7
WAGRAM

Sixteen months were to pass between Marie's departure from Paris and her next meeting with Napoleon. They were testing months for the Emperor, overshadowed by the ill-fated Spanish adventure, which was rapidly engulfing his forces, and by the gradual disintegration of his much-hoped-for alliance with the Tsar. Little evidence has survived of his correspondence with Marie during that period, but he must have kept in touch with her, though intermittently, as much as his constant travelling allowed. He spent most of that year's spring and early summer in Spain and returned there again in October, after his summit-meeting with Tsar Alexander at Erfurt.

In Marie's absence, her countrymen did their best to remind the Emperor of Poland. In October the three newly formed Polish Lancers' regiments reached Spain after a long march from Warsaw to Paris and then south, through Lyons, all the way down to Bayonne. With the exception of a few officers, none of them had ever before left Poland. The march through France in the full glory of its autumnal landscape had been exhilarating, but Spain presented an entirely different emotional picture. The simple patriotism of the Spanish people, who rose in a spontaneous uprising against the invading armies, which threatened their existence as a nation, could not fail to appeal to the Poles. 'I like these people,' wrote an officer in the Lancers to his wife back in Poland. 'They are proud, attached to their old customs, strong on family ties and – though they can be very cruel at times – they command respect because of their unaffected dignity. They deserve a better government than they've got, but I wish we did not have to fight them.'

On his arrival at Bayonne, Napoleon found his armies disorganized, camping behind the River Ebro after their forced evacuation from Madrid, and King Joseph, his ineffectual brother, whom he had recently planted on the Spanish throne, greatly dispirited and anxious. In order to recapture Madrid and bring the war to what he hoped would be a decisive and speedy conclusion, Napoleon threw into the campaign an additional 150,000 of his best troops. Following his usual system of moving great masses of men and material swiftly from place to place, he rapidly defeated the Anglo-Spanish army of General Blake on his left flank, followed by Palafox's on his right, and went on to attack Burgos, defended by the Army of Estramadura. Marshal Bessière, assisted by Marshal Lasalle with the Poles under his command, took Burgos, pushing the retreating enemy south towards Madrid. But the way to the capital remained barred by the mountains of Guadarrama, a wild, impassable chain with only one narrow road to the top, through a pass called Somosierra; thirteen thousand Spanish infantrymen, reinforced by artillery, guarded the access to the pass. With gun-positions entrenched along the way and the main force dug in on the summit with a sweeping view all around, this gateway to the capital commanded an invincible position.

On the morning of 30 November 1808, Napoleon rode out of camp at daybreak to survey the enemy positions: before him, seemingly unconquerable, the amphitheatre of mountains emerged menacingly from the mists. After a moment's reflection the Emperor decided that the road through the pass had to be secured at all costs. Berthier, the Chief of Staff, supported by other commanders, argued that it was an impossible undertaking – even if human casualties were to be totally disregarded. 'Impossible?' the Emperor is reported to have said. 'I don't know the meaning of that word. I will tell you who is going to do it – the Poles will. Yes – *laissez faire les Polonais* – let the Poles do it! Now.'

Why did Napoleon choose the Poles for what was obviously a near hopeless, suicidal assignment? There were several regiments of his Old Guard on the spot, better trained than the newly arrived Polish Lancers, as well as several thousand of his veteran infantrymen. Yet he chose the relatively inexperienced Poles, for he knew that every man in that squadron looked upon himself as a representative of his country and would stop at nothing to prove his courage, particularly in front of the Emperor. As a result they were almost senselessly reckless and far more likely to secure the unconquerable pass than his own men, who knew what danger awaited them. 'Tell my Poles to attack,' the Emperor told Louis Philippe de Ségur, shrewdly assessing their mood.

'The moment we received the Emperor's order,' writes Captain Niegolewski in his Memoirs, 'we re-formed and hurriedly moved uphill on the narrow pass, four abreast, gathering speed as we went, unsheathed sabres in one hand, pistols held in the other, reins gathered between the teeth. . . . We flew towards the amphitheatre with the speed of wind shouting '*Vive l'Empereur*', oblivious of the murderous enemy fire from above. . . .'

The distance to the top was two miles, and only a fraction of the men reached the last Spanish gun-emplacements, but the lightning effect of the charge broke the lines of the enemy infantry, causing chaos. When Benito San Juan, the distinguished Spanish commander, tried to stop the retreat, his men summarily shot him.

Napoleon, who had watched the charge in deep silence, bared his head before the handful of surviving heroes. 'You are as brave as my old regiments of the Guard – I salute you.' The Polish Lancers wept with joy. The road to Madrid now lay open and on 3 December the city capitulated and King Joseph returned to the throne.

The attack on the pass of Somosierra captured the imagination of contemporary soldiers in the same way as the assault on Monte Cassino some 130 years later was to do. It was immensely brave, swashbuckling, but, from the Polish point of view, useless. For Napoleon it opened the way to Madrid. For Poland it wiped out the flower of her officers, the nucleus of the future leaders of the land. Their deaths, thousands of miles from their homeland, proved to be completely in vain. It was said that they died happy, with the cry of '*Vive l'Empereur*' on their lips.

The Imperial Order of the Day, extolling the supreme courage of 'the Second Regiment of Lancers', evoked proud enthusiasm throughout Poland. Few people asked themselves why the casualties had to be so staggeringly high, and only the families of the dead did not share in the general euphoria. The heroic leader of the charge was Captain Kozietulski, Marie's neighbour and friend, whose mother lived in the country, some nine miles from Kiernozia. Wounded eleven times in the assault, Kozietulski somehow survived his multiple head- and leg-injuries, and after a lengthy stay in the field hospital at Aranjuez, where, as he wrote to his mother, he 'almost died of starvation', he managed to recover in Madrid and hoped to rejoin the regiment in the New Year. There was much rejoicing at the news in the district, for the widow Kozietulska from Kompina was a well-known and popular figure in the county. Like Marie's mother, she had been widowed in the Polish-Russian war and left to run her property single-handed, which she did with considerable energy and acumen. The dashing, dark-eyed, effervescent Hipolithe was the apple of her eye and the only son she had left. The altar of the local church was covered with votive offerings for his safe return from the wars.

According to contemporary Polish diarists, Marie received a letter from Napoleon, written from Valladolid in Spain in the first half of December, shortly after the Somosierra engagement, congratulating her on the courage of her countrymen. The letter has not survived, but it is more than likely that Napoleon would have written to her on this occasion; with the approaching New

Year he would also have wanted to send her holiday greetings, to which he knew she attached great importance. The traditional Polish Christmas – the carol singing, the Yule log, the lighted tree, hay under the snow-white tablecloth in remembrance of the child in the manger, the festive meal with its usual dozen fish courses and array of poppy-seed cakes, the magic of the Midnight Mass on Christmas Eve – all came and went.

In the meantime Marie's mind must have wandered to the mountains of Spain, where Napoleon's armies were pursuing the British General Moore and his troops, whose retreat towards Lisbon Napoleon was trying to prevent at all costs. 'There were times', recounts General Marbot in his Memoirs, 'when it was impossible to advance because of the driving snow and glacial wind in our faces. The Emperor, hoisted astride a cannon – a grotesque sight – personally led the advance through the mountains. "*Foutu métier* – dreadful profession", he swore, when the going got particularly rough. . . . "Forced labour would be preferable to *this*," murmured some of our veteran soldiers. . . .'

Their hardships were suffered in vain, for the elusive General Moore managed to escape from the trap. In January Napoleon gave up the pursuit. By then the political horizon in France was clouding over : a war with Austria was about to erupt, and his presence in Paris was essential. He went back, driving furiously in a light, speedy conveyance, leaving the best units of his army in Spain, to carry on a war they all hated – one they knew could never be won.

While the Emperor was in Spain. two former antagonists, Talleyrand, his former Foreign Minister, and Fouché, the Minister of the Interior, had come together to plot his downfall. Their objective was peace, which they felt would never come as long as Napoleon ruled France. 'Let us prove to Europe that, although the genius of Napoleon can add lustre to France, his presence is not esential to repulse the enemy,' said Fouché, whose idea was to substitute Marshal Murat for Napoleon.

Talleyrand went much further. At Erfurt the previous October he had systematically set about undermining the Franco-Russian alliance. While Tsar Alexander conferred with Napoleon during the day, offered effusive greetings and embraces, reviewed troops, attended innumerable festivities in an outward show of affection, he also spent long evening hours *tête à tête* with Talleyrand, who, aware of Alexander's ambition, appealed to him to save Europe from Napoleon's war-mongering. The words fell on fertile ground. The Tsar of All the Russias found the role of 'Saviour of Europe' most appealing.

The first test came when he refused to intervene in Austria's preparations for war and remained consistently vague when it came to committing his country to a joint military action in the event of Austria's going to war against France.

It seems strange at first glance that Austria, already three times defeated by Napoleon in the past, should embark on another military campaign against him; the Spanish adventure was at least partially responsible. Napoleon's high-handed treatment of the Spanish Bourbons caused fear in Vienna lest the Habsburgs' turn should come next; the Spanish insurrection was a challenge to Austria's national self-respect and sparked wide anti-French sentiment in several parts of Germany. But another reason was the fact that the Austrian army, reorganized and rebuilt since its defeat at Austerlitz three years earlier, now felt capable of delivering a severe blow to Napoleon. Though technically at war with England, Austria had entered into secret negotiations with London, who had promised (after hostilities had begun) that a British expeditionary force would be landed in northern Europe to create a second front. Metternich, the brilliant young new Austrian ambassador to Paris, primed by Talleyrand, argued in his reports to Vienna that half of Napoleon's army was tied up in Spain, the majority of people in France were tired of war, and that prominent Frenchmen, such as Talleyrand and Fouché, would welcome a check to their Emperor's adventures.

While Napoleon was returning to Paris from Spain at breakneck speed, covering as much as seventy-five miles in twenty-four hours, the Austrian mobilization was quietly proceeding apace. On 12 April 1809 the Austrian armies invaded Bavaria. Two days later another contingent, under the command of Archduke Ferdinand, crossed the old Polish border with directives to occupy Warsaw. Prince Joseph Poniatowski found himself in a very difficult situation: the greater part of his troops were either in Spain or scattered about France and Germany on assignments with individual French army corps. All that remained to him were reserves – about fifteen thousand men, mostly untrained volunteers and older people – barely enough to oppose an enemy force twice the number. No one, not the least Napoleon, had expected the Austrians to attack in the east. If they did, it would be up to France's ally the Tsar to engage them in fighting.

But things had changed considerably since Tilsit, and the Tsar, in spite of his formal treaty of alliance with Napoleon, had not the slightest desire to intervene. Russian troops, massed along Polish borders, looked on with interest as the greatly outnumbered Poles, under the command of Prince Joseph, fought a desperate battle with the Austrians a few miles outside Warsaw at Raszyn. Though the Austrians prevailed, Prince Joseph was able to negotiate a truce which allowed him to evacuate his troops to the eastern bank of the Vistula, while the Archduke Ferdinand occupied Warsaw. The government of the Grand Duchy fled to Thorn, a small town in the north-western part of the country, once famous as Copernicus's birthplace. They were followed by a number of prominent citizens whose pro-French sympathies were well known. Among them was Marie Walewska.

The archives of the Quai d'Orsay mention an exchange of telegrams between Champagny, the then French Minister of Foreign Affairs, and Serra, the French Resident Minister in Warsaw, who was asked, as a matter of 'great urgency', to keep an eye on the Countess Walewska and 'regularly report on her welfare'. It was a great comfort to Marie to know that, in spite of the military campaign now in full swing, the Emperor's thoughts had not totally deserted her. He was naturally anxious that she remain out of Warsaw. It would never do for Marie to be taken hostage by the Austrians.

In a series of swift, brilliant manœuvres, Napoleon and his marshals overcame the much superior Austrian forces. On 13 May 1809 – a month after the hostilities had begun – the Emperor entered Vienna and installed himself in the palace of Schönbrunn. The Viennese garrison had put up a show of resistance, and for a period of two days the city had been bombarded with cannon-fire. Among the terrified citizens who rushed to take refuge in their cellars was the composer Joseph Haydn, then aged seventy-seven. The shock of the experience had been too much for him and he died two weeks later – the most illustrious casualty of the 1809 war. Among the mourners who followed him to the grave were hundreds of French officers.

On 18 May, from his study in Schönbrunn, Napoleon wrote to Marie:

Come to Vienna. . . . I want to see you and give you new proofs of the tender affection I have for you. You cannot imagine what a tremendous importance I attach to everything that concerns you. . . .
Many tender kisses on your lovely hands and just one on your beautiful mouth.

Napole.

But, before they could be together, the Austrians had to be decisively overcome; so far they had only been pushed back, not defeated. The loss of their capital did not make the Austrian commanders sue for peace, and in Poland Archduke Ferdinand's forces barred the way out for Marie. The victory of Wagram was still almost two months away in the future. Impatient as she was to rejoin the Emperor, the only thing Marie could do was to wait.

In the meantime, having been forced to surrender Warsaw

to the Archduke's overwhelming forces, Prince Joseph Poniatowski led the remainder of his army south into Polish Galicia,
gathering new recruits as he went. The objective was to recapture Cracow, the ancient capital of the Polish kings, which
Austria had annexed in the partitions. This would create a much
needed diversion on the Austrians' southern flank and enable
the Poles to link up with Napoleon's forces on the Danube.

Enthusiastically welcomed by the populace, Prince Joseph
was well on the way to recapturing the whole of this formerly
Polish province when Russian troops moved in from the east,
blocking his further advance. It was a strange situation, for
officially the Russians were France's allies, expected to attack
the Austrians the moment hostilities were declared. But instead,
all through April and May they deliberately avoided coming to
grips with the enemy, waiting for the outcome of the military
contest to become clearer. At one point, after the battle of
Essling, in which Napoleon lost nineteen thousand men in casualties, including Marshal Lannes, his closest friend, and when it
seemed as if victory was to go to the Austrians, the Russian
armies withdrew back to their borders.

They decided to intervene in the war only when it became
clear that Prince Joseph was about to occupy the whole of the
southern province of Galicia. From then on it became a race
against time as to who would be the first to enter Cracow. The
Poles beat the Russians to it by two days, and on 14 July, a
week after Napoleon's victory at Wagram, a Polish general
accepted the Austrians' capitulation. Polish and French flags
flew over the medieval castle of Wavel and the fifteenth-century
arcades of the old Rynek, the market square.

On the morning after Cracow's surrender, Prince Joseph,
accompanied by his staff, arrived on the Vistula bridge, just
below the castle of Wavel, to make a ceremonial entry into the
city. He found his way barred by a detachment of General
Golitzin's burly guards, who had sneaked into the outskirts
overnight to arrange for the city's occupation by the Russians.
According to eye-witness accounts, there was a moment of

stunned silence; but Prince Joseph did not hesitate. He spurred his huge chestnut gelding and in one powerful leap landed right in the midst of the Russians, knocking several of them to the ground; the others respectfully moved aside, and the Prince and his escort rode on.

Though Cracow and the western part of Galicia were now under Polish command, General Golitsyn's troops remained in the vicinity, ostensibly as allies of the French, hoping to partake in the spoils now that the war with Austria had been won.

Following the victory of Wagram and the signing of the armistice, Archduke Ferdinand's forces left Warsaw. Marie was now free to travel to Vienna. The roads, though clogged with military transports, were now safe and patrolled by detachments of Polish and French mobile squadrons.

She had been preparing for this journey for nearly two months, ever since she received Napoleon's letter from Schönbrunn in May. Thanks to the good offices of Monsieur Serra, the ebullient French Resident Minister in Warsaw, Marie was kept informed of developments and was one of the first in Poland to hear the news of the splendid victory at Wagram and of the armistice that followed.

Two days later she was on her way, ostensibly to take the waters at Bad Gastein, near Vienna, as she announced to her friends. With her were two members of Anastase's family, Josephine and John Witte, who rather incongruously volunteered to act as Marie's chaperones.

Josephine Witte was a woman in her late thirties, good looking and sparkling with vivacity. Born into the great Lubomirski family, she first married Adam Walewski, one of Anastase's nephews, to whom she was already related through her mother. She lived with him at Walewice and became a friend and confidante of Marie's in the early years of her marriage. In the general turmoil following Napoleon's campaign in Poland, she fell in love with the handsome John Witte, the future governor of Warsaw, and married him, much to the annoyance of her family, who disapproved of the newly introduced divorce laws. Unkind rumour had it that, even after the divorce, Josephine managed to share her favours equally between her two husbands. But the serious and scholarly General Witte adored her, and Marie, so romantic and reticent by nature, found pleasure in the company of this volatile, gay, rather superficial woman, who had always shown her affection and had proved to be an unusually reliable friend.

Travelling fast, they stopped only one day in Cracow, to see friends, continued through what is now eastern Czechoslovakia and reached the Austrian capital in four days. Vienna was a familiar place to Marie. It had always been the Polish gentry's favourite city – closer to Poland than Paris, more sympathetic than Berlin. This is where smart young men dashed off to partake in the gaieties of the carnival season, where they ordered their riding boots, smart uniforms and shooting clothes. One always stopped in Vienna for a *séjour* on the way to the waters at Bad Gastein, to attend the opera and the theatre and visit friends and relations, for there was much intermarriage between the Poles and the Austrians.

Affection for the city persisted even after the partitions of Poland, for out of the three occupying powers Austria was the most benevolent and easy-going. And, though a century had now passed, there was still the lingering affinity born out of the common struggle to defend Christendom against the Turks. In 1683 the Polish King John Sobieski, in one of those outbursts of Polish heroism recurrent in Polish history through the ages, had led his armies in a breathless march over the mountains to rescue the Habsburg Emperor, and with him continental Christian Europe, from Sultan Suleiman, with 'half the East at heel', battering at the weakening defences of the near-starving city. It had been a close run. A delay of two or three days and the Turks would have taken Vienna. Would they have raced all the way west, across the great European plain to the Channel, and pitched their tents in sight of the white cliffs of Dover? And what would present-day Europe be like had they done so? It is an interesting speculation.

A charming house had been reserved for Marie in the lovely old village of Mödling, about ten miles from Schönbrunn, away from prying eyes and the bustle of the military. In the midst of a war-ravaged countryside, where most of the houses had been burned, Mödling, with its surrounding vineyards, its Benedictine abbey dating back to the twelfth century, was an oasis of peace and an enclave of absolute privacy. Mödling is a delightful place even now. Marie's residence was torn down at the end of the last century to make room for a modern villa, but there are other early-eighteenth-century houses in the beautiful ancient village which suggest its appearance. It must have had at least four or five bedrooms, a fine square sitting-room and a dining-room with a terrace overlooking the hills of Hietzing and the vineyards. Though it was Napoleon who had ordered that a house be found, one detects Marshal Duroc's thoughtful care and his evident sympathy for Marie in choosing a retreat that was sure to delight her.

After the battle of Wagram [writes the valet Constant], the Emperor took up residence at the palace of Schönbrunn. As soon as it was possible, he arranged for Madame Walewska to join him; he ordered a house be found and furnished for her, and a truly charming one was selected . . . not too far from Schönbrunn. . . . I used to go and collect her there in a closed, unmarked carriage, accompanied by only one servant. I used to bring her to the palace through a special door which was the Emperor's private entrance. The journey, though not very long, was not without its dangers, particularly when it rained, because of the mountainous terrain and the pot-holes in the road. The Emperor used to say: 'Be careful, Constant – remember it has been raining today, the road might be slippery. . . . Are you quite sure of your coachman – is he experienced? Is the carriage in good condition?' and other similar questions, which showed how much he cared for Madame W. As a matter of fact, he was quite right to be concerned, for one evening, shortly after we had left Madame W.'s house, the carriage overturned, as the coachman, trying to avoid a particularly deep pot-hole, came too close to the edge of the road. Luckily it tilted on to the right side, so I was able to act as a cushion for Madame W., who escaped unhurt. She thanked me with this unique amiability and charming grace which was so characteristic of her. Though I was slightly concussed, any pain I might have felt disappeared as a result of her kindness, and we were both able to laugh at the accident. As soon as we arrived at Schönbrunn, Madame W. told the Emperor what had happened, and he thanked me for protecting her. . . .

The palace of Schönbrunn, begun in the seventeenth century in the age of flamboyant Baroque, was completed by the Empress Maria Theresa in 1754 in the classic eighteenth-century style, copied from Louis xiv's Versailles. It had 1,440 splendidly furnished rooms, 139 kitchens, vast gardens, laid out on Le-nôtre's classical pattern, a botanical garden, a zoo 'with several elephants, kangaroos and one lion', and a museum of precious stones (of which the most famous exhibit was a 130-carat diamond called 'the Florentine', which had at one time belonged to a duke of Burgundy). One of the first lifts in Europe, designed for Maria Theresa, a so-called *chaise volante*, had been installed next to the Empress's famous blue bedroom decorated with frescoes by Guillelmi. On the same floor, in a suite of rooms of exquisite beauty – all red and gold, known as the Japanese apartment – the victorious Napoleon made his headquarters. By a strange twist of fate they were the same rooms in which, twenty-three years later, his son the King of Rome, lived and died a virtual prisoner.

Marie's first view of the palace came as her carriage turned into the long, straight avenue of chestnut trees, set between orchards and in undulating parkland; it led up to magnificent wrought-iron gates, surmounted by gold imperial eagles, which are still there to this day. In the light of a late-summer evening the pale ochre classical palace, framed by its two obelisques, set between playing fountains, the enormous Grande Place, big enough to accommodate seven to eight thousand marching men, must have seemed like an operatic stage-set. She came to know Schönbrunn intimately in the next two and a half months.

Though Napoleon was supposed to be resting at Schönbrunn (his contemporaries called his stay there '*le repos du lion*'), his days, as at Finkenstein, were filled with the usual affairs of state, correspondence, daily military reviews in the immense court-yard of the palace and preparations for the signing of the peace treaty with Austria, which would officially put an end to the state of hostilities between the two countries. The Emperor and his staff were also engaged in another, more mundane activity: the sorting out and despatch to France of mountains of loot.

Monsieur Denon, Director of the Museums of France, is here [wrote Guillaume Peyrusse, the Treasurer of Napoleon's Household]. His presence is bound to cost the Emperor Francis several of his best pictures and various antique objects. It would not surprise me at all if the splendid marble bust of Joseph II soon started on a journey to St Cloud, also the sculpture of Marie Antoinette, aged eight, together with the fire-screen embroidered by Maria Theresa.... I know the Emperor has his eye on several sculptures by Canova – a whole stack of aquarelles, views of Vienna ... and other objects.

'I only have a few moments before the departure of the courier for Paris,' wrote Monsieur de la Bouillerie, Treasurer of the Empire, to his wife. 'Am sending you the rolls of wallpaper you requested. Vienna is famous for them.'

The pillage must have been appalling. Yet, barely six months later, the Austrian Emperor agreed to add his own daughter to the mountain of spoils Napoleon had already collected.

At Schönbrunn, as at Finkenstein two years earlier, and again in Paris the year before, Marie's day was conditioned by Napo-leon's schedule, communicated to her by Duroc, who remained the established link between them. Schönbrunn did not afford the same privacy as Finkenstein, and at first she saw the Emperor only at night and during the long, light evenings of the summer. But soon he wanted to have her near him all the time – between audiences, in his study, while he dictated correspondence – ready to leave at a moment's notice for a secret walk with him in the park or for a drive in an unmarked carriage along the Danube in the Prater.

In those days the old ramparts and glacis still circled the inner part of the city. The great Ringstrasse, as we know it today, which in the latter part of the nineteenth century incorporated the suburbs and swallowed up the vineyards on which most of Vienna's old fame had rested, had not yet been built. The Prater, the vast park, spread along the Danube, with its magnificently planted alleys and winding walks, was the playground of Vienna's multi-national population.

On summer evenings in the Prater [wrote Guillaume Peyrusse, who was spending July and August of 1809 in Vienna], you could see Greeks, Turks, Bohemians, Hungarians, Jews, Cossacks, even Tartars, walking arm in arm, alongside the local Viennese, enjoying themselves and ogling the fashions.... Only one problem spoiled the fun – the insects. There were always millions of them in the Prater – and they attacked the pedestrians so fiercely that many were forced to retreat. The Viennese called them a 'celestial police'.... Without the insects, they said, love would wreak real havoc during the twilight hours.

We can only conjecture on how many occasions Napoleon and Marie must have driven along the alleys of the Prater. They may have followed the banks of the Danube; like the Roman Emperors before him Napoleon was fascinated by this great river. What we know, on the basis of contemporary accounts, is that he spent as much time with Marie as he could; there was no other woman in his life at that time. He even liked what he called her 'reasonings' – political arguments – something he refused to tolerate in other women. He put it down to her intense patriotism, which he respected. 'I have news for you, Marie,' he once said. 'Poland will get western Galicia in the treaty; it will add ten new departments to the Duchy of Warsaw – aren't you pleased?'

'Oh, only western Galicia?' she queried. 'We conquered the

entire province, why not the eastern part as well?' How could he explain to her that he did not dare to antagonize Tsar Alexander, uncertain ally that he was, that the thorn in this shaky alliance he did not dare to endanger *was* Poland? A time would come when, he hoped, even Russia would be brought under his control. Then, perhaps, Marie's dream of an independent homeland could become a reality, but the time was not ripe for it yet.

On the days when the Emperor was away – in Hungary or inspecting his troops in the field, Marie visited the Wittes in Vienna or held small gatherings at Mödling for friends from among the Polish Lancers, who were quartered between Hietzing and Schönbrunn. She was seen at the theatre, at the opera and at parties among Vienna's fashionable circles.

'Last night at the theatre I paid a call on Josephine and John Witte in their box and saw Madame Anastase Walewska, who told me much about Warsaw, which she left a few days after the departure of the Austrians,' reported Thomas Lubienski, a captain in the Polish Lancers, writing to his wife in the last days of July 1809.

The presence of her husband's relations at her side and the pretence that she was on her way to take the waters at Bad Gastein lent an aura of respectability to Marie's stay in the capital, though she would have been naïve to imagine that anyone in the gossipy Viennese society of the time had any illusions as to the real reason for her visit.

With the advent of peace, the Austrian capital resumed its rich cultural life, bolstered by an influx of French and Italian actors and opera-singers, imported on Napoleon's orders. Guillaume Peyrusse, the music-loving treasurer of Napoleon's household, noted in his Memoirs that 'during one month alone' he saw: *The Barber of Seville*, *Griselda*, *La Cosa Rara* and *Matrimonio Segreto* – all performed at the Vienna Opera House, as well as 'a charming rendition of *Nina* at the theatre in Schönbrunn. Not bad for a newly occupied city,' he noted.

Marie's friends who saw her in Vienna that summer all commented on the 'extraordinary blossoming of her looks'. She had always been considered beautiful, but there was now a kind of glow and radiance about her, more pronounced because it had been stored for so long. The weeks at Finkenstein had awakened her as a woman; she had longed for Napoleon's presence and for his touch during the long, solitary nights at Kiernozia. She had been absolutely faithful to him, and her meeting with him now, after a parting of sixteen months, had been everything she had hoped for. Again she was a woman fulfilled, and her appearance became that of the Marie Walewska passed down to us in the drawings of Isabey and in Lefèvre's sketches.

She was arrestingly beautiful [wrote a contemporary of her own sex, who saw her at the opera in Vienna that summer]. As it was a hot night, she was dressed in a light blue and white flowing dress, gathered under the bosom, fully revealing the figure. . . . Her complexion was of the most wonderful freshness – the tissue of the skin so fine that you could almost see the circulation of her blood – she blushed easily, and then she became truly ravishing. . . . She is very much admired here not only for her looks but also for her extreme modesty, which in her situation is remarkable.

This opinion, general in Viennese society, was widely shared by the members of the Emperor's household who came into contact with Marie. Duroc in particular had been her devoted admirer since Warsaw, and even General Berthier, the Chief of Staff, who disliked the Poles in general ('They are too impulsive', he used to say), smiled in affectionate sympathy whenever he met Marie in one of the great rooms at Schönbrunn.

With the approach of September, as the first mists of autumn swept down from the Danube over Schönbrunn, muffling the murmur of the fountains in the park, Marie realized that she was pregnant. She had been happy in the lovely Japanese room at the castle, where she and Napoleon lay in the big golden bed with red hangings, while Constant mounted guard outside. She had been happy in her sunny little house at Mödling, where vineyards reached to her front door.

But now Marie felt elated. Not only was she carrying a child by the man she had worshipped for so long but she knew that for Napoleon this meant the reassurance he had so desperately longed for through the years. Generous by nature and suffused with selfless love as she was, she probably never stopped to think where it left *her*. The journey to Finkenstein, daring and unconventional as it had been, now seemed a trivial episode compared with the magnitude of this event. Marie did not think of herself as a Louise de la Vallière, and this was not Louis XIV's Versailles, where illegitimate royal children were publicly paraded and acclaimed. In her strictly Catholic and still very conventional world, an illegitimate child had no place, even if fathered by Napoleon. She already had a husband and a son. Who was going to be a father to this child – even if the Emperor acknowledged it as his own? She would have been less than human if she had not at that moment passionately hoped for some miracle that would make Napoleon marry her. She could not face any more long separations. He was now her entire life, 'my present and my future', as she expressed it in one of her letters that autumn.

Napoleon was jubilant. He immediately summoned Corvisart, his personal doctor, from Paris, to examine Marie and confirm. The cheerful, benevolent Corvisart, with the most perfect bedside manner in Paris, arrived in a rapid *diligence*, escorted by two Imperial Guard officers. His verdict left no doubt: the Countess Walewska was pregnant, and her child would arrive in early May.

Never had the Emperor been as attentive and solicitous of Marie as he was at Schönbrunn that autumn. And never again would the two of them be so close. Constant, who saw them daily during that period, wrote:

I could not even begin to describe the loving care the Emperor lavished on Madame Walewska, now he knew she was pregnant. . . . He was reluctant to let her out of his sight, even for a short time, and insisted she return to Paris with him. . . . Madame Walewska was happy. . . . 'I belong to him now,' she told me, '. . . my thoughts, my inspiration all come from him and return to him . . . always.'

Their intimacy was complete: she totally depended on him, and he – in his own fashion – truly loved her and had every reason to be immensely grateful for her removing once and for all his haunting fear of sterility, refuting the allegations of impotence that Josephine's mocking taunts had implanted in his mind years ago. For *this* child was conceived by Marie, his Marie, his Polish wife, here under his own roof at Schönbrunn. No shadow marred the Emperor's supreme pride in his father-hood.

It would have been natural if his concern at that moment had gone to the lovely woman at his side, who had given him this priceless gift, whose 'present and future' he had become, and to Poland, her country, whose soldiers had sustained his conquests with their lives. But Napoleon was unlike any other man. 'Yes, I am in love,' he wrote to Joseph, his brother, 'but always sub-ordinate to my policy. And though I would like to crown my mistress, I must look for ways to further the interests of France through my next union.' That meant a dynastic marriage. There was no room for his Polish Countess in such a scheme. Holding Marie in his arms, with her child stirring within her, Napoleon's mind roamed over Europe's royal Houses, selecting a suitably nubile princess. Josephine, his wife of thirteen years, had ceased to matter; he felt that it was now his duty to divorce her.

Viewed from an historical perspective, it strikes one as supremely ironic that Marie's pregnancy, such a wholly femin-ine achievement, should have become her one most important political action, with far-reaching consequences for all Europe. Little did she realize at the time that neither she nor her country would benefit from the new political re-alignments this would cause.

With Napoleon's watchful eye on her health, and keeping her secret jealously to herself, Marie divided her time between the Emperor's quarters at Schönbrunn and her own little house at

Mödling. Autumn is the most beautiful season in Austria. The hills between Mödling and Schönbrunn had turned crimson with golden shafts of sunlight between them; the air was invigorating and clear, like the young *heurigen* wine gaily drunk all over the lovely countryside around her. It was grape-gathering time: women in short brown pleated skirts trimmed with ribbons, and yellow waistcoats with rows of silver buttons, men in shirt-sleeves, black braces and large round felt hats, carrying enormous baskets overflowing with luscious bunches, smiled at the beautiful blonde woman as she drove by in her carriage, responding to their traditional greeting, *'Grüss Gott'*. The war seemed all but forgotten, as French, Austrian, German and Polish soldiers toasted each other in new wine.

Hipolithe Kozietulski, hero of the charge of Somosierra, often dropped in for a visit at Mödling, bringing other Polish officers with him. The Lancers were now stationed at Schönbrunn, as part of the Emperor's body-guard. It was a great honour, slightly marred by constant dissension in their ranks. 'These men only know how to fight,' Napoleon once remarked after news of some inter-regimental intrigue had reached him. 'They need an outstanding leader in peacetime, but in war there is no one to equal them.' Marie was sometimes asked to arbitrate in her countrymen's disputes, but there is no record of her ever having done so. Nor would she intercede with the Emperor. It would have been useless if she had, for Napoleon would never permit a woman to influence a decision. But she must have enjoyed having those spirited fellow-countrymen around her. They shared her devotion to the Emperor and lovingly spun long campaign tales, woven around his person, filling in the details she craved for. And though they must have suspected her latest secret, she knew she could count on their sympathy and support when the time came for her to return home.

In October, with negotiations for the Austrian peace treaty completed, Napoleon's departure from Vienna drew near. For Marie the problem now was where to go. Should she return to Poland and face a further long separation from the Emperor, the father of her child to be born, just at a time when she most needed his presence? Or should she follow him to Paris and wait? But what about Anthony, her son, now aged four, staying at Walewice with his father, surrounded by a bevy of possessive aunts, just as in the first year after his birth? Would she ever see him again? And how would Anastase react, once he realized what was happening? No doubt he would be informed soon enough. Would the news jolt him out of his curious state of benevolent apathy? Would there be a scandal? And her mother, who had loyally supported her for so long – would her forbearance extend even to this latest event? These were problems in which even the omnipotent Emperor could not help her.

Corvisart had suggested to the Emperor that after the first ten or twelve 'delicate weeks', during which it was advisable not to travel, Marie should proceed at a leisurely pace to Paris to her house in the rue de la Houssaye, where he could keep an eye on both her and the child. Napoleon must have encouraged the idea, for Marie set about her preparations for an immediate journey to Paris. She asked Josephine and John Witte, who had accompanied her to Vienna from Poland, to travel to Paris with her – a suggestion which the fun-loving Josephine received with great satisfaction. But Marie felt torn and uneasy – on one hand loath to be away from Napoleon, yet uncertain as to whether she was right to absent herself from Poland for so long.

A few days before Marie's departure from Vienna an incident occurred which decided her to follow Napoleon to Paris. Come what may, she could not face being away from her lover, who seemed to be in imminent danger. The incident had a very different effect on Napoleon.

Every day, at ten o'clock in the morning, a military review took place in front of the palace of Schönbrunn, on the large esplanade, flanked by the two obelisques. On the morning of Thursday 12 October, as Napoleon came down from the reviewing platform, a blond, handsome young German suddenly moved close to the Emperor, claiming that he had come a long way in order to deliver a petition. Napoleon was about to receive him when something about the young man's behaviour and 'his odd, fixed gaze' attracted the attention of an aide, who ordered that the petitioner be searched. They found a long, sharp kitchen-knife, wrapped in red paper, on which the so-called petition was supposed to be written. The man's name was Frederick Stapps; he was the son of a Lutheran clergyman, and he admitted that he had come to Vienna with the express intention of murdering Napoleon, because, as he said, 'Without him Europe would finally be at peace.'

In the course of a long interview with the young man, the Emperor tried to persuade himself that the assassin was mentally deranged, but the man refused to recant and went to his execution proclaiming, 'Death to the tyrant'. The encounter made a great impression on Napoleon. That a civilized young man – not an agent of the Bourbons but one of the educated middle classes – should want to assassinate him, the champion of enlightenment and of freedom, was shocking, but even worse – puzzling. Was there a new spirit stirring in Europe? How many potential murderers were awaiting their cue in the wings? If any one of them was successful, the Empire would collapse. Was it then not a matter of extreme urgency to marry into a legitimate dynasty and swiftly produce an heir who would carry on his life's work?

While Marie sank to her knees thanking God for her beloved's escape, Napoleon drafted a secret memorandum to his Court Chamberlain, preparing the first step towards divorce from Josephine: he ordered that the communicating staircase between his rooms and the Empress's apartments be walled off. The act of divorce would take place the moment he returned to the capital. Josephine, his gracious consort, the Creole wife whose supple body he had so passionately desired in his youth, and Marie, his adorable 'Polish wife', the one woman he had loved in his mature years, were to be sacrificed on the altar of dynastic necessity.

'I want to marry a womb,' Napoleon announced. 'It matters

not what she looks like, as long as she comes from royal stock.'

Two days after the Stapps incident, the treaty with Austria was signed. It turned out to be ruinous for the Habsburgs. The Emperor Francis was forced to cede Salzburg and the surrounding districts to the King of Bavaria, western Galicia to the Grand Duchy of Warsaw, eastern Galicia to Russia (though her help in the war had been minimal); Carinthia, Croatia and Trieste went to France, to be joined to the Illyrian provinces. In all, the Austrian Emperor lost more than three million of his subjects and had to agree to reduce his army to a mere 150,000 men; on top of that, Austria paid an enormous indemnity in hard cash – an onerous condition to exact from a country with a highly inflated currency.

The treaty was a bitter personal humiliation for Emperor Francis. After Austerlitz he had been obliged to change his title from 'Francis II, Holy Roman Emperor' to 'Francis I, Emperor of Austria', thereby renouncing his succession to the throne of Charlemagne. Vienna wags now nicknamed him 'Francis Zero', and the streets of his capital city blossomed with cruel caricatures of the imperial family on their knees before 'the little Corsican'.

As soon as the official ceremonies were completed, Napoleon got into his carriage and started on the return journey to Paris. He was escorted by a detachment of Polish Lancers, whose company he enjoyed because of their 'spirited singing during breaks in their journey'.

One of the Polish officers who escorted the Emperor from Vienna to Strasburg on that journey described it in his Memoirs:

The Emperor always travelled in a green four-wheel carriage drawn by four sturdy horses; he preferred the limousin breed, but those were not always available. The Emperor always sat in the back on the right with Duroc on his left side; the entire front seat was piled high with reports and dispatches. As they bowled along at great speed, Duroc opened the sealed envelopes and threw them out of the window, handing over the contents to the Emperor, who often just glanced at a paper, shrugged his shoulders and promptly discarded it also; we travelled in a blizzard of paper, flying out from both sides of the carriage.

Marie, accompanied by the agreeable Witte ménage, had left Vienna a day or two earlier, travelling at a leisurely pace through Munich and Stuttgart and on to Strasburg. In years to come, she would remember that journey through Napoleon's realm and the long month in Paris that followed, before harsh reality ripped off the delicate fabric of her dream. It was – as she was to recall later – the happiest period of her life.

For all of us there is a time which belongs to our dreams and our visions – a silkier kind of time; separate and unconnected with the world in which we move in the routine of everyday life. All through the post-Wagram golden weeks Marie carried a vision in her mind: of living with Napoleon for ever – not as an empress (splendour had little meaning for her) but as a wife; of together watching their child grow; in touch with Napoleon during the day and physically close to him at night. She had never yet been fully happy, and this was the first time in her life that she had allowed herself to contemplate a blissful future.

On the last day before her departure from Schönbrunn she presented Napoleon with a ring, a gold and enamel band with a lock of her hair entwined under the surface and inscribed: 'When you have stopped loving me, remember that I love you still.' It did not cross her mind at the time that their idyll was nearing its end.

Did Napoleon encourage her to hope that one day she would share her existence with him? It is possible that for a very brief moment the more human part of him wished for it. Napoleon's concept of marriage was an essentially bourgeois one, in the mould of his Corsican past. Marie suited him perfectly in daily life; he was proud of her lovely looks and her noble ancestry, and his family instinct rejoiced at the prospect of the child to be born. But such moments could only have been ephemeral.

Though he had once confided to Lucien, his brother, that he

would 'like to crown his mistress', he never seriously considered it. Even in the intimacy of Schönbrunn's bedroom, Marie's beautiful, loving face was obscured by the distant image of the yet unknown Russian Grand Duchess he hoped to secure for a bride.

And what if, in exchange for her hand, he was asked by the Tsar to sacrifice Poland – Marie's homeland? It would be sad if it happened, but he would have to comply. After all, it would be a small price to pay for the glory of the Bonapartes' dynasty.

8

ALEXANDER

Wagram was a great victory, but it failed to re-establish Napoleon's overwhelming prestige. At Eylau in 1807 and again at Essling in May 1809, only two months before Wagram, he had skirted defeat. He was the victor, but no longer invincible. The war in Spain was continuing, the English still occupied Portugal, and Austria, after the conclusion of the peace treaty, was neither crushed nor exhausted. Russia remained a doubtful ally, but her co-operation was essential if the fight against England was to go on.

In this complex political situation, Poland was the ace in the pack. Recreated as an independent state, it would have been an ideal counter-balance to Austria and a barrier to Russian expansion. But to recreate Poland meant a rupture with Alexander; to allow it to be swallowed up by Russia spelled danger to the advance echelons of the French army in eastern Europe.

What could be done? How could Russia's co-operation be secured without sacrificing too much in return? Some risks obviously had to be taken, and there was only one way of forging a strong link with the Tsar – the old traditional alliance through marriage. The Grand Duchess Anne, the Tsar's sister, though not yet fifteen years of age, would indeed be a suitable bride for the Conqueror of the West. But what if this meant abandoning Poland? Napoleon decided to risk it – he was playing a game with high stakes, so let the chips fall where they may. The idea first came to him in October, even though Marie was still with him at Schönbrunn. In December, after Josephine had been repudiated, Champagny, France's Foreign Minister, advised the Tsar in St Petersburg that, in exchange for the hand of Grand Duchess Anne, 'His Majesty was prepared to see the words "Poland" and "Polish people" disappear from all current political transactions.' In January 1810 Caulaincourt, Napoleon's new ambassador to Russia, made the deal even more explicit and added the shameful clause: 'His Majesty would agree that the kingdom of Poland will *never* be restored.'

Having signed the cynical codicil, Caulaincourt asked for the hand of the Grand Duchess. What he got was excuses and endless procrastination. Alexander was not against the idea – securing Poland was certainly worth his sister's hand – but he counted without the opposition of his mother, the Dowager Empress Marie, who, like most of Russian society of the period, detested the *parvenu* and – as gossip had once told her – impotent Bonaparte. It was out of the question that 'the monster' should marry her youngest daughter. Caulaincourt was informed that, as the Grand Duchess Anne 'had not yet achieved puberty', the decision would have to be postponed for 'at least two years'. The delay suited the Tsar; he wanted to have ample time gradually to reveal to the Poles the extent of Napoleon's treachery. It was a skilful game, but it failed to take into account Napoleon's impatience to get married and his extraordinary sixth sense. Through Caulaincourt's communiqué he guessed Alexander's intentions and promptly halted the negotiations; the offer of Poland was withdrawn and he later denied that it had ever been made.

At this eventful time a powerful new participant entered the political arena, a man who was to dominate the European scene for the next forty years: Prince Clement von Metternich, Austria's ambassador to Paris and later his country's Foreign Minister.

'You are very young, Monsieur, to be representing the oldest monarchy in Europe,' Napoleon remarked to the newly arrived Ambassador, then aged thirty-three. as he presented his credentials at the Tuileries. 'Sire,' answered the handsome blond Prince, bowing deeply, 'I am exactly the same age as was Your Majesty at the battle of Austerlitz.' The remark passed into history.

Nominated Austria's Foreign Minister in the autumn of 1809, after the signing of the Treaty of Schönbrunn, the young diplomatic genius, like his older friend Talleyrand at the Congress of Vienna five years later, succeeded in turning Austria's military defeat into a political success. At the perfectly right psychological moment, when the prospect of a Romanov bride had become embarrassingly uncertain, Metternich offered Napoleon a Habsburg archduchess, the daughter of the defeated Emperor Francis and Marie Antoinette's great-niece. What better link with the past could there be? The deal was settled at once. Even Napoleon found the prospect of a family alliance with the most prestigious of European monarchies quite dazzling.

In April, in a ceremony of golden splendour, the Emperor married Marie Louise of Austria. Marie Walewska learned about the event from the newspapers. She was back in Poland by then, living at the castle of Walewice, as in the first years of her marriage – invited there by her husband, to await the birth 'of a Walewski descendant'.

How did this surprising reversal come about? Walewice was the last place Marie had expected to return to for the birth of Napoleon's child. She had planned to have the baby in Paris, but after a few weeks in the French capital she sadly came to the conclusion that it would be less painful for her to withdraw from the scene and return home to Kiernozia. The truth was that she had become an embarrassment to Napoleon.

Captain Thomas Lubienski, who in his Memoirs had noted that Marie had left Vienna, does not mention why she cut short her stay in Paris. It should not be too difficult however to imagine the circumstances that led her to take this painful decision.

F

The process of divorcing Josephine was undoubtedly a terrific strain on the Emperor. It took him a month from the day of his return from Vienna to bring himself to tell his wife that she was no longer wanted. In the meantime he deliberately avoided her, inflicting a long period of agonizing suspense on the poor woman. There was also the accumulation of work and the business of taking up the reins of government after his absence of four months. But most important were the delicate negotiations with the Tsar for the hand of the Grand Duchess Anne. Even for a cold realist and a cynic like Napoleon, Marie's presence at his side would have been embarrassing. No man wants to be faced daily with his conscience.

Poor Marie. She of course knew all about the Emperor's preparations for a divorce from Josephine and understood the strain it must have caused him, but it was a long while before she became aware of his future matrimonial plans. It is possible that Marshal Duroc, who always had Marie's interests at heart, might have given her some useful advice. Gradually, as her elation subsided, returning to Poland must have seemed the only dignified way out of the situation.

She arrived in Warsaw in the first part of December, probably in very low spirits, for on the 18th of that month Napoleon was writing to her from Trianon: 'Madame – I have received your letter; I note with pleasure that you have safely arrived to Warsaw. Take care of your health, which is very precious to me; chase away the black thoughts – you must not worry about the future. Tell me that you are happy and content.' The letter was signed 'Napole'; it was affectionate enough, but it had been a long time since he had addressed her as 'Madame'. The relationship was about to change – and she knew it.

Preoccupied as he was with his quest for 'a nubile princess', Napoleon nevertheless did think of Marie's future. It would clearly be best for both her and their child if the marriage to Walewski continued and the baby was born legitimate. How was it to be arranged?

The indispensable Monsieur Serra, the French Resident Minister in Warsaw, who so often in the past had acted as post-box and intermediary between Napoleon and Marie, was now faced with a tricky diplomatic assignment. He was asked to see Anastase Walewski and delicately review matters with him. Contemporary diarists suggest that in this peculiar diplomatic *démarche* Serra was helped by Henriette de Vauban, Prince Joseph Poniatowski's mistress and Anastase's old friend. Such was undoubtedly the case: Monsieur Serra would indeed have been wise to avail himself of Madame de Vauban's good offices; she was still a power in Warsaw, with her finger firmly planted on the pulse of the capital; successive French Ministers found her advice invaluable through the years – and of course she had watched the romance from the very beginning. Also, the old Chamberlain seldom acted without consulting 'his dear friend Henriette'.

It is not known how Serra broached the delicate subject to Anastase, and what Walewski's reaction was to his approach, but knowing the old Chamberlain's vanity, Serra must have flattered him with 'a personal request from the Emperor'. All his life Anastase had lived in obsessive fear of family scandals: his three unconventional nieces, whose marriages always seemed to go wrong, had worried him for a long time. Marie's departure had undoubtedly been a severe blow to his pride, though in moments of candour he admitted that it would have been worse had she gone off with 'some unimportant young guards officer'. Besides, he was getting on in years – his seventy-third birthday had just passed and not much remained for him of the future. Here was a great opportunity: with the Con-queror of the World asking him for a favour, it would be gratifying to appear generous. But first he had to consult the eldest son of his first marriage, now aged fifty, to whom the estate had been made over (though he did not appear to be living at Walewice), and his own sister Jadwiga, who ran the house, and the three nieces, all of whom were delighted at the prospect of having Marie back with them.

In the memoirs of the period there is much talk of 'a dignified and matter-of-fact letter' which Anastase was thought to have dispatched to Marie, suggesting she return to Walewice, as 'the right place for a Walewski child to be born'. Several versions of this letter have been quoted, but so far no original has been found. It may or may not have been written. What is certain, however, is that one morning in the first days of March Princess Jablonowska, Anastase's niece, ordered her carriage to be made ready and, braving the ordeal of the spring floods, drove along the poplar-lined, rutty road to Kiernozia, returning to Walewice the next day with Marie.

The move came at a propitious moment, for something had to be done to lift Marie's spirits and get her out of the state of depression she had lately fallen into at Kiernozia – a natural reaction after the peaks of euphoria of the previous autumn. Napoleon must have guessed her mood from her letters and from reports Serra had undoubtedly been forwarding to Duroc, for we find him writing an almost stern letter to her on 16 February, at the time when the negotiations for the Russian Grand Duchess's hand were suddenly interrupted and a Habsburg bride proposed. As in the December note, he addresses her as 'Madame' – a new departure.

Madame – I received news of you with great pleasure, but I regret the black mood you seem to be in; it does not suit you at all. I don't want you to be depressed. Let me know soon that you have given birth to a fine boy, that your health is good and that you are happy and gay. Never doubt the pleasure I will always feel at seeing you and my tender interest in everything that concerns you. *Adieu*, Marie, I confidently await your news.

Napole

It was just as well that Marie decided to go to Walewice, for it is doubtful whether this note – so typical of the kind of letters countless men must have been writing in similar circumstances through the ages – would have done much to cheer her.

The comfortable, sprawling house was full of flowers. The

family greeted her with open arms (her husband had tactfully gone abroad); no questions were asked; no curious neighbours were allowed to disturb her privacy; she was made to feel welcome and secure. Everything appeared to be exactly as when she had left it three years earlier. Were it not for her memories, the Emperor's secret ring and the medallion with his likeness which she now wore under her dress, she might have convinced herself that she was about to bring into the world Walewski's offspring.

It was late winter when she moved: the streams were still frozen; the countryside was hushed and barren. A month later the long-awaited Polish spring had burst forth with a richness of life one had forgotten to expect in those northern latitudes during the interminably long winter months. On 4 May 1810, at four o'clock in the afternoon, Alexander Florian Joseph Colonna Walewski, a perfectly formed, robust little boy, opened his eyes on a world in which he was to enjoy a prominent and tempestuous career.

'I was born at the castle of Walewice, in Poland, in the middle of a thunderstorm,' the future Foreign Minister of France wrote in his Memoirs some thirty-five years later. 'Thunder and lightning accompanied my birth – a good omen, my mother was told, and an indication that my life would be far from ordinary. Following an old superstition, two beggars stood by the font in the church during my christening; this was to guarantee me luck in my lifetime.'

A more formal – indeed an official – presence at young Alexander's christening was Monsieur Serra, representing the French Government. A glimpse at Alexander's birth certificate in its original Polish version affords interesting reading:

Taken at Walewice, on 7 May 1810 [it runs]. Before me, the parish priest and civil official of Bielawa, in the district of Brzezina, Department of Warsaw, appeared the high-born and respected Anastase Colonna Walewski, *staroste* of Warek, residing at the castle of Walewice, aged seventy-three years, and showed me a child of masculine gender, born at his castle on the fourth day of

May 1810 at four o'clock in the afternoon. The above mentioned high-born Anastase Walewski declared the child as being his issue and that of Marie Laczynska, daughter of the *staroste* of Gostyn, aged twenty-three, his lawful spouse. He further stated his wish to confer upon the said child the following names: Florian Alexander Joseph.

All the above being attested in the presence of the following witnesses: Squire Stanislaus Wolowski, administrator of the domain of Walewice, residing therein, aged thirty; Doctor Joseph Ciekierski, aged thirty-two, consulting physician to the Institute of Surgery and Gynaecology in Warsaw, consulting physician to His Majesty King Frederick Augustus of Saxony and Reigning Prince of the Duchy of Warsaw, residing at no. 302 at the mansion he currently owns on Nowy Swiat, in Warsaw.

The above document, after careful perusal by each of the individual witnesses is duly signed hereto:

Jan Wegrzynowicz, parish priest of Bielawa and official recorder in the district, Joseph Ciekierski, physician, and Stanislaus Wolowski, administrator of the domain of Walewice.

The birth had been easy, and Marie soon recovered her strength, but the eminent gynaecologist Ciekierski suggested that she give up nursing Alexander; her kidneys, he said, needed watching; she must find a wet-nurse for the baby. Years later he was to repeat the advice, but both times his warning went unheeded.

All through that summer and early autumn Marie remained at Walewice surrounded by attentive relatives and her two children. Anastase left for Bad Gastein a few days after the christening. She appeared contented and serene; Alexander's birth brought her a semblance of peace. She knew she could never have Napoleon, but at least she had his son, that part of him which carries through generations; there was a purpose to her life after all. She had suffered when she learned of the Emperor's engagement to Marie Louise of Austria, and of his delight in his 'fresh German bride', all meticulously relayed by candid friends. The long period of wedding festivities in Paris, during which Napoleon 'appeared radiant' must – even at a distance – have been an ordeal for her. But after the baby was born, these images stopped haunting her. Just as well, for it seemed that, for the time being at least, the Emperor had forgotten his son.

The news of Alexander's birth was relayed to Paris by Serra, and Napoleon who was touring Belgium at that time with the Empress, responded with an affectionate message and a gift of Brussels lace for Marie. He had always known, he told her, that she would give birth to a boy. But for three months afterwards silence descended. Gossip had it that he was totally absorbed in his new bride.

Finally, in September, came a letter: it was brought back from Paris by Theodore, Marie's twenty-four-year-old brother, who had been commissioned into the French army and attached to the staff of Duroc at the time of Marie's stay in Schönbrunn; Napoleon thought it an additional way to maintain contact. Written from St Cloud on 3 September 1810, the letter was brief and concise, but it told Marie what she wanted to hear – and it opened a new phase in her life.

Madame – I want to tell you what a great pleasure it was to have direct news of you through your brother. Assuming you are now completely recovered, I desire you to come to Paris in late autumn, where I would very much like to see you. Never doubt my interest and the affectionate feelings I have for you, of which you must be well aware.

Napoleon.

In the last week of November an imposing collection of carriages drew up in front of the great colonnaded entrance at the castle. Marie, with her two sons, accompanied by Anastase's handsome nieces the Princess Jablonowska and Madame Bierzynska, two nurses, three personal maids, two cooks and other attendants, prepared to start on the ten-day journey to Paris. Supervising all the arrangements, in charge of a flock of his female relatives and their stupendous mountain of luggage, was Theodore Laczynski, captain in the French army and Marie's favourite brother. From now on he would replace his much older brother Benedict as his sister's confidant and right-hand man.

In the year 1811 Paris was at the height of its brilliance. The whole of Europe paid homage to the glory of Napoleon's Empire: *'l'Europe à genoux devant Napoléon,'* as contemporary newspapers put it.

Not even in Russia did I see such luxury at the Court, or such magnificent displays of military uniforms [wrote Count Oginski, a visiting Polish nobleman]. There were so many pearls, diamonds, emeralds everywhere that they ceased to impress one. It was quite a spectacle to watch the crowned heads of Europe in attendance on the Emperor of France – and even more impressive to witness the daily parades of French, Italian, Polish, German, Dutch, Portuguese, Spanish troops, as they marched past the reviewing stand at the Invalides.

In the preceding two years the mood of the Parisians had been sombre. Even Wagram had failed to lift the general atmosphere of depression. There was little rejoicing at the new conquests. People by then had learned that new conquests usually brought new wars in their wake.

The Emperor's second marriage failed to evoke much enthusiasm. Josephine, infinitely graceful, generous to a fault and naturally elegant, had always been very well liked. 'He shouldn't have left his old girl,' said the Parisians. 'She brought him luck.' In the country at large, Austrian archduchesses had never been popular with the people, after all, they had decapitated the last one. Spontaneous acclaim failed to materialize as the new Empress, riding in Josephine's coronation coach, passed by the Arc de Triomphe – which was then in the process of construction – descended the Champs Elysées, slowly crossed the Place de la Concorde, full of tragic memories of Marie Antoinette, the last queen, her great-aunt, and entered the palace of the Tuileries, followed by a brilliant retinue of pages and dignitaries of the realm.

To placate the Parisians, various popular amusements were arranged: free concerts, free theatre performances, displays of acrobatics, and games of all sorts. Along the Cour la Reine by the Seine, where fountains were spouting wine, twelve gigantic buffet-stands were erected, groaning with food: five thousand pâtés, two thousand legs of lamb and roasts of beef, three hundred turkeys, four hundred capons, five hundred chickens and thousands of sausages from Alsace were the succulent prizes in a feast-cum-lottery organized by the city. This public-relations exercise turned out to be so popular that for many of the citizens Napoleon's second marriage must have become inextricably linked with memories of acute indigestion.

To most Parisians the new Empress's pink and white face and her round, porcelain-blue eyes appeared rather ordinary, but her 'fine child-bearing figure', as Dubois, the Prefect of the Seine, described it, seemed a good augury for the hopes of the nation. An heir, it was said, would guarantee peace. A year later people's hopes were fulfilled.

It was about 10 a.m. on 20 March 1811 [recalled the writer Stendhal, who was living in Paris at the time]. I was still in bed with Angéline when we suddenly heard the booming of the cannon. We counted up to nineteen, when mad cheering broke out in the streets. We then realized that we had missed the first three salvoes while asleep . . . it was to be twenty-one for a girl and 101 for a boy – the cannon went on booming. It was a boy all right . . . a young prince had been born. All around us people went wild with joy. . . . My wig-maker in the rue St Honoré told me that he had seldom seen such enthusiasm, not even when a favourite actor appeared in the street. It is a happy event for us all, for it spells peace.

Stendhal reflected the mood of most Frenchmen, irrespective of age, political preference and social status. Even those hostile to Napoleon welcomed the birth of his heir. With French and Austrian blood in his veins, the tiny François Charles Joseph,

King of Rome, personified the alliance between Austria and France which was to guarantee peace for a generation.

To his former wife, Josephine, who sent her congratulations, Napoleon replied: 'My son is plump and healthy. He has my chest, my mouth and my eyes.'

The Empire was at its height; the conqueror of the world had reached the summit of his happiness; the rumblings of the impending catastrophe were still more than a year away. No wonder that Paris was at its most dazzling.

In the glamorous social life of the imperial capital at its zenith, the ladies of the Walewski family assumed a leading position. For Marie this was a very different stay from her last two visits to Paris, during which she had tactfully remained in the background, content to be seen occasionally at the theatre or riding in an unmarked carriage to the Tuileries, to be smuggled through a secret door into the Emperor's presence. That period was at an end. From now on, Paris was to be her permanent home, and she would lead a life appropriate to a lady of her rank. But emotionally, too, things had changed. For the first time in three years, Napoleon – in the throes of unaccustomed marital bliss – did not want her love as a woman. Painful as the knowledge was to her, she had to face it. At least she knew that it was thanks to her that he now stood confident of his powers as a man, as a lover and as the founder of the Bonaparte dynasty. But even if, for the time being, this particular side of their relationship had ended, much remained between them. There was their son Alexander, and great mutual understanding and affection. Napoleon gave Marie all the affection of which he was capable. And of course there would always be Poland. Marie had to remain in the Emperor's orbit – if only to remind him of Poland.

He ordered that she be received at Court and treated as a distinguished foreign friend, and of course it was right, according to the custom of the day, that he should handsomely provide for her and their son.

As if to compensate Marie for the change in their relationship, Napoleon saw to it that she was installed in Paris in princely fashion. The house in the rue de la Houssaye was re-furnished in elegant Empire style, and a country residence was acquired for her by Duroc at 7, rue de Montmorency in Bou-logne, a pleasant and fashionable suburb within reach of the Emperor's country residence at St Cloud. According to the French historian Masson, Napoleon himself chose furniture for the villa. As in years past, Duroc was entrusted with the task of looking after Marie's wishes, and Corvisart, her old friend, Napoleon's personal physician, visited her regularly to keep watch on her own and baby Alexander's health. Free tickets to all Paris theatres were put at her disposal, and she had her own special box at the Opéra and the Théâtre Français. She was also granted free entry to the various museums in town, a privilege that sounds odd in our day but which was a very special favour at the time, as museums were the exclusive domain of the sov-ereign, and right of entry was restricted to only a selected few. According to the records of Napoleon's Private Purse, she received a monthly allowance of ten thousand francs, a hand-some allowance by all standards, when one considers that the pension paid to a high-ranking officer war-veteran in those days came to about 8,000 francs a year. She could live on it very com-fortably. It was a considerable change from barely four years ago, when a blushing and indignant Marie had rejected Napo-leon's gift of a brooch hidden in a bouquet of flowers. The shy, innocent girl had become a woman of the world, and the mother of the son of an emperor. She would never become grasping: greed was not in Marie's nature. But if Paris was to be her permanent home from now on, her life would have to be led according to Napoleon's wishes, and the Emperor had ordered that the Countess Walewska be installed 'with dignity and style'. This was also the view of her Walewski cousins and her brother Theodore, whose careful management talents and thrifty nature were to prove of much benefit in years to come. Marie also believed that she had, in a sense, to represent Poland in Paris by providing a rallying-point for her compatriots in exile. Throughout her long sentimental attachment to Napoleon, she never ceased to be on the alert for an opportunity to remind him of Poland, and now that there was a living link between them, she hoped he would instinctively think of her country. Napoleon must have been conscious of it, for during one of the winter receptions at the Tuileries he remarked to Princess Jablonowska, Marie's cousin, 'Don't worry about the little boy. He is a child of Wagram and one day he will become king of Poland.'

Did he see much of his child? It is impossible to know, for such visits would not have been recorded. According to Constant's Memoirs and Marchand's notes, he visited them several times at the rue de la Houssaye, shortly after Marie's arrival in Paris, and they were brought to see him in his study at the Tuileries. It is likely that there were also visits from the villa at the rue de Montmorency in Boulogne to St Cloud. Napoleon loved children, and little Alexander, with his curly blond hair and his father's light olive complexion and lovely skin, must have been a very appealing boy. But no matter what his attraction, he would have been pushed into the background by Napoleon's fascination with his heir, the newly born King of Rome. If one is to believe contemporary memoirs – and Marie, though reticent by nature, talked to one or two of her friends, who in turn recorded her confidences – Napoleon remained in frequent contact with Marie, but they did not see much of each other except at official receptions until the spring of 1812 when, with a new war looming on the horizon, the Emperor decided to make long-term financial provision for his son's future.

What, then, was Marie's life in the last carefree year of an empire whose ruler still dreamed of conquering the world? No matter how deeply disappointed in love, she would have been less than human had she not derived some measure of satisfaction from her worldly successes. For she had become one of the most popular and admired women in Paris.

'Paris was full of young, beautiful and coquettish women in that year,' wrote Madame de Chastenay, recalling the 1811–12 season, 'but the one remarkable not only for her looks but for her grace, dignity and distinction was the young Polish Countess Walewska, who it was said had borne a son to the Emperor.' And Anna Potocka, not known for her kindness to women, looking back on that period, recalled:

During her stay in France, Madame Walewska has become an accomplished woman of the world. She possesses rare tact and an unerring feel of proprieties. She has acquired self-assurance but has remained discreet, a combination not easily arrived at in her sensitive situation. Conscious of Marie Louise's jealousy, she somehow managed to conduct her social life in such a way that, even in this gossipy capital, few suspect that she still remains in close touch with the Emperor. It does not surprise me at all that she is the only one of his loves that so far has survived the test of time and of the Emperor's recent marriage.

This was high praise indeed, particularly as it came from a habitually hostile source.

We can imagine Marie, elegant in Leroy's lovely clothes (a lilac-coloured floating tunic, hem trimmed with green laurel leaves – 310 francs, as listed in Leroy's invoices), at Madame de Bassano's ball, which was such a success that 'carriages stretched all the way from the rue du Bac to the Concorde.' We see her at Queen Hortense's ball, taking part in an exclusive quadrille, 'dressed as a nymph', and floating across the ballroom at one of Pauline Borghese's famous balls to the lilting tunes of the newly-introduced waltzes, or excelling in a mazurka, the Polish dance which had become the rage in Paris, beloved particularly by the women because of the 'lovely sound of clicking spurs, and their partners' gallant postures'. She was painted by Lefèvre wearing a *décolleté* cream-coloured gown with a silk scarf in her hair. Her portrait by Gérard, the most fashionable painter of the day, in a dark blue high-waisted dress of Lyons velvet, hair adorned with precious jewels, became the rage of Paris. 'Will you allow me to accompany you to Gérard's studio tomorrow morning?' wrote Count Charles de Flahaut to the same Anne Potocka. 'Everyone is rushing there to admire Madame Walewska's portrait.'

Accompanied by her cousin, who herself presided over a lively political salon, Marie visited the Paris museums – Napoleon's special pride. It was part of Napoleon's 'ceaseless dream' to make Paris the true capital of a Europe united under a *Pax Napoleonica*. He wanted to force every king in Europe to build a large palace for his use in Paris, 'and when the Emperor of the French is crowned, these kings shall come to Paris, and they shall adorn that ceremony with their presence and salute him with their homage'. By 1810 his scheme for the adornment of Paris still remained largely in the planning stage, except for the Louvre, or the Musée Napoleon, as it was then called. With virtually all the greatest art-treasures of Europe transported there and united under one roof, it was the richest collection the world had ever known and symbolized the splendour and the power and the glory which was then the exclusive prerogative of France, all of it embodied in her emperor.

The director of this treasure house was Vivant Denon, the Empire's famous 'cultural Tsar', a charming man of perfect taste and sunny disposition. An aristocrat by birth, he was a diplomat-turned-collector and engraver. He had met Josephine during the Directory, and it was she who had introduced him to the then General Bonaparte, whom he accompanied to Egypt as a cultural adviser and draughtsman. He became Director of the Medallic Mint under the Consulate; the inscription 'Vivant D' appears alongside Napoleon's signature on Napoleonic medals. Next he became Director of the Musée Napoleon to which he brought masterpieces captured from enemy cities or 'borrowed' from servile states, including the Apollo Belvedere and the Madonna from the Sistine Chapel. Vivant Denon was always one of the first state officials to arrive in a capital city in the wake of a Napoleonic victory, to 'make his selections'. Unfortunately his job came to an abrupt end with the Abdication; great was his despair when, under the terms of the Congress of Vienna, he was forced to restore all the loot to its rightful owners. He retired from public life after the Bourbon Restoration. Although Denon is mostly remembered as the Director of the Musée Napoléon and as an arbiter of taste, he is even more lastingly important for the encouragement he gave to the living artists under the Empire.

A charming story which appears in a Polish memoir of the period tells of a visit by Marie Walewska to the Louvre to lunch with Denon, who enjoyed entertaining beautiful ladies. After lunch, as Marie was leaving the building, one of the armed soldier-guards at the door barred her exit with the words, 'Madame, I am here to guard the Venus and to prevent her escape.'

Marie was also presented at Court, which made her social position unassailable but could not have been a particularly enjoyable experience. She would have much preferred to avoid meeting Marie Louise. Her sponsor was the Duchess of Montebello, wife of the late Marshal Lannes, with whom Marie had already come into contact in Warsaw four years before. The widow of the Marshal was one of the most beautiful ladies at Court and was at that time a lady-in-waiting to the Empress. She had married Jean Lannes, a farmer's son from Gascony, after he had divorced his first wife on his return from the Egyptian campaign, when he heard that she had borne him a son, though he had not been near her for fourteen months. Madame Lannes had her own well-attended salon in Paris, and her kindness and beauty went a long way to help bring together the recently created aristocracy of the Empire and the still somewhat reticent families of the old Faubourg St Germain.

In 1806 Napoleon had begun to create kings and to distribute kingdoms to his family. In 1808 he gave the title of 'prince' to all great dignitaries (a measure that resulted in many grotesque situations), and created a new nobility, dukes, counts and barons, all of whom he endowed generously with revenue-producing property in various parts of his empire. During the Polish campaign, for example, Napoleon's generals were given titles and property in Poland,* much to the despair of former land-owners, just as many of the Polish officers in the French army in Spain were given the title of 'baron of the Empire' and endowed with life-time pensions. The old French nobility were not officially restored to their former titles, but as time went on, more and more among them were eager enough to accept new ones and flocked to fill offices at the Emperor's bidding: first at Josephine's Court (who had worked enthusiastically to bring about a reconciliation), then at Marie Louise's. They became chamberlains, gentlemen ushers, ladies-in-waiting and the like. By 1810 only an obdurate nucleus of the strictest of the Faubourg St Germain families remained aloof – and even their opposition was constantly undermined by their children. Their sons, either by desire or through conscription, were by then all fighting in Napoleon's army. 'Who could resist the chance of serving under the greatest general of all times?' wrote de Ségur, while their daughters pined to join the scintillating world of the Court balls, 'where all the eligible men were to be found'. It must have been a frequent source of friction between the old Faubourg's parents and their daughters, and the generation-gap must indeed have yawned wide, as Victorine de Chastenay, herself a reformed member of the Faubourg, recalls: 'The unfortunate young girls, to whom attendance at the Emperor's Court balls was forbidden because of their parents' prejudice, led a very dull life and complained bitterly at being barred from so many glamorous occasions. There were no other parties in town they could go to. How were the poor girls ever to find husbands?'

By contrast, the Court was the centre of life: the glittering, exuberant uniforms, the jewelled swords and the medals, the golden eagles, the dazzling balls, the clattering cavalcades, the military dash of the men strutting like peacocks in their plumes

---

* Napoleon gave his generals Polish lands worth about twenty million francs. He announced that the Poles ought to be delighted because it would mean that his generals would take an interest in their country.

and gold braid and skin-tight breeches, the famous marshals, whose very names bore an aura of legend, the women in their high-waisted, intricately embroidered dresses, moving across the sumptuous ballrooms to the music of orchestras. It all provided a spectacle and created a mystique that the young, no matter what their persuasion, found intoxicating. To some the effect, when viewed at close range, might appear theatrical, even tawdry. Next to elegant, naturally distinguished women one came across the wives of some of the marshals, gauche and fussed, unused to social conversation and the sophisticated surroundings of the Court and hating it. The same applied to their husbands, whose splendid uniform, so striking on a parade-ground, contrasted with their rough speech and brusque manners. It was like a pageant staged by a dramatic genius, with himself as the focal-point of the show, dressed in his simple grey riding-coat, surrounded by his generals and marshals, by the kings and the princes he had created; he commanded obedience with one look of his imperious gaze.

It is not known on what day Marie was presented at Court, but it must have been sometime in the late spring or early summer of 1811, as Marie Louise did not hold any official receptions for two months after the birth of the King of Rome in March. Led by the kindly, protective Madame Lannes, Duchess of Montebello, she was ushered into the presence of the new Empress, who, stiff and doll-like, in spite of her ravishing Paris clothes, greeted her with a set smile and a few perfunctory remarks. The ritual called for three consecutive deep curtsies, which Marie executed with her usual grace. She then had to withdraw, moving backwards all the way into the next drawing-room – mindful of the long train of her Court dress – under the gaze of the bracketed lorgnettes of the experts on Court etiquette. This was the test of good breeding and graceful manners. It is unlikely that Marie would have had an opportunity for a private word with the Emperor on this occasion. Court presentations at the Tuileries took place at about noon and were always exceedingly brief. Napoleon usually retired after a few moments, leaving the guests to Marie Louise and her ladies. All Marie could hope for was that he would soon send a message summoning her and their son to his presence. The presentation was, however, an important milestone in her life: it established her, in the Court Circular's parlance, as 'a distinguished acquaintance of both the Emperor *and* the Empress'.

Like all those who had known Napoleon at his physical peak, Marie must have been conscious of the change that had come over him since Warsaw days. He had put on considerable weight; his complexion was now of an unhealthy yellow pallor; his movements had become slow; he who used to be so brief, often abrupt in conversation was now almost garrulous, and though his famous 'grey, steady gaze' was unchanged, it was rumoured that he was often irritable and depressed and that the famous concentration he had always applied to his work had almost vanished. The Emperor was now forty-one years old; unknown to Marie and to those around him, he was entering a period of failing health, just at a time when he was about to embark on the greatest challenge of his life. For by the summer of 1811 Napoleon had made up his mind that war with Russia was inevitable.

What happened to the spirit of Tilsit? It had never been a natural alliance. The two Emperors' interests were too divergent: each in his own way wanted to dominate Europe, but the two insuperable problems between them were the so-called 'Continental System' and Poland.

The Tilsit commitment to join the Continental blockade against England prevented Russia from exporting grain, flax, hemp and other agricultural products in exchange for cheap manufactured English goods. The arrangement was ruinous to Russian commerce. French luxuries, such as perfumes, Lyons silks, wines and cheeses, which flooded the country because of low tariffs, were no adequate substitute – too few Russians appreciated them. As trade suffered, the French alliance became progressively more unpopular, and the Tsar was made keenly aware of it.

Poland was an even more intractable problem. At one point, during the negotiations for a Franco-Russian marriage, her future was to be bartered for the hand of the Grand Duchess Anne. But once Napoleon had decided on an Austrian bride, the talks – still at a tentative stage – were broken off, and the problem remained.

The Grand Duchy of Warsaw was a source of great irritation to the Tsar. For here, on the very frontiers of his empire, the egalitarian principles of the Napoleonic civil code were freely promulgated and widely put into practice: political rights for the Jews, freedom for peasants to own land, independent rights for women – even divorce. What if these explosive ideas started to seep into Holy Russia, where millions of ill-fed serfs, tied in perpetuity to the soil, lived lives of subhuman existence?

Tsar Alexander, the supreme autocrat of all the Russias, was not in fact a free agent. He had to take into account the views of the nobility and of his Court. He had ascended the throne over the body of his murdered father and remained haunted by guilt. When the nobles urged him to seal off the seepage of 'hostile principles' from the West by annexing Poland and turning her into a Russian satellite with himself as king, and to repudiate the detested 'Continental System', he at first resisted the idea, for he knew it would antagonize Napoleon. But the nobles charged him with being 'pro-French and a traitor'. He was warned that, unless he changed his political views, he would end up like his father – strangled.

At the end of December 1810 the Tsar issued his famous *ukase*, opening all Russian ports to neutral shipping, and imposed high tariffs on French imports. The move enraged Napoleon. Coming on top of reports of Russian re-armament and of large-scale concentrations of troops on the frontiers of Poland, it convinced him that Russia was bent on war and a return to the English alliance.

As the stage was gradually being set for a confrontation

between giants, Poland, on whose territory the war was going to be fought, became the object of intense rivalry. Poor Poland! For a people as passionately attached to freedom as the Poles, their weakness was the geographical position of their country: it made their co-operation a vital factor. It had been barely a year since the two Emperors had talked about 'erasing the name of Poland from the map'; now each of the two protagonists in the conflict was prepared to return the country to its former splendour, if only she consented to go to war on his side. 'They promised the Poles resurrection, providing they died for their cause,' observed a sceptical Swedish statesman, reporting to the former French Marshal Bernadotte, then Crown Prince of Sweden.

Tsar Alexander moved first. His plan was to proclaim Polish independence with himself as king, throw in an army of a hundred thousand men with an equal number of reinforcements and call upon the army of the Grand Duchy of Warsaw to join him. He hoped that within a few days the two armies, reinforced by friendly Prussia, watched benevolently by neutral Sweden, jointly numbering over a quarter of a million men, would reach the Oder. If Austria could be persuaded to come in (and the Tsar had skilfully prepared the ground with Metternich), the combined armies would roll back the limits of Napoleon's empire before its master had time to mount a counter-offensive.

It was a good plan, but its success depended on the co-operation of the Poles. Should the Grand Duchy of Warsaw remain loyal to Napoleon, its army would fight and would certainly slow down Russian progress, thus allowing the French troops in Germany to regroup and strike back.

At this point Tsar Alexander consulted Prince Adam Czartoryski, the intimate friend of his youth, a Polish magnate who had always believed that Poland's future lay with Russia. 'I cannot start a war against France until I have received guarantees of Polish co-operation,' Alexander told him. He intimated that the reward was to be Poland's independence.

But the Poles refused to be bought. Prince Joseph Poniatowski, the glamorous commander-in-chief of the army of the
Grand Duchy, indignantly brushed aside Czartoryski's suggestion. He had sworn allegiance to Napoleon, and so had his
soldiers; Poles were not traitors, and treason was too high a
price to pay even for freedom.

It must have been an extraordinary interview between two
very remarkable Poles, both patriots, scions of great families,
one a statesman of international reputation, the other a soldier,
romantic and recklessly brave and a charismatic leader of men.
They were both in their forties and famous for their good looks.
But, though related by blood, they represented two diametri-
cally opposed points of view. Prince Adam was a long-standing
enemy of Napoleon; he had managed the seemingly impossible
feat of being both a Polish patriot and a Russian Deputy Foreign
Minister; personally devoted to Tsar Alexander, he believed that
Poland's future lay with Russia. Prince Joseph, on the other
hand, was bound to the French Emperor by his military oath
and sentiments of 'loyalty, gratitude, confidence and fear'. His
answer required no hesitation. As a result, Czartoryski's mission
failed, and so did Tsar Alexander's plan of a surprise grand-scale
offensive on the Oder. While Prince Adam retired to his country
estates, Prince Joseph left hurriedly for Paris to acquaint Napoleon with the situation. He left Warsaw astir with rumours of
the coming of 'a second Polish War for Independence', in the
throes of passionate patriotic fervour and generous willingness
for sacrifices – ideal human material for exploitation, as the
next two years' campaigning at the side of Napoleon were to
show.

'The Poles are all the rage in Paris these days,' remarked a
contemporary chronicler in the early months of 1812. As the
prospect of war with Russia drew nearer, Napoleon left no
stone unturned to fan the patriotic fires in the easternmost out-
post of his realm. A steady stream of visitors from Poland's most
influential families made its way to the French capital to pay
their respects to Napoleon and to assess his intentions for their

country. Steeped in French culture since childhood, speaking the language perfectly, they felt very much at home in Paris, and many of them owned houses in the fashionable quarters of the city. There were no restrictions on the transfer of capital in those days, and even at the height of a war a private citizen could purchase property in any country he wished.

Though the visiting Polish magnates could always count on being well received at Court, many of them were sceptical of Napoleon's promises to recreate Poland. Several, like Prince Adam Czartoryski, believed that Poland's future lay with Russia; others favoured an Austrian solution; but all of them feared the effect that a new war, fought across the vast Polish plain, would have on the severely depleted economic and human resources of their country. They demanded firm guarantees from Napoleon before they committed themselves to his side, but he continued to evade giving them.

Marie Walewska's houses at the rue de la Houssaye and the rue de Montmorency in Boulogne were centres of lively gatherings. Polish memoirs of the period abound with numerous testimonials to the prominent position Marie occupied among her compatriots at the time. She was treated with universal admiration and respect – 'almost like a queen', some said. In her salon one met the most influential personalities of Napoleon's France: ministers, politicians, Court dignitaries, famous marshals, as well as artists such as Gérard and Isabey. She was on terms of close friendship, going back to old Warsaw days, with the Duke of Bassano, Davout and of course Duroc, who was a frequent visitor in her house; she was liked by Napoleon's sisters Caroline, the Queen of Naples, and the Princess Borghese, the beautiful, graceful Pauline; even Queen Hortense of Holland favoured her with her affection. It was Queen Hortense who introduced Marie to her mother, the former Empress Josephine, whom she was to visit regularly at Malmaison over the next year.

Marie was generally acknowledged to be beautiful and graceful, good at conversation and admirably generous to her friends. But two traits in her character made her particularly outstanding: one was her modesty, the other her straightforward nature. Considering how close she was to 'the centre of power', she remained endearingly unaffected by it. In a city swirling with intrigues at all levels, she scrupulously kept her own counsel. 'She helped whoever she could, quietly, remaining as much as possible in the background,' wrote her old childhood friend from Kiernozia, Captain Skarbek, who visited her several times in Boulogne. Her commitments were her son, the Emperor and Poland. She devoted much time to little Alexander. This gay, handsome, exuberant little boy was all hers; he was not going to be whisked away from her by jealous relatives, as her first-born had been. She observed, with a pang in her heart, his growing resemblance to Napoleon. What would be his destiny? How would he accommodate within him the unusual mixture of his Slav and Corsican blood?

When she was not entertaining in Paris, Marie spent much time in her country house at 7, rue de Montmorency in Boulogne. This charming property still exists (it is now a school), and so does a lease signed by Marie Walewska on 1 April 1811 'for the sum of fifteen hundred francs for the duration of one year – until 1 April 1812'. The house was owned at the time by a Monsieur Grenier, a rich silk-merchant from Paris. It is a spacious, two-storey, eighteenth-century building, with a terrace overlooking a large garden and a fruit orchard. The adjoining stables have been demolished since Marie's time. A record of the furniture has survived: most of it remained intact until the beginning of the First World War, but in November 1914, according to a municipal report: 'Eleven lorries, full of rare Empire furnishings, were sent to the local auction-house and disposed of.' Monsieur Grenier's *acte de vente* (he sold the house to another rich Paris merchant) described in detail the contents of one of the rooms, presumably Marie's bedroom. It is a high-ceilinged, large, square room, light and airy, on the first floor, with French doors opening onto the terrace and the vast garden beyond. Boulogne is still, even now, a quiet, residential, leafy suburb, and change has not obliterated the former countrified atmosphere: it is not very different from what it must have been in Marie's time. It is easy to see what her room must have looked like, with its Empire-style bed, painted in grey and gold tones, and its fine silken bedspread with a gold and grey fringe. The room itself was 'dove grey' with crimson and white touches to the panelling; the curtains were of grey silk with white borders; there was a fine Empire dressing-table with a mirror. surmounted by a golden eagle, a writing desk in *acajou*, a marble table with a golden pedestal, four armchairs painted grey with gold touches, and a delightful chaise-longue, covered in pale-grey satin with yellow cushions. The fine parquet floor is still there. It is a sophisticated room, evoking memories of perfect taste, warm and exceedingly feminine. It was an appropriate background for Marie, a temporary refuge from the storms which were to buffet her unremittingly in the remaining few years of her life. She must have been very happy in Boulogne.

It was either at Boulogne or at nearby Mons sur Orge, the home of Princess Jablonowska, that Marie received the visit of the revered Polish patriot General Kosciuszko, the hero of the last Polish uprising against the Russians. He had left Poland after the last of the partitions and was now living in France. Nesselrode, Tsar Alexander's special Envoy in Paris records the visit in his Memoirs and interprets it as a special sign of respect for Marie on the part of a man who had always disliked Napoleon.

It was indeed a particularly significant tribute to Marie's patriotism, for Kosciuszko had always mistrusted Napoleon and obstinately refused to throw his influence and prestige behind Napoleon's crusade in Poland. 'He thinks of nothing but himself', he used to warn his compatriots. 'He detests every great nation and he detests even more the spirit of independence. He is a tyrant.'

That this venerable Polish patriot should, in spite of his dislike for the Emperor, decide to call on Marie and wish her well in her forthcoming journey to Poland was a mark of the esteem in which she was held by her compatriots.

As Paris danced, flirted and fed on endless rumours, and while Polish magnates gathered in Marie's drawing-room discussing the coming of 'the Second Polish War', the tempo of events was quickening. All through the vast Napoleonic Empire, from Spain to Warsaw, armies were again on the march. France's mobilization-machine was swinging into high gear: a gigantic army of French, Dutch, Belgian, German, Italian, Polish, Illyrian, Danish, Prussian and Austrian troops was being raised. There was even a Spanish regiment, whose soldiers thought they were taking part in a crusade against the infidel 'king of Turkey'.

The Emperor called for books from the libraries describing Charles XII of Sweden's campaign in Poland and Russia at the beginning of the eighteenth century and ordered topographical studies of Russia's rivers, of its endless marshes, forests and nonexistent roads.

Most Frenchmen viewed the prospect of another war in the East with apprehension. Veterans of the last wars remembered only too well the hardships of the Polish campaign of 1807 and the horrors of Eylau, when vast armies were swallowed up in the freezing, merciless, snowy desert. The ever-increasing levies of conscripts added to the general unease. It had been a difficult year: a severe crop-failure that summer, due to unusually rainy weather, led to famine in the late months of 1811 and the winter of 1812. While the Emperor was poring over his maps, long lines of his hungry subjects formed queues at Paris street-corners in front of the government-organized field-kitchens, which doled out platefuls of soup to keep the citizens from starvation.

As if to add to the general atmosphere of alarm, strange, unexplained portents appeared in the European sky that winter. From the northern tip of Scotland to Moscow and as far south as Portugal, people watched in superstitious wonder a comet blaze in the heavens. Its 'white radiance and long, uplifted tail' were visible to the naked eye, even in daytime. 'Brook's Comet', as it was later named, fascinated astronomers but filled the masses with fear. For centuries the appearance of a comet was believed to be a portent of disaster – a great war, a famine or a plague. John Quincy Adams, then US Ambassador to Russia, tells in his memoirs how in St Petersburg people believed that they were seeing two comets in the northern sky, and that Tsar Alexander, who was fascinated by the phenomenon, had re-marked that, if there were two comets, 'their mischief would operate mutually against each other and so offset the evil they might foreshadow'.

Throughout the spring Napoleon's Grand Army continued to grow large, devouring class after class of recruits, while in the huge, mute Empire to the east, regiments of troops marched westwards and people filled the onion-domed churches to pray for victory over 'the Anti-Christ'. Tsar Alexander pledged him-self that he would sooner retire to Kamchatka than yield one province to Napoleon.

'*Mon absence sera immense*,' Napoleon announced to his Court. He looked worried and pensive in those days and was frequently absent-minded in the midst of all the receptions, the dances, the amateur theatricals, which on his orders continued in Paris unabated. He was uneasy – a new departure for him – and it was said that he almost hoped that some miracle would make the war go away. In late April Tsar Alexander arrived in Wilno, the capital of Polish Lithuania, to supervise the prepara-tions personally. He sent Napoleon an ultimatum, demanding 'immediate evacuation of Prussian and Swedish Pomerania and all territories east of the River Elbe', a demand he knew Napo-leon could not possibly comply with. The situation was fast moving towards the inevitable climax.

As the moment of his departure for the front drew near, the

Emperor turned his mind to settling personal affairs. On 5 May, at St Cloud, in Marie's presence, he signed a lengthy legal paper safeguarding young Alexander's future.

It was an amazing document, reminiscent in spirit of Louis xiv's provisions for his own illegitimate family. Its dry, official language put into historical perspective the importance of the Emperor's Polish romance, and its particular emphasis on safeguarding the rights of the mother made it different from the prevailing legal documents of the day. The original is today in the Walewski family archives. At the time it was kept among Napoleon's personal papers and on his orders was removed from the Ministry of Justice files, as well as from the State Archives, where it belonged. It was to remain private for all time.

Dated 5 May 1812 at the palace of St Cloud, it reads:

We Napoleon, Emperor of France, King of Italy, Protector of the Confederation of the Rhine, mediator of the Confederation of Switzerland etc. etc. have decreed what follows:

DECREE

Article 1

The estates listed below situated in the kingdom of Naples forming part of my private domain are granted by this decree to Count Alexander Florian Joseph Colonna Walewski to form an entail which we hereby establish in his favour and to which we attach the title of Count of the Empire.

Article 2

The above estates will be transmitted by inheritance to the direct and legitimate male descendants also natural or adoptive by way of primogeniture of the said Count Walewski.

Article 3

If Count Walewski should die without leaving a male descendant, we command that his daughters, if any, issued from a legitimate marriage, be free to benefit from the estates forming the above specified entail and to divide them in equal parts among themselves.

Article 4

In the case described in the preceding article a part of the above-mentioned estates which come into the possession of any of Count Walewski's daughters will be transmitted together with the attached title of Count to the direct and legitimate natural or adopted male descendant of the said daughters by way of primogeniture.

Article 5

In conformity with our statutes of 1 March 1808 the estates forming Count Walewski's entail will return to our private domain in any of the following eventualities:

1) If the said Count Walewski dies without leaving an heir.
2) If his male line becomes extinct.
3) If the male line descending from any of the daughters of the said Count Walewski, who by the provisions of Article 3 benefit from inheriting the estates, becomes extinct.

Article 6

We command that until the coming of age of the said Count Walewski, his mother Marie the Countess Walewska, born Laczynska, be the full beneficiary of all the revenues of the said estates; that they be kept at her disposal to provide for the education and the upkeep of her son and for herself as she sees fit; that she be able to administer the said estate as would the head of the family; and that the said Countess Walewska be excused from submitting any accounts as to the moneys which had been placed at her disposal.

Article 7

From the moment of Count Walewski's coming of age and his full assumption of the rights of his entail, we command him to pay his mother, the said Countess Walewska, a yearly pension of fifty thousand francs.

Article 8

In case, as stated in Article 3, whereupon due to death of the said Count Walewski without male descendant, the entail would revert to a daughter or daughters of the said Count Walewski, each one of them will be responsible for the payment of a part of the above-mentioned yearly pension.

Article 9

In case the entail should return to our private domain, we command that the Countess Walewska retain until her death the full use of all the revenues and privileges connected with this entail.

Article 10

The title to the estates forming this entail of the said Count Walewski will be forwarded, together with the present Decree, to our cousin the Prince Arch-Chancellor of the Empire, so that, for the benefit of Madame Walewska, he may prepare the necessary forms and letters of patent as well as papers connected with the investiture which we authorize Countess Walewska to take up in the name of her son according to current laws and customs.

Article 11

After the execution of our letters patent and the investiture of Madame Walewska, the General Superintendent of our private domain will forward the title of ownership of the estates to Countess Walewska in the name of her son.

Article 12

Our cousin the Prince Arch-Chancellor of the Empire and the General Superintendent of our private domain are hereby charged by me to carry out the execution of the present Decree.

Little Alexander's endowment consisted of sixty-nine farms near Naples with an annual income of 169,516 francs 60 centimes. On 15 June, in Königsberg, at his military headquarters in East Prussia, Napoleon signed the 'letters patent' creating Alexander a Count of the French Empire.

The Walewski family crest conferred by the letters patent, together with the hereditary title of Count of the Empire, was a combination of the Walewski and Laczynski insignias. It consisted of a golden column on a bright blue (azure) background, to which was added a sword with a golden handle, through which intertwined a silvery scarf, tied around in a bow with the ends falling straight through the handle.

Cambacères, the Arch-Chancellor, counter-signed the document on 13 August, making it operative. By then Marie had returned to Poland, leaving the children in Paris with her cousins.

On 9 May 1812 the official *Moniteur* announced that His Majesty the Emperor 'left today to rejoin his armies on the Vistula'.

9
THE RUSSIAN NEMESIS

In the last days of June, when the war had already begun, Marie also left Paris. She travelled through Belgium with her cousin Princess Jablonowska, who was on her way to Belgium to take the waters at Spa, then continued through Dresden to Warsaw over roads clogged with military transport, all of it heading east.

The official motive for her journey was to be 'present at the resurrection of Poland' and to help Napoleon's new ambassador in Warsaw, the Abbé de Pradt, to 'fan Polish enthusiasm for the new war'. 'I want all of Poland mobilized', Napoleon instructed his ambassador. Marie was expected to assist him in this task.

Those were the political motives resulting from the Emperor's instructions. But Marie also had a powerful private reason for her journey – to obtain a divorce from her husband.

For some time now she had worried about the worsening financial plight of the Walewice estates. Because of the prevailing poor economic conditions in the Grand Duchy of Warsaw, the slump in farm prices and Anastase's profligacy, Walewice had become heavily mortgaged. Under the laws of communal property there was danger that the income from Napoleon's gift to young Alexander might, during his minority, be swallowed up in the general avalanche of the old Chamberlain's debts. It was imperative to secure her son's future, as well as her own, particularly as she now intended to reside permanently in Paris.

On 16 July the couple drew up a separation agreement in which Marie declared her intention to separate legally from her husband and undertook to assume financial responsibility for her two sons, and to set up a trust for Anthony – her older boy – from the moneys given to her previously by her husband as part of their marriage settlement. The agreement was the price that the old Chamberlain was exacting for his consent to a divorce.

On 18 July Marie petitioned the Warsaw courts – both civil and ecclesiastical – for a legal separation from her husband. The petition was based on the claim that Marie had been 'coerced into marriage' by her mother and her older brother Benedict at a time when her health was impaired, and that she had suffered 'extreme mental cruelty from her husband in the two years immediately following their union.'

The court would not have been so receptive to her claim in the old days, but Marie was benefiting from the provisions of the recently introduced Napoleonic civil code, which made divorce easier for women to obtain.

Benedict, Marie's brooding, ambitious older brother, recently appointed brigadier, delayed his departure for the Russian front (it was rumoured that he had been ordered to remain in Warsaw to testify) and submitted a convincing affidavit to the court on how he 'had dragged his young sister, well under the age of consent, half fainting to the altar to marry a man fifty years older than herself'. Anastase, by now quite senile, was prevailed upon to sign a declaration stating that he had entered into an understanding with his wife that 'she need not be faithful to him'!

On 24 August 1812, six weeks after the petition was submitted – an astonishingly short time for a court to make a decision – the Walewski marriage was dissolved. Legally Marie was now a free woman, in control of her own and her son's destiny. Though Anastase was to live for another two and a half years, her connection with him was now severed. She may have been legally free, but such was the strength of her Catholic upbringing and tradition that, as long as Anastase was alive, she would continue to look upon him as her husband.

All around her, other women, freed by the new divorce laws, were shedding unsatisfactory partners and rushing into new matrimonial ventures, oblivious of the teachings of the Church. But Marie's situation was different. Even if she had felt free to re-marry, she would have found it impossible, for she was firmly bound to Napoleon by her son and by her country, Poland, whose future he held in his hands. It was to be some time yet before she would finally realize that she too had a right to a measure of personal happiness. But by then the whole of Napoleon's world would have crashed to pieces around her.

The remarkable speed with which the divorce decree had been granted might have had something to do with the official French government's presence, which hovered over Marie's divorce proceedings just as it had over little Alexander's christening two years before. This time the French Minister in Warsaw was the Abbé de Pradt, a somewhat incongruous choice for a post which everyone had expected to go to Talleyrand. Considering that the success of the war against Russia would, to a large extent, depend on the support the French armies could obtain from the Poles, the post of French Ambassador to Warsaw was deemed one of great responsibility, requiring vast diplomatic experience and consummate skill. Only one man in France possessed the necessary qualifications, Talleyrand, and everyone expected the Emperor to offer the post of ambassador to him. He never did so. Talleyrand had in fact started to prepare for the journey and was buying Polish currency when the news of Monsignor Pradt's nomination reached him. He was first surprised, then amused, and predicted that the mission would end in failure – which was exactly what happened.

His Excellency Dominique de Pradt, Archbishop of Malines, was squat and ugly ('*figure du pêché vieilli*' – 'personification of old sin') and exceedingly pompous. No one knew why this slightly comical ecclesiastical figure, a relative newcomer to diplomacy, had been sent to a post in which Talleyrand would have excelled. The most likely reason must have been Napoleon's desire to win over the clergy of Poland to his cause. Then, as now, Poland was an intensely Catholic country, with the Church holding sway over the mass of the people. And the clergy of Poland were disturbed. They wholeheartedly condemned the Code, Napoleon's provisions for civil divorce and were horrified by the Emperor's treatment of Pope Pius VII, the news of which, in spite of strict censorship in France, had managed to seep through to Poland from Rome. Napoleon's excommunication by the Pope hit them like lightning from heaven. 'Are we right to ally ourselves with a religious outcast?' asked the bishops of Poland in their councils. Monsignor Pradt's first duty on arrival was to allay these fears and explain the complex political reasons behind Napoleon's annexation of the Papal States. But the Ambassador's most important instruction was to turn the Grand Duchy of Warsaw into another Vendée – a province in revolt – to inspire a nationwide uprising, mobilize every resource and enlist the co-operation of every citizen from the lowest peasant on the land to the magnate in his castle. '*Toute la Pologne à cheval.*' 'Let every Pole mount his horse and ride at the side of the French into battle,' was the Emperor's stirring order. But he still stubbornly refused to commit himself to the establishment of an independent Poland. It seemed impossible that any ambassador could fail in such a mission, for, in spite of the vagueness of Napoleon's promises and his open conflict with the Church, the prevailing mood of the country was overwhelmingly on the side of the French; the faith of the Poles in Napoleon was touching. Yet, by his love of intrigue, his pomposity and lack of tact, Monsignor Pradt succeeded, during the seven months of his tenure, in antagonizing not only the clergy but all factions and shades of opinion in Poland. Napoleon had every reason to regret not having appointed Talleyrand, and it would also have prevented him from plotting against the Emperor in his absence from Paris.

One of Monsignor Pradt's instructions was to 'look after Countess Walewska in Warsaw'. This semi-official communication to the Ambassador is interesting as evidence of how much importance the Emperor attached to Marie's well-being. With the deplorable lack of tact which was to plague his entire mission, the Abbé Pradt managed to embarrass Marie by his over-zealous show of affection. His so-called 'courtship of Madame Walewska' is amusingly described by the tireless Anna Potocka, back in Poland after her recent triumphs in Paris.

His Excellency Monsignor Pradt treated Madame Walewska as if she were the Empress herself. He insisted she take precedence over all other women present – no matter what their age or distinction. She always sat on the Ambassador's right hand and was always served first; he concentrated his attention on her, to the exclusion of all other guests – much to the fury of old dowagers and to the intense amusement of the younger set, who watched with great merriment the lecherous old Archbishop ogling, through his lorgnette, Madame Walewska's splendid shoulders and her shapely white arms.

Annoyed and made uncomfortable by the Ambassador's undiplomatically conspicuous behaviour, Marie decided to leave Warsaw temporarily and retire to her mother's home at Kiernozia, to await news from the battlefield.

In the blistering heat of summer, Napoleon's gigantic multinational army was advancing deeper and deeper into Russia through the empty, devastated countryside in pursuit of the phantom-like Tsarist troops, who forever refused to give battle. They kept retreating, burning everything around them – and inexorably drawing the Grand Army to its doom.

With them marched a corps of forty thousand Polish troops under the command of Prince Joseph, while the Second Regiment of Polish Lancers – the heroes of Somosierra – as usual escorted the Emperor. From a small farm in the north-eastern corner of the Grand Duchy, on the day before the hostilities began, Napoleon issued his famous Order of the Day proclaiming the beginning of 'the Second Polish War':

Soldiers, the Second Polish War has begun. The first one ended at Friedland. At Tilsit Russia swore eternal alliance to France and war on England. Today she breaks her oath. Destiny must run its course. We are still the soldiers of Austerlitz. Let us march beyond the Niemen and carry the war into her territory. This Second Polish War will be as glorious for our French armies as was the first one. Our victory this time will guarantee peace for at least fifty years.

There was no mention of independence for Poland, a promise Napoleon obstinately refused to give as long as there was a remote chance of bringing Tsar Alexander to the negotiating table. But never mind, the outbreak of war was greeted with wild enthusiasm by the Poles.

Next day the Emperor, travelling in his carriage drawn by six sturdy horses, surrounded by pages, adjutants and a well-armed detachment of his Polish Lancers, reached the Niemen, well ahead of his army. On reaching the bank of the powerful river, recently swollen by floods, he got out of his carriage, put on a Polish uniform so as not to be recognized by the enemy, carefully inspected the crossing, then ordered an immediate advance. At daybreak on 24 June, the day of the Feast of St John, the huge multi-lingual army, 'the walking Babel of tongues', flowed out of the Lithuanian forests that had been concealing it until now and split up in three parts to cross the Niemen by three bridges. The faces of the men were happy at the commencement of a long-awaited campaign; and they enthusiastically cheered the solitary, grey-coated figure who stood watching them from a nearby hill.

That afternoon an incident occurred which vividly illustrated the extraordinary dedication of the Poles to Napoleon. Men from a Polish cavalry regiment – one of the first to cross onto the Russian side – were camping on the banks of another river, the Wilia, a tributary of the Niemen and a natural barrier to the Grand Army's further advance, as all the bridges on it had been blown. The Emperor, riding a grey horse, pulled up beside the men on the bank and sat down on a log, propping his field-glasses on the back of a page. He surveyed the boiling, treacherous river for a moment, then sent an urgent order to the Poles to find a fording-place. In an excess of zeal, both unnecessary and heroic, the regiment re-formed and, to the sound of trumpets, plunged into the water without bothering to look for a ford. It was cold and dangerous in the rapid current. The soldiers clung to each other and to their stirrups; many horses were drowned; so were several of the men. Others struggled to swim across, clinging to their horses' manes, and though the ford was less than half a mile away, they were all proud to be swimming and drowning before the eyes of the Emperor, their idol. But the idol, raising his eyes from the map spread at his feet on the logs, spared only a cursory glance in the direction of the struggling men, and a shrug of displeasure at what seemed to him an act of senseless self-sacrifice. Several soldiers were drowned, in spite of boats sent to the rescue, but the majority clambered on to the opposite bank, drenched but happy, shouting '*Vive l'Empereur*' and looking back at the opposite bank in the hope of seeing the figure in the grey coat still standing there. But Napoleon had ridden away long before.

Such was the mood of the Poles at the outset of a war which they hoped would restore their independence. Napoleon cast the same powerful spell over them as he did over his own regiments of the Guard. The German poet Heine, who was present at a review of the troops as they passed through Germany on their way to Russia, recalled, in memorable words:

For ever I see him, high on horseback; the eternal eyes set in the marble of that imperial visage, looking on with the calm of destiny at his Guards, as they march past. He was sending them to Russia, and the old grenadiers glanced up at him with so awesome a devotion, so sympathetic an earnestness, with the pride of death: *Ave Caesar, morituri te salutant!'* [Hail Caesar, those who are about to die salute you!]

In Warsaw the proclamation of the war was received with delirious enthusiasm. For the time being at least, all doubts about Napoleon's intentions were swept away. Strangers stopped each other in the streets and openly wept with joy. White-and-red Polish flags with the two-headed eagle appeared everywhere. People brought out their family silver to be melted for coinage to pay for the upkeep of the army. The monastery of Czestochowa, the most holy of Polish places of worship, which houses the shrine of the miraculous Black Madonna, donated its centuries-old treasure-chest of gold and precious jewels to help with the expenses of the war. To mark the historic occasion, the government of the Grand Duchy ordered festive illuminations in the capital. These unfortunately did not last long: there was such a shortage of cooking-oil in Warsaw at the time that people simply extracted the oil from the lamps and carried it home to their kitchens.

For Marie this was the repetition of the mood of the winter of 1806 – the joyous hope, the utter commitment with, strangely, no undercurrent of fear or doubt. It had been almost fifteen years since the Poles first threw in their lot with Napoleon's legions in Italy, but their faith in his star was still blazing.

Until Moscow the bulletins were superb. The colossal difficulties of getting supplies to the troops, the wastage of men, horses and material, due to the lack of food, disease and the enemy's policy of 'scorched earth', were glossed over. The enemy was forever retreating, and in Warsaw this was interpreted as good news. The Abbé de Pradt continued to entertain on a grand scale; he had now moved to the lovely eighteenth-century Brühl Palace, Warsaw's grandest residence, and Warsaw's society, eager for news of the war, flocked to his receptions. There members of the Grand Duchy's government, French diplomats, military men and assorted visiting dignitaries passed evenings discussing the latest bulletin from the front, political gossip from Paris, the Grand Duchy's worsening economic situation – while doing honour to the Ambassador's famous Chambertin and good cuisine. If no news came, it was put down to the state of the roads. Only a handful of die-hard pessimists forecast possible disaster, but they were made to feel unpopular. The prevailing mood in the capital was one of optimism and anxious anticipation.

Marie, though she did not like the Abbé Pradt, returned from the country in early autumn and attended his receptions because of her longing for news. It is probable that, on Napoleon's instructions, she used the Ambassador's good offices to communicate with the Emperor during his long stay in Moscow. One or two references in contemporary memoirs make one suspect that she contemplated joining him there, since at one point Napoleon was expected to spend the entire winter in Moscow. After Finkenstein and Schönbrunn, why not the Kremlin? It would have been in keeping with the past. But this time the journey was not to take place.

As in the winter of 1806, Marie joined the ladies of Warsaw at work in preparing space in the hospitals. Warsaw was the main evacuation-base for the wounded. They made lint, sewed sheets, tore bandages, and assembled stocks of medicines and food supplies. This was a difficult task because of the lamentable economic state of the country, drained by the inexhaustible demands of the Grand Army, which had taken three months to march through Polish territory on its way east and had stripped it of more or less everything. In 1812 everyone in Warsaw was incomparably poorer than they had been five years previously.

Among Marie's friends of that first winter, the lovely Elizabeth Grabowska had married a prominent politician and was now one of Warsaw's most popular hostesses; she and Marie were still close. The sultry, flirtatious Emily ('the siren with the face of an angel'), now reluctantly entering middle-age, was in Vilna, the capital of Polish Lithuania, where she entertained the advance echelons of the army and succeeded in enticing into matrimony Captain Abramowicz, a dashing Polish Guards officer, more than twenty years younger than herself. Madame de Vauban was still there, much aged, badly affected by her rheumatism, but continuing to attend an occasional dinner-party at the Abbé de Pradt's residence. Like all Warsaw, she anxiously awaited bulletins from the battle-field, and particularly any mention of Prince Joseph.

The first inkling that something was wrong was the news of the burning of Moscow, which reached Warsaw in the middle of October. After that, all communications suddenly ceased. A dreadful sense of foreboding descended on the Polish capital. Every family in Warsaw had a husband, a son, a brother or some more distant relative at the front; people hardly dared to look at each other for fear of hearing the worst. But not even the most gloomy of forecasters could have predicted the dimensions of the catastrophe. And it was just as well that they did not know what was happening. This time, reality would outstrip imagination.

The Poles could not see their idol the Emperor as he stood at a window in the Kremlin, watching the blazing city of Moscow with 'extreme agitation – so that one would have thought he himself was being consumed by the fire around him'. They did not witness the surrealistic spectacle which, after the fires had abated, greeted the returning troops. It was a sight vividly recorded by General Count de Ségur, a scion of an aristocratic family, who had joined the imperial army for the glory of serving under Napoleon's command.

Enormous fires had been lit in the middle of the fields, in thick, cold mud, and were being fed with mahogany furniture and gilded windows and doors. Around these fires, on litters of damp straw, ill-protected by a few boards, soldiers and their officers, mud-stained and smoke-blackened, were seated in splendid armchairs or lying on silk sofas. At their feet were heaped or spread out cashmere shawls, the rarest of Siberian furs, cloth of gold from Persia and assorted silver dishes in which they were eating coarse black bread baked in the ashes and half-cooked bloody horseflesh.... The disorder and licence in the city were past belief. All the loot of Moscow was spread out in the smouldering squares and traded among the soldiers. Gold, being easier to carry, was bought at a great loss for silver, which the knapsacks would not hold. . . . Soldiers were seated in the midst of the finest wines and liqueurs, trying to trade them for bread.

Napoleon lost five precious weeks waiting in Moscow for a reply to his peace-overture to the Tsar. But his letter remained unanswered. And then – in the third week of October, when the Russian winter was about to descend, the armies began their ill-fated retreat. In the first days of November the snow fell, and everything in sight became vague and unrecognizable. 'We walked without knowing where we were,' recalled one of the participants, 'or what lay ahead.'

As the soldiers collapsed, overcome by hunger or cold or because they had tripped on some obstacle – a branch or the body of a fallen comrade – the snow instantly covered them, and only 'low white mounds showed where they lay.' 'Our road was strewn with such hummocks like a cemetery,' says Ségur. Numbed by the cold, men dropped their muskets, broke rank, fell behind in small groups of stragglers and were then mercilessly slaughtered by the Cossacks.

After the crossing of the Berezina, in which Napoleon lost over twenty-five thousand men, the army disintegrated. While Marshal Ney – 'the bravest of the brave' – and his cavalry, covering the rearguard, fought heroic battles every day to hold off the enemy, the wretched army – now more like a rabble – dragged itself through the snows towards the Lithuanian and Polish borders. On 3 December only about nine thousand men remained in formation. The Emperor himself, sometimes riding in his carriage but mostly walking with a stick among his Guard, 'suffered terribly from the cold'. That day at Molodechno he dictated his famous 29th Bulletin in which he announced the annihilation of the *Grande Armée* and listed all their sufferings and disasters. It concluded with the famous words: 'His Majesty's health has never been better.'

Two days later, accompanied by Caulaincourt, he got into a carriage and, leaving the army in charge of Marshal Murat, which turned out to be a disastrous decision, he began his head-long dash toward Paris to assume control of the situation at home. In his absence there had been an attempted *coup* by a former general, Malet.

In Warsaw the Abbé de Pradt somewhat forlornly continued to give splendid receptions and even once criticized a Warsaw lady who came wearing a black mourning-dress. But slowly the truth began to emerge in all its horrifying implications : the war was lost, and so was Poland. Napoleon had led his armies to destruction; the Conqueror of the World had been defeated.

Marie was back at Kiernozia with her mother, who was awaiting news of her eldest son, Benedict. (He eventually returned from Russia unhurt.) On 10 December – a day of extreme cold (−23°C), made worse by a biting east wind – the Emperor, travelling in a small sleigh with Caulaincourt, the former French Ambassador to Russia, unexpectedly arrived in Warsaw. Once across the Praga bridge on the Vistula, he got out to stretch his legs. No one recognized the well-wrapped figure in a fur-lined green velvet cloak with gold braid and a large sable hat walking up the Krakowskie Przedmiescie (Cracow Faubourg), a graceful street of eighteenth-century houses, gently curving toward the large esplanade where he had often held his parades in the past. Installed at the Hôtel d'Angleterre, he summoned Ambassador Pradt and members of the Polish Government.

'Why doesn't he stay at the palace?' the bewildered Abbé Pradt asked Caulaincourt.

'He does not want to be recognized in this city.'

'And where are you going?'

'To Paris.'

'Where is the army?'

'It has ceased to exist.'

To the venerable Polish statesman Stanislas Potocki, who rushed in to inquire of his health, Napoleon announced that 'he had never been better'. He quoted Voltaire's line from the death of Caesar : 'From the sublime to the ridiculous is only one step.'

He then went into what he called 'practical matters', to urge the raising of an additional ten thousand Polish cavalrymen to continue 'waging the war'. After a short rest and a meal, and having taken on board a supply of Monsignor Pradt's Chambertin, the Emperor got into his sleigh and sped off west into the blizzard.

Gliding over a blanket of deep snow, he arrived that afternoon at Lowicz, a small town a few miles away from Marie's home. With the Emperor at the time was his Polish interpreter and ADC, Colonel Wonsowicz, who later married Anna Potocka. According to his account, Napoleon, who at all times was informed of Marie's whereabouts, suggested to Caulaincourt that they make a small detour via Kiernozia, but Caulaincourt dissuaded him, arguing that this was no time for private matters and that the news of the Emperor's visit to Countess Walewska at a time when his army was being harassed by the Russians would have a fatal effect on the morale of his soldiers. According to Colonel Wonsowicz, the Emperor 'looked annoyed' but agreed that they had better continue on to Posen.

There exists another account, which may also be true; it could have happened later that day a little way beyond Lowicz, where they might have stopped to have supper. It appears in a book by a Belgian traveller, Alexandre Gley, *Voyage en Allemagne et en Pologne*, published in Paris in 1816. Gley apparently retraced Napoleon's footsteps in Poland a few months after the Emperor's abdication, and reported a conversation Napoleon allegedly had with a lady from a neighbouring estate, who knew the Walewski family. She, of course, had not recognized him, dressed as he was in a Russian peasant's pelisse and a curious-looking green velvet coat. When asked about old Count Walewski, she chatted amiably, recounting how 'the old Chamberlain's debts had been paid by the Emperor of France' and how Madame Walewska, his wife, had spent the entire autumn in Warsaw 'worrying about the fate of the armies and wanting to join the Emperor in Moscow'. Napoleon never revealed his identity.

Whether the conversation took place or not, it is certain that Napoleon did not make a detour to visit Marie. And it is not surprising that he did not. He had by then been travelling continuously for six days in atrocious weather conditions, obsessed by the thought of what he would find back in Paris, where General Malet's conspiracy to overthrow him had been discovered. He was exhausted and feverish, certainly in no mood for romance or even friendship. Marie's safety was not immediately endangered. She had received her instructions: she was to pack up her things and go to Paris. The Russian army would soon be marching into the Grand Duchy of Warsaw.

Before leaving Poland, Marie went to Warsaw one last time, to pay her respects to Prince Joseph Poniatowski, who returned with the scattered remnants of his army. It was hard to recognize the dashing Prince Pepi, the adored commander-in-chief of the army of the Grand Duchy of Warsaw, in this haggard, emaciated man, racked by fever and unable to walk because of a bad wound in the leg. He had set off in June with a splendid corps of forty thousand men; now fewer than a thousand were left, pitiful wrecks in tattered uniforms, wrapped in stray bits of fur, odd coats, some in pilfered church vestments – anything to keep from freezing in the snow. Though most of their comrades were now dead and their military formations disbanded, they had managed to bring back all the regimental standards, which they now gathered at the feet of their leader, who had to be carried out on a stretcher to address them.

Did Prince Joseph regret his loyalty to Napoleon? He could not but recall Tsar Alexander's entreaties to him to abandon the Napoleonic cause. Even at the very last moment – a few days before the hostilities began – the Tsar had sent out a secret emissary offering to make Prince Joseph the effective ruler of an independent Poland if he 'changed sides and marched with the Russians'. But Poniatowski had refused.

And even now, though the horror of the catastrophe had become fully apparent, Prince Joseph talked only of rebuilding his army and continuing to support the Emperor of France, no

matter what sacrifices were called for. In the end, before a year
had elapsed, he was to make the ultimate sacrifice – that of his
own life.

Vilna, the woodland capital of Lithuania, built on hills and
circled by lakes, was to be the last refuge of the Grand Army. It
housed masses of stores, bulged with food and supplies. But no
sooner did the famished French army get there than they were
fallen upon by the Cossacks, who had followed them in pursuit
across the frontier. Instead of being a refuge, Wilna became a
nightmare. Those who did not die of hunger or cold perished at
the hands of the Cossacks or were trampled to death in the
narrow streets by their own comrades frantically searching for
food. One of the casualties in the town, though not at the hands
of the Cossacks, was the American Minister in Paris, Joel
Barlow, who had been sent by President Madison from Paris to
Wilna to 'discuss a new commercial treaty with Napoleon'.
Communications between Washington, Paris and the front
could not have been very efficient if Barlow had hoped to find
Napoleon residing in Wilna. He arrived in mid-December on a
day when the temperature was − 23°c. He promptly contracted pneumonia and died on 24 December 1812 – the first
war-casualty in the history of the young American Department
of State. He was buried on a hillside in Wilna, a long way from
his native Maryland, and his name appears at the head of the
State Department's Roll of Honour tablet in Washington.

When the indomitable Marshal Ney led the rearguard of his
men over the Niemen into Lithuania and the stragglers re-
grouped, it was seen that fewer than forty thousand men of the
initial Grand Army of over half a million had survived.

As the fatal year of 1812 drew tragically to its close, a
muffled sob could be heard throughout Poland – a lament for the
lives that were lost, for the hopes that remained unfulfilled, for
the love that died on the frozen plains, for the dreams that had
proved to be a mirage. The nation watched with mounting
horror the emaciated men painfully trudging home from the

white hell; they remembered the distant silhouette of the Emperor speeding away in his sleigh. Their army had melted away; they were left alone and defenceless in the face of the onrushing hordes from the east.

10

PARIS IN 1813

The year 1813 found Marie back in Paris, settled in the rue de la Houssaye house with her two sons, her brother Theodore and her sister Antonia, who had travelled with her from Poland. Little is known of Antonia. Uruski's *Book of Polish Nobility* gives her birth-date as 1794, which makes her eight years younger than Marie, and lists three consecutive marriages, all to military men. A rare mention in one of the contemporary memoirs describes her as 'fair of skin, a bit stout, bearing a distinct family resemblance to Marie, but with none of her beauty'. It is likely that Antonia's first husband, young Lasocki, was with the Polish Lancers at the time, serving either in France or in Poland, and that she planned to rejoin him at some stage when his regiment returned to its military depot at Chantilly. In the meantime she remained in Paris with Marie throughout the year and later accompanied her to Elba.

Thanks to Napoleon's generous endowment, Marie was now a rich woman. Since the previous October, money from Alexander's Neapolitan estates had started to accumulate in her account. Just before she left Poland she advanced the large sum of fifteen thousand francs and seven thousand sovereigns to Prince Joseph Poniatowski to help re-equip the Polish army. It was ironic that this money, which came from Napoleon's private pocket, should have been given at a time when Maret, France's Foreign Minister, who had just arrived in Warsaw from Vilna, was exerting strong pressure on the Prince to raise a new army but refusing at the same time to grant the impoverished Grand Duchy of Warsaw a loan from the French government. Napoleon's private purse was proving to be more generous than his government's. The loan was duly noted in Prince Joseph's personal archives and repaid to Marie's descendants some years after his death.

The Countess Walewska was now twenty-six years old and at the height of her beauty. With her looks, social standing and newly acquired wealth, she was in an enviable position, particularly when her fate was compared with that of the majority of Polish women back home, for whom the future looked dark and uncertain. She had her two children with her, and though her mother had refused to leave Poland, with Antonia, Theodore and Benedict in France she was surrounded by her family. And she had great security, something that her fellow-countrywomen would lack for generations to come.

How did she feel about life? Most of Marie's activities between the time she returned to Paris from Poland and the fall of the Empire took place in the houses of friends or in her own house in the presence of friends and relatives. These activities are haphazardly recorded in the journals of those friends and acquaintances, some of whom were enthusiastic – though variously accurate – scribblers. They convey a picture of a woman living a quiet and dignified family life, appearing in society and Court circles, fashionably dressed by Leroy (two Court *toilettes* supplied in the winter of 1813 – one of black velvet, embroidered with gold, and another in white tulle – are listed among many other items), attending the opera and the theatre, visiting friends, dining at the fashionable Very's restaurant near the Palais Royal. As she confided to an old friend at the time, 'There is no point giving up all pleasure in life because of the suffering of my country – but you will understand that I find it difficult to be *really* happy these days.'

For a young, rich and beautiful woman, no matter how patriotic, the state of her distant country could not have been her sole reason for sounding wistful. Marie wanted to love and be loved, and she longed for a normal relationship with a man. She had always been essentially monogamous: having given herself body and soul to Napoleon, having discovered the delight of the senses, having felt his child stir in her body, she was then abruptly shunted aside at a moment when she loved him most passionately. Early in the year 1810 she was in a state that we would describe today as approaching a nervous breakdown. Only the birth of her child saved Marie from sinking into the deepest depression. The long months following the birth, with practically no word from the Emperor but with plenty of rumours and comments about his 'marital bliss' – each of them a stab of pain to her heart – were, in spite of her joy in Alexander, a period of cruel agony. Seeing him in Paris at rare intervals, solicitous as a friend but unwilling, out of loyalty to his new wife, to answer her desperate longing for him, was at first a tremendous blow to her pride. Only during the infrequent occasions when they were alone with their son could she feel the old intimacy creeping back. For the rest of the time he left her to her own devices. And yet the Emperor always knew whom Marie saw, with whom she dined, who accompanied her to the theatre, who had partnered her at a ball. Surveillance was a feature of life in Napoleon's Paris. Fouché's (the Minister of Police) and later Savary's agents always seemed to hover in the distance whenever she ventured out on a social engagement away from home. Even if she had desired it, a new romance would have been difficult to contemplate.

But Marie was not yet ready for another man, nor did she want to break out of the circle of Napoleon's custody, which, though confining at times, meant that he still cared about her; strangely, she had always approved of his semi-oriental, proprietary attitude to his women. She was familiar with his bourgeois concept of marriage, and it made it easier, though not necessarily less painful, to understand his absorption in the new Empress and their son. But above all she still loved the Emperor as a man; even now, though his appearance had changed and he had become 'puffed up with a protruding belly', (the result of an over-indulgence in rich food), as his portrait painted in 1812 at St Cloud shows. No matter what his appearance, Napoleon could always cast a powerful spell over people, and for Marie the old magic still held.

As the winter progressed, two new, widely different persons came into Marie's life – one of them a woman. Unexpectedly one day a messenger appeared bearing a charming letter from the former Empress Josephine, in which she asked Marie to pay her a visit at Malmaison. Marie's reaction was a mixture of surprise and vague embarrassment. She recalled the time – more than six years earlier – when Josephine had been jealous of her and upset at not being allowed to rejoin her husband in Warsaw. She had rightly suspected that Napoleon had refused her permission to travel because of his infatuation with Marie. The two women had never met.

It was probably Hortense, Queen of Holland, Josephine's daughter, who suggested the meeting. Since the annexation of Holland by Napoleon, Queen Hortense, now separated from her husband, had been living at the Tuileries in close contact with the Empress Marie Louise. Hortense was very fond of Marie and only a few weeks previously had asked her help in organizing a dance she planned to give at the Tuileries at Napoleon's request. The idea was to counteract the general atmosphere of deep gloom. Dances were infrequent in those days, as the capital was tense and anxious – unlike the glittering, dancing Paris of previous years.

It was spring. The discarded Empress, now forty-nine, with much of her beauty and grace left intact, was living at Malmaison, the delightful country retreat near Paris which she and Napoleon had bought in the first years of their marriage. The gardens she had so lovingly created were bright with lilac, irises and gillyflowers.

During the anxious days before Napoleon returned from Russia, Marie Louise had got into the habit of showing her husband's letters to Hortense. It was an uncharacteristically kind gesture on her part: she knew that Hortense would pass on the news to her mother. Josephine was grateful to her but in her anxiety still needed some closer link with her ex-husband. With her infallible sixth sense, she was convinced that a catastrophe was about to engulf 'my Bonaparte'. She asked Hortense to invite Marie to Malmaison with her small son. The first meeting, in spite of some reticence on Marie's part, was a success, and others followed. Mademoiselle Avrillon, Josephine's lady-in-waiting, recalled in her memoirs that 'the ex-Empress developed great affection for Madame Walewska. She often talked of her unusual qualities and went to great lengths to stress that this woman, so essentially kind and good-natured, had never caused her any pain. She sent her frequent small gifts and showered presents on the little boy, whose features so reminded her of the Emperor.'

We can imagine the two women walking in Malmaison's lovely gardens among the massed borders of roses, which were Josephine's gift to France and to Europe. Before she introduced the new varieties from Persia, the roses in France were small and fragile and bloomed only for a few days. Josephine planted over two hundred varieties, and from them cultivated the tea-rose which went on blooming for weeks; from the tea-rose she bred the 'hybrid perpetual'. Most garden roses today stem back to Malmaison.

A picture comes to mind of the two of them: the former Empress, in a loose-flowing dress, gliding with ethereal grace about the lawns, talking in her languorous voice with the haunting Creole inflection, and the young, willowy, blonde Polish woman with the enormously expressive blue eyes, dragging a lively little boy by the hand. They had both loved the same man; this man's good fortune had left him when he deserted both wife and mistress. Married to Josephine, 'Notre Dame des Victoires', as the Parisians called her, he had fought triumphantly from the first Italian campaign to Wagram, and at the time of their divorce he was the virtual master of Europe. He could have retained Marie at his side, restored Poland, united Europe in peace by abandoning further conquests, but instead, blinded by his dynastic ambitions, he had forfeited half a million men in Russia and was preparing to spill ever more and more blood.

That spring Josephine had only one more year to live: she died two months after Napoleon's abdication, following a chill she contracted walking in her gardens in late evening. Marie was to survive her by only three years.

The other new friendship in Marie's life was with a man, a Corsican soldier, cousin of the Emperor (related to the Bona-partes through his mother's family). Philippe Antoine Ornano, newly promoted to general, was two years older than Marie, good-looking in a dark, Italian way and, according to con-temporary accounts, 'of an irreproachable character and great charm'. Ornano had begun his military career at the age of eighteen, when, as adjutant to General Leclerc, he sailed with the French forces to San Domingo (present-day Haiti), to restore the colony to France after Toussaint l'Ouverture's insurrection. Ornano was one of the few Frenchmen who escaped the ravages of yellow fever and returned to France unharmed. There was a Polish contingent with General Leclerc's forces, and this was where Ornano came into contact with the people with whom his life was to be intertwined from then on. Serving as one of Napoleon's ADCS in Warsaw during the first Polish campaign of 1807, he first met Marie at the house of her married sister, the Countess Ledochowska; later, at the famous Talleyrand's ball, he witnessed Napoleon's infatuation. A nice but rather improb-able story was bandied about at the time to the effect that Ornano was on guard at Napoleon's apartments at the castle when Marie was ushered in 'sobbing', and that he offered to protect her from the Emperor. Whatever the truth may be, their paths did not cross again. Ornano spent the subsequent years on the Spanish front and from there was ordered to Russia whence he returned wounded but covered with decorations and newly promoted to general. In a letter dated 17 January 1813, Madame Letizia Bonaparte, the Emperor's mother, wrote to Pauline Borghese, her daughter, 'During the last days of 1812 we saw

General Ornano, almost recovered after being given up for dead on the battlefield.' It was not difficult for Marie and Ornano to meet again. They were both well-known figures in Paris, and Marie was a celebrity; it was undoubtedly pleasant for her to have this dashing young general, the Emperor's cousin, to escort her around town. The fact that he was related to the Emperor and that Napoleon sanctioned the friendship silenced potential gossips on the subject. For some reason never explained, probably a private joke between them, Marie called her young admirer Auguste and addressed him so in the few friendly and rather detached letters she wrote to him after he left Paris for the front in the spring of 1813, when Napoleon's new campaign re-opened.

The remnants of the *Grande Armée* could not be expected to defend East Prussia, Polish Lithuania or even the Grand Duchy of Warsaw, from where Polish troops were obliged to withdraw to the Austrian-occupied zone and Cracow. The flamboyant Marshal Murat, whom Napoleon had left in command of the army, deserted the cold of the north after two weeks and made his way back from the frontiers of Russia to his warm kingdom of Naples. Josephine's son, Eugène de Beauharnais, the Viceroy of Italy, who took over from Murat, had to give up the line of the Oder, evacuated Berlin and fell back behind the Elbe in the face of the inexorable Russian advance. In late February the King of Prussia, so despised by Napoleon, signed a formal alliance with the Tsar and declared war on France. In contrast with its state in 1806, Prussia was now a formidable enemy, with a newly reformed and modernized army longing to avenge the humiliating string of past military defeats. And beyond the borders of Prussia, German nationalism was stirring, with poets and philosophers proclaiming the cause of German freedom – an ominous threat to the future existence of the Confederation of the Rhine, on which Napoleon's domination of Europe depended. Austria, though still an ally, was secretly negotiating with Tsar Alexander. Napoleon was aware of it but firmly refused to believe that the Emperor Francis would ever fight against his own son-in-law; his faith in the strength of the dynastic connection proved to be one of the factors that contributed to his eventual downfall. In the meantime, to emphasize the family tie, he conferred upon Marie Louise the title of Regent during his absence from France.

In the spring of 1813 Napoleon succeeded in raising another army in France, this time of three hundred thousand; most of his recruits were barely out of childhood. To them were added units from Germany, Poland and Italy but, with the exception of the Polish contingents, none was fully reliable. To add to the difficulties, Bernadotte, a former marshal of France, now Crown Prince of Sweden, joined Napoleon's enemies, concluded an alliance with England and landed Swedish troops in Pomerania.

Napoleon rejoined his army at Erfurt on 25 April. He led off the campaign with a victory at Lützen, near Leipzig, but he had so little cavalry for the pursuit of the enemy that the victory proved to be an empty one. As the Russians and the Prussians fell back, the Emperor's troops occupied Dresden and won another victory at Bautzen. But two great losses marred this military success. At Lützen Marshal Bessières, Duke of Istria – the most brilliant cavalry commander after Murat and much loved by the army – was killed by a sniper's shot. And even worse, on the first day of the battle of Bautzen, Géraud Duroc, the Grand Marshal of the Palace and Napoleon's most intimate confidant and closest friend, was mortally wounded – disembowelled by an enemy shell – as he galloped beside the Emperor. Napoleon's grief for Duroc was terrible; some historians compare it with Alexander the Great's agony after the death of Hephaistos. It induced strangely uncharacteristic behaviour on the Emperor's part: he called off the action and would see no one for the rest of that day and night. Later he bought the farmyard where Duroc died and had a monument erected on the spot.

Marie too was shaken by the news of the Grand Marshal's death. Duroc had been part of her life since the early days of 1807. It was he who had sat next to her in the carriage which took her to the castle in Warsaw for her first rendezvous with Napoleon. It was Duroc who had held her hand quietly when she trembled with fear at the Emperor's outburst of rage because she failed to wear the jewels he had sent her. It was Duroc who had made her laugh at the private sign-language between him and the Emperor. And it was Duroc who, for the last six years, had provided the link with Napoleon and who at all times had given her excellent advice and moral support. She knew how essential he was to the Emperor, for no other man could be trusted with so many important secrets as Duroc.

Her letter to Napoleon commiserating with him after Duroc's death has not survived, but it must have been eloquent, for it elicited a short, affectionate reply. Like Marie, Géraud Christophe Michel Duroc, Duke of Friouli, was one of the handful of people who loved Napoleon for himself as a man and not as an Emperor.

After Bautzen the Emperor agreed to an armistice that was to last until 20 July that year. In consenting to the truce, his main motive was the desire to conclude peace before Austria, whose stand had become equivocal, changed sides. But his calculation went wrong, for there was wide dissension among the enemy sovereigns, and the armistice proved to be an unhoped-for gift from Heaven. It certainly gave Austria a chance to prepare her about-face and enabled treacherous Bernadotte's troops to reach the zone of combat in time. Metternich, the diplomatic genius, whose family estates on the Rhine were occupied by revolutionary France in 1794, assumed the role of mediator between France and her enemies. He intended to force Napoleon to give up all his gains in Europe and return them, including the Metternich estates, to the old Teutonic Empire. To begin with, the Grand Duchy of Warsaw was to be partitioned and suppressed, a condition to which Napoleon could not honourably agree, though he tried to devise a compromise. Northern Italy was to be given back to Austria, the Confederation of the Rhine to be dissolved, Prussia to regain the left bank of the Elbe. All in all, the French Empire was to be dismembered and its frontiers pushed back to the Rhine. In spite of his two victories, Napoleon was being asked to give up three-quarters of the gains he had made since 1800 and was told that, if negotiations came to nothing, Austria would join the other powers in war on France.

Metternich represented the old order, with all its privileges and tradition. In Napoleon's eyes the French Empire was the new order, embodying the rights of man and social and political development brought about by French ideas, French genius and force of arms. As he expressed it in his writings, Napoleon saw western Europe as a patrimony he held in trust, that no man had the right to disperse. He firmly believed that it would be wrong to make peace at any price. His interview with Metternich at the Marcolini Palace in Dresden lasted nine hours; at the end of it the break was complete. The two men never met again, and in the subsequent confrontation the old order won over the new.

From then on events moved rapidly to a climax. Austria rejoined the anti-Napoleon coalition, and on 12 August the Emperor Francis, 'a skeleton whom the worth of his ancestors had placed on the throne', declared war on his son-in-law. So much for Napoleon's trust in dynastic connections. Next, Bavaria defected from the French alliance, and from Spain came the news that Wellington had routed King Joseph. From one end of Europe to the other, nations were arrayed against a weakening conqueror. But Napoleon still hoped for a great battle which would turn the scales in his favour.

Marie was in Paris when the battle of Leipzig, 'the Battle of the Nations', as it was called – because so many different nationalities took part in it – started on 14 October; it lasted four days, costing the French 73,000 men killed and wounded. Napoleon was defeated by the so-called Allied armies – Russian, Prussian and Austrian – that had joined together to rout him. In the confusion of the retreat through the city of Leipzig, the one remaining bridge over the Elster was blown up too soon, and a rearguard of over twenty thousand men was trapped. Covering the French armies' retreat was the Polish contingent commanded by Prince Joseph Poniatowski, who only a few days before had been made a Marshal of France 'to give encouragement to the Poles in the great battle which was about to be fought'.

Back in Warsaw after the disastrous Russian campaign, Prince Joseph, in a feat of organizational wizardry, had managed to raise a new army to add to the shattered remnants of his corps. It consisted mainly of peasants and country folk mounted on fast, diminutive mountain horses indigenous to the province of Cracow. They proved immensely effective, particularly in combating the Cossacks. Napoleon called them 'my pigmy cavalry' and loved to see them in action. When the Russians occupied the Grand Duchy, Poniatowski withdrew his forces to Cracow. Again strong pressure was put on the Prince to change sides and endorse Tsar Alexander's plans for the creation of a Russian-ruled kingdom of Poland. He refused. He still had faith in Napoleon. For Prince Joseph it was a matter of military discipline. He was the commander of a unit which technically formed a part of the Grand Army: therefore he felt under obligation to rejoin it. Desertion, betrayal, changing sides – this was not the Polish way of waging war; as always, his soldiers were behind him. In late spring, in spite of threatening objections on the part of the Austrian military who controlled the territory between Cracow and Dresden, Prince Joseph led his small army of fifteen thousand men out of Poland and rejoined Napoleon's headquarters in Saxony.

'Prince Joseph was pensive and sad while in Dresden, quite unlike his usual high spirits,' recalled one of the officers on his staff. 'He looked as if he had some premonition of doom, and his mood communicated itself to all of us.' He was right. For the Polish Bayard – the *'chevalier sans peur et sans reproche'*, as he was generally called in the French army – the shadows were lengthening.

On Monday 18 October, the third day of the battle of Leipzig, when the pontoon bridge on the River Elster was prematurely blown up by a frightened sapper of the French Engineers Corps,

Prince Joseph, wounded three times, was covering Marshal Macdonald's retreat through the suburbs of the city. But the enemy was in such strength that he and his men could do nothing. As the Prince's horse was shot from under him, he and his men walked towards the river through the muddy back-gardens of Leipzig under constant enemy fire. They found him a horse, and he rode on, but he was bleeding heavily from his wounds and growing weak in the saddle. 'His companions begged him to surrender,' related an eye-witness account, 'but he shook his head, uttering some words about honour and Poland – he already had death in his face.' At the approach of enemy infantry, he spurred his horse and leaped into the River Elster. An enemy bullet pierced his left lung; he slid off his mount and went under. From a nearby hill, Prince Schwarzen-berg, the commander of the Austrian forces and boon com-panion of Prince Joseph in his youth, watched with sadness as his friend, but enemy in battle, the commander-in-chief of the Polish forces, was swallowed up by the muddy waters of the Elster. Years before, when they were camping together in the Hungarian *pushta*, a gipsy had warned Prince Joseph: 'Beware of magpies.' *Elster* is the German for magpies.

With the death of Prince Joseph, the dream that had so mes-merized the Poles, who saw their country recreated and happily existing in Napoleon's orbit, irrevocably came to an end. Late that evening the Emperor, inspecting the dismal battlefield in the rain, came across a group of Polish officers who were sadly discussing the loss of their leader. Most of them were now plan-ning to return to Poland from Leipzig. '*Messieurs les Polonais*,' Napoleon addressed them, as he stopped by their bivouac fire, 'I never had anything to reproach you people, neither as an emperor nor as a general. You must do what you wish. Return to your country if you must, but I would like you to come back to France with me, *Messieurs les Polonais*.' The men looked at each other in silence. Even after a defeat Napoleon could still cast a spell, for suddenly a great cry arose: '*Vive l'Empereur!*' Leipzig was near the borders of Poland; it would have taken them less than a day to return home, but instead most of the Polish contingent turned around and marched west, to follow Napoleon to the end. It had been seven years since the victorious Emperor arrived on the banks of the Vistula as the Saviour of Poland. Now the Poles were crossing the Rhine to help him save France.

Throughout most of the gloomy summer months Marie was at Spa, a health resort in Belgium, trying to repair her fragile health, undermined by the nervous exhaustion she had suffered during the Moscow campaign. Ornano's letters from headquarters kept her in touch with events. She answered rarely, unwilling to encourage a commitment which she was not yet prepared to reciprocate. She was back at her house in Paris when news came of Prince Joseph Poniatowski's death. That too was a severe shock. She had liked and admired Prince Joseph from the early days of her childhood, when to every teenaged girl in Poland he represented Prince Charming. She had watched him grow in stature as a statesman and as a national leader and attain his present popularity. He had always been a figure of which dreams are made, and though he had now taken a place in the Pantheon of Polish heroes, Warsaw would never be the same without him. Little did she know that in less than five years Prince Joseph's residence, the palace of Pod Blacha, a famous Warsaw landmark she knew so well, would become the private property of Tsar Alexander, the man whose blandishments the Prince had so valiantly rejected.

The Polish Bayard left a very modest fortune behind him – he had lived fully and well. One of his specific bequests was to his soldiers, to spend 'a happy evening drinking to my memory'. An equestrian statue of the Prince by the Danish sculptor Thorwaldsen was erected by public subscription in the main Warsaw square. It was destroyed by the Germans during the last war, but a new one, cast from the original mould preserved in the Thorwaldsen Museum in Copenhagen, was put up near the place where his palace used to stand.

When Napoleon returned to Paris on 9 November, his empire was in a state of collapse. The new army he had raised at the beginning of the year had shrunk to a mere sixty thousand men. Italy, Holland and the states of the Confederation of the Rhine were in ferment, asserting their independence.

In a way they were being ungrateful, for Napoleon had given them social justice, an excellent code of law and the beginnings of self-government. But they had learned patriotism from the French and now wanted to be independent themselves. They were also tired of the economic isolation imposed through the Continental blockade and were determined to have access to England's industrial expertise and her cheap manufactured goods, woollens, cottons, cutlery, razor-blades and all kinds of machinery. One by one the German states deserted France. Holland recalled the Prince of Orange, and Northern Italy joined the Austrians. Napoleon was faced with the necessity of defending the frontiers of metropolitan France itself, and the country was frightened; there was an ominous feeling of impending catastrophe in the air.

In December, just before Christmas, Napoleon sent for Marie, 'to discuss her financial affairs'. Marshal Murat, the King of Naples, was about to change sides. After accompanying the Emperor in the hurried retreat from Leipzig, Murat had made up his mind that Napoleon's cause was hopeless and in order to safeguard his kingdom decided to accept Metternich's offer to defect to the Austrians. He knew that, if he delayed any longer, his defection might not be worth buying. Such a move would annul Alexander Walewski's endowment in Naples, as Napoleon's writ would cease to run in the kingdom: the estates would undoubtedly be confiscated. Some other arrangement had to be made.

It is remarkable that, in the face of an avalanche of preoccupations, as his empire was about to collapse, Napoleon still found time to attend to young Alexander's future. In January 1814 a document was prepared making over to him an income of fifty thousand francs (about 300,000 new francs at today's value), derived partly from shares in property and navigational rents from the canals of France and partly from the *grand livre*, a state register of pensions. Monsieur de la Bouillerie, the Treasurer General of the Empire, was asked to draw up the necessary legal documents forthwith. On 8 February 1814, on the eve of the battle of Champaubert, we find the Emperor urgently writing to de la Bouillerie from Nogent: 'I have received your letter relative to young Walewski's affairs. I leave you a free hand to settle it. Please do everything necessary but do it *now*. My first interest is in the child, the mother comes second. Napoleon.'

The last sentence was put in for the benefit of history. It was more appropriate, perhaps, that on the eve of a battle the Emperor should occupy himself with his son's future rather than with the fate of the woman he had loved.

Earlier in January Napoleon had given orders that a new house be purchased for Alexander. By a strange coincidence one was found – the Hôtel St Chamans, at the rue Chantereine (present 48, rue de la Victoire) – next to the charming, countrified little house where Napoleon himself first started his married life with Josephine. The house, which still exists today (it is now the Crédit Industriel et Commercial), square and two-storeyed, lies between a courtyard and a garden. The ground floor consisted of several drawing-rooms leading out of each other, a dining-room and a library; overhead must have been the bedrooms, all on the garden-side facing south, with a wide view of trees. There were several small lodges housing a porter, stables and a laundry – altogether a nice roomy residence, ideal for bringing up children. Marie was to occupy it until her death.

She had just completed the purchase when, in late January, Napoleon took the field again to play out his last gamble. 'The Emperor left this morning,' she wrote to Ornano. 'I did not have a chance to say goodbye to him. . . . I wonder whether he has noticed . . . my nerves are in a very bad state.'

In late December the Russian and Prussian armies began to cross the Rhine into France. With the Austrian forces advancing through Switzerland, and Wellington marching north from the Peninsula through the south-west, they had more than half a million troops and fifteen hundred guns, a formidable concentration of firing-power in those days. To oppose them, Napoleon could muster an army of less than a hundred thousand soldiers, most of them new recruits, boys of sixteen or seventeen, nicknamed 'the Marie Louises' after the Empress, who again was made Regent, together with Napoleon's brother Joseph. The Treasury was empty, the country utterly weary of war, and, with every Frenchman yearning for peace, conscription was widely evaded.

In a brilliantly fought campaign Napoleon's genius flared up once more in a final astounding blaze. Wellington said afterwards that the study of the campaign of France had given him a greater idea of Napoleon's genius than any other. But in spite of this it was too late to save the Empire. The odds were too overwhelming. The circle was closing in. Neither the marshals nor the ministers had any stomach left for a fight. The Paris Stock Exchange was dropping alarmingly, and there was the beginning of a panic in the capital: rich ladies, afraid of being raped by the Cossacks, were leaving hurriedly, their jewels sewn in the hems of their skirts. The Emperor was surrounded by treachery and an atmosphere of deceit.

On 30 March the last battle was fought at Montmartre, and that night Marmont signed the capitulation of Paris. On 31 March Tsar Alexander and the King of Prussia rode down the Champs Elysées at the head of the victorious troops, the first time since the Hundred Years' War that a foreign army had entered the French capital. The Tsar took up residence in Talleyrand's house, and together they planned Napoleon's abdication.

On the day the victorious enemy made his entry into the capital, the Emperor arrived at Fontainebleau – the old Renaissance palace of Francis I and Henry IV, where Pope Pius VII had recently been imprisoned. Napoleon loved Fontainebleau, which had for centuries been used as a weekend retreat and hunting-lodge by successive kings of France. At night in its vast forest, it was said that, 'the ghost of a huntsman descended from an old picture on the wall and, clad in black, rode all night in the forest, surrounded by invisible companions.' Napoleon still had troops and the remnants of his Old Guard at his disposal; for a time he even entertained the idea of further fighting, but he ran into a wall of protest from his marshals. They urged him to abdicate. As the painful negotiations progressed, more and more of his entourage slipped away. After ten days, only a handful were left.

On the afternoon of 14 April, with the rain beating furiously at the windows of the palace, a veiled lady stepped out of a carriage which pulled up in the Cour du Cheval Blanc. There was no one to receive her in the deserted château. She hesitantly made her way through the long Francis I Gallery, where Court balls had been held in the past, to the west wing, where to her joy she encountered Constant, Napoleon's valet, her old friend, who led her to the Emperor's apartments. She sat in a small library directly adjoining his bedroom and waited.

Lying on his four-poster bed, hung with green Lyons velvet, adorned with imperial bees, topped with a golden eagle grappling laurels, the Emperor was in a state of deep torpor. He had signed the document of abdication – a humiliating treaty for a man who had ruled Europe from Spain to the borders of Russia – and was now being offered the sovereignty of a small Mediterranean island. He knew not only that he had lost France but that at that moment his wife and son were on their way to Austria; he suspected he might never see them again. The night before Marie's arrival he had tried to kill himself by taking poison, a mixture of opium, belladonna and white hellebore (also called 'indian poke'); he had carried it on his person from the days of the Russian campaign. But the phial of poison must have lost its potency, or his body had reacted too violently, for after a night of acute pain and vomiting, he survived. But he was physically and morally drained, suspended between reality and nightmarish dreams.

When the valet announced that Countess Walewska was

waiting, he either did not hear him or did not realize the identity of the caller. For days he had seen no one but Caulaincourt and his personal staff, some of whom had already deserted. According to the ever loyal Caulaincourt, 'The Emperor alternated between feverish exaltation and what seemed like total withdrawal from the present.'

Marie waited. She watched the rain-soaked clouds move to the west, the mists rise, enveloping the forest and the park; she heard the distant rumbling of carriages in the courtyard and the anxious footsteps of the valet on duty in the adjoining gallery. Still no summons. Napoleon was no more than twenty yards away from her; should she go in? It would have been natural for her to be with him now, when he was just a solitary man, suffering. But no one dared to penetrate into Napoleon's presence unbidden – so she waited. At her request Constant tiptoed into the room again; he reported that the Emperor was now awake but 'lost in thought'. He did not dare interrupt. Hours passed.

'I could not bear to watch her grief,' recalled Constant, 'so I went away and walked in the gallery.' As dawn broke, the Countess Walewska, anxious to keep her visit a secret, decided to return home. 'Less than an hour after this gracious lady's departure,' wrote Constant, 'the Emperor appeared in the door and asked for her. I told him all the circumstances of her visit . . . hiding nothing.' The Emperor was deeply moved. 'Poor woman, she must have been very upset,' he said, 'I must explain it to her.' Whereupon, according to the valet's testimony, Napoleon rubbed his forehead and murmured, 'I have so many, many problems these days.'

It took Marie all of that day and most of the following night to reach Paris over roads clogged with refugees, military vehicles and troops marching in every direction. The armistice had been signed, French troops were returning to headquarters, but there were still enemy detachments in Paris and some highways were being patrolled by the Cossacks. Luckily, just before entering Paris, the most dangerous point in the journey, she came under the protection of the Polish Lancers, who were returning to their military barracks in Paris (the Ave Maria barracks, near the Champ de Mars). Although, according to the terms of the armistice, Polish units serving with the French army now came under Tsar Alexander's jurisdiction, Napoleon had insisted on a separate deal for 'his Poles'. The regiments were not to be disbanded but to reassemble in Paris and regroup; then – fully armed – they were to begin their march across Europe, back to Poland.

The Lancers escorted Marie's carriage all the way to the Champ de Mars. As they approached the centre of the town, she saw that the news of the abdication was plastered over all the official buildings in Paris, and she noticed the preponderance of white cockades in the crowd. It did not take the Parisians very long to switch their allegiance to the Bourbons. Even the Garde Nationale now sported the white pennants of Louis XVIII, who was about to return from exile but had to delay his ceremonial entry into Paris because of a serious attack of gout. In the meantime the Parisians greeted with tumultuous enthusiasm – which even he found astonishing – the return of the Comte d'Artois, the brother of the restored king.

Next morning Marie dispatched a farewell letter to the Emperor. He replied on 16 April:

Marie – I have received your letter of the 15th and it has touched me deeply. When – after you have arranged your affairs in Paris – you decide to take the waters at Lucca or Pisa, I will see you with great and tender interest, as well as your son. My feelings for you remain unchanged. Keep well; don't worry. Think of me with pleasure and never doubt me.

Yours
Napoleon

There is a touching warmth and intimacy about this letter. The reference to Lucca and Pisa makes one suspect that earlier that year Napoleon must have discussed with Marie, either personally or by letter, the possibility of her travelling to Naples to

207

H

sort out young Alexander's inheritance. In the present circumstances, such a journey would also afford her an opportunity of visiting him on Elba.

In the meantime, alone in the palace of Fontainebleau, the deposed Emperor spent the rest of the week waiting for Caulaincourt to settle his financial affairs, as well as a multitude of personal details connected with his leaving Paris. On his journey to Elba, Napoleon was to be escorted by four Allied Commissioners.

On the morning of Wednesday 20 April, a cold day, the Grenadiers of the Guard, in dark-blue uniforms faced with scarlet and black bearskins adorned with red tassels, stood lined-up in two serried ranks in the Cour du Cheval Blanc, later named the Cour d'Adieu. Behind them glowed the pinkish façade of the palace of the Capetian kings. Napoleon (followed by the Allied Commissioners and a handful of his faithful generals, who had travelled from Paris on that day – including two officers of the Polish Lancers) came down the famous Ducerceau double staircase. The farewell scene was charged with emotion. When, after a short speech, he embraced the flag and the eagle in a moving farewell to glory, 'the grizzled warriors, who many a time had watched unflinching while their own blood trickled from wounds, could not restrain their tears.'

After the Guard had presented arms for the last time, Napoleon, who by then was anxious to leave, briskly entered his carriage, where Bertrand, Chief of the Imperial Household, was waiting for him. The coachman whipped the horses to a gallop, past the wrought-iron gates, left onto the Fontainebleau forest road, then onto the main highway leading south. The Emperor departed into exile.

So many of the Guard had volunteered to accompany him to Elba that the agreed number of four hundred had to be increased to a thousand. Among them were 120 Polish Lancers.

All that day Marie tried to reach Fontainebleau, hoping to join the crowds outside the wrought-iron gates of the château, gathered to witness the Emperor's departure. She had set off

Above Napoleon's house, Il Mulini, on the island of Elba

Below The Hermitage at Madonna del Monte, where Napoleon received Marie Walewska on her arrival on Elba

Above The arms of Alexander Walewski, Count of the French Empire, bestowed on the Walewski family by the Emperor Napoleon

Below Two views of the ring given by Napoleon to Marie Walewska after the Battle of Dresden in 1813, made from a piece of enemy shrapnel

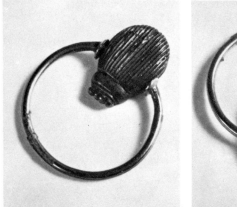

Above The Empress Josephine at Malmaison (detail from an engraving after Pierre-Paul Prud'hon)

Below left Pauline Borghese (née Bonaparte) by Robert Lefèvre. The painting now hangs at the British Embassy in Paris, once her home

Below right Caroline Murat (née Bonaparte), Queen of Naples, with her four children, painted by François Gérard

Alexander Walewski, son of Marie Walewska and the Emperor Napoleon,
at the time of his appointment as Ambassador to the Court of St James's

early that morning from Paris, accompanied by Alexander, Princess Jablonowska and her sister. But they only managed to get to the edge of the forest, for the guards posted by the Allied Commissioners had barred the approach to the palace. Perhaps it was just as well, for it would have added to Marie's grief had she seen that the officer in command of the royalist detachment, escorting Napoleon into exile, was her friend the young General Ornano, who had recently offered his services to the Bourbons.

With the signing of peace between France and her enemies, ending the twenty-two-year-long period of Napoleonic wars, all prisoners of war were released. Among them was Marie's eldest brother, Benedict, who had been taken prisoner by the Prussians a year before. He arrived at his sister's house one morning, determined to enjoy freedom before returning to Poland with his regiment. In spite of Benedict's help in the formalities connected with the divorce, Marie had never been close to her older brother; she had always found him loud and overbearing. But this time the much maligned Benedict could be useful in assessing the situation in Naples, before she herself undertook the long journey. Benedict had been to Naples before. He spoke Italian, having served in Bonaparte's Polish legions at the time of the Italian campaign, and he would welcome the prospect of being away from Paris on 7 June 1814, the date fixed for the departure of the Polish contingent from France; the trip would be a welcome excuse for him to remain abroad a little longer. Unlike Theodore, who was a regular officer in the French army, Brigadier Laczynski needed the excuse of 'important family business' to justify extending his stay in France.

After consulting the distinguished firm of solicitors of Maître Thibert & Co., Marie authorized her older brother to travel to Naples and 'carry out business' on her behalf. Benedict was away for almost two months; he returned at the end of June, bringing discouraging news. King Murat was about to abolish the Walewski entail together with other Napoleonic donations of the period. The only hope was for Marie to intervene personally with Murat, through his wife, Queen Caroline, who had always been a good friend to her.

Marie decided to go first to Florence, take stock of the situation out there, get in touch with the Emperor through his agents (an entire network had by then sprung to life in Tuscany), then proceed to Naples by boat, a journey less tiring and less dangerous than overland.

In the first days of July, having left Benedict and attorney de Joly in charge of her Paris affairs, the young Countess Walewska, her son Alexander, sister Antonia, brother Theodore and two maids departed for Italy by way of Lyons, Geneva and Genoa. After a visit to Elisa Bacciochi, Napoleon's sister and ex-Grand Duchess of Tuscany, now living in retirement in Bologna, and a brief stay at the waters of Lucca, Marie and her entourage reached Florence in the last week of July. At Elisa Bacciochi's suggestion they rented a house in the hills, above Florence, to escape the heat of the city, and it was there that Marie now awaited a message from the Emperor.

II

ELBA

1 September in Elba was a luminous day, one of those brilliant Mediterranean days when the languid heat of the summer gives way to the early crispness of autumn, when the sea glimmers and all the trees, rocks and reeds stand out in sculptured, glossy outlines.

On a hill dominating the fishing village of Marciana stood the Emperor, scanning the sea through his field-glasses, looking towards the Italian coast-line, visible that day in minutest detail. Coming from the direction of Livorno, a small brig was making its way towards Elba in the direction of Portoferraio, the main port, about eighteen miles from Marciana. It was some way off yet, sailing briskly before the wind, and it would be several hours before it came into port. As an eye-witness reported, 'The Emperor seemed very attentive to its progress.'

It had been nearly four months since that day in early May when Napoleon himself had sailed into Portoferraio on board the British frigate *Undaunted* and hoisted a new flag in the fort with the emblems of the imperial bees added to the old Elban standard with the Medici arms on it. Early next morning he was off on horseback to survey his new kingdom. 'I have never seen a man in any situation in life with so much activity and restless perseverance,' wrote Neil Campbell, the British Commissioner who guarded Napoleon on Elba.

For a man who had ruled an empire bigger than Charlemagne's, the lovely, mountainous island, eighteen by twelve miles, populated by 112,000 people – most of them very poor, must indeed have seemed restricted. (The British press indulged in puns such as 'lack of Elba room'.) But Napoleon set to work to organize his new kingdom with the same extraordinary energy he had applied to administering Europe. Within the ten months of his stay, he succeeded in totally transforming the island, leaving an indelible imprint which marks it to this day. He planted trees everywhere, checking erosion; he reclaimed agricultural land, built up vineyards and fisheries, developed Elba's famous marble quarries, set up a network of roads, got rid of flies. He introduced a silk industry by planting mulberry trees. He even colonized a new island, the Pianosa – eight miles south – and restored it to the cultivation of wheat, which had not been grown there since Roman times. He was up from the early hours of the morning, building, planting, always the indefatigable innovator. No detail was too insignificant. The powerful brain which had evolved the most modern legal code, now applied itself to organizing the collection of refuse in Portoferraio. Sanitation on the island was non-existent. Napoleon ordered that each house, under penalty of taxation, be provided with a disposal-bin; rubbish-collectors with large wicker baskets on their backs went through the town blowing trumpets, a signal for the housewives to rush out and empty their rubbish. Thus the flies were defeated. He paved the streets, lighted them by putting up lamps every ten yards and ordered that benches be set along the quays for the enjoyment of strollers. So much progress achieved in a short time impressed the inhabitants. 'A new era has dawned on Elba,' wrote Pons de l'Herault, a former Jacobin and Bonaparte's old foe, now turned a passionate admirer. 'We all walk taller these days . . . industry is humming once again . . . ships plough the sea bringing new materials to the island, and our wealth is growing each day.'

The man of whom these admiring words were written lived in a small, two-storeyed house by the sea called Il Mulini (The Mill), at Portoferraio, in the shadow of the fifteenth-century

fort. It was added to and rebuilt according to his precise instructions. In this modest town-residence he was surrounded by a
tiny military and civilian household, which even in these
reduced circumstances observed all the punctilio of the Court
of the Tuileries. It was hard to get decent furniture, household
fixtures or, for that matter, many other necessities in Portoferraio, and Napoleon was obliged to send out regularly for
them to the mainland.

Preserved in the files of Il Mulini, which is now a museum, is
a little-known memo from the Emperor to Bertrand, Chief of
the Imperial Household, dated 27 July 1814, concerning the
sailing of his brig the *Abeille* to Livorno; it lists all the shopping
to be done, as well as other, more personal commissions:

The *Abeille* is to sail tonight for Livorno. The Marine Commissioner will give her the list of what is to be purchased in the way of
equipment needed for my rowboats, e.g., sailcloth, compasses, etc.
She is also to bring reeds suitable for ceiling construction. . . .

You will deliver in Florence at the address given to you by
Cipriani [Napoleon's personal agent in Florence] a message for the
Countess Walewska; you will tell her that we have learned with
pleasure of her arrival in Genoa, and subsequently in Florence, and
you will ask her to send news of herself and her son through the
intermediary of someone you will suggest to her in Livorno. She
should address her letters to you.

The note goes on to command that the *Abeille* also bring
'some necessary equipment for the stables, such as whips,' as
well as 'two or three hundred colour-glasses for outdoor illu-
mination, a few alabaster vases for the garden and a little
chandelier of Bohemian glass from which others could be copied
here on the island'.

The mention of Countess Walewska is an indication that
since earlier that summer Napoleon had been preparing to
receive Marie on the island. She must have written to him from
Genoa, and later from Florence, in the first days of July. In
answer to the message delivered by the *Abeille*, Theodore,

Marie's brother, travelled to Elba in early August. He returned to Florence with a letter in the Emperor's handwriting, dated 9 August 1814.

Marie, I have received your letter; have talked to your brother. Go to Naples to settle your affairs. I will see you here with the same pleasure as always – either now or on your return from Naples. I will be very glad to see the little boy, of whom I hear many nice things, and look forward to giving him a good kiss.
Adieu Marie.

Your affectionate
Napoleon

Theodore spent several days on Elba with Napoleon. It appears from the records of the Emperor's correspondence that, on his return from the island, he was also entrusted with a letter to Marie Louise, who, under the name of Duchess of Colorno, was taking the waters at Aix. In the letter Napoleon again urged her to rejoin him on Elba. Tactless as such a choice of messenger would seem, it is not impossible that the Emperor, suspecting that letters to his wife were censored or held and delayed, would have taken advantage of a person of absolute trust such as Theodore. By travelling to Aix – before he set off for Elba with Marie – Theodore would have realized that the Empress had no desire to join her husband on Elba. She was happily ensconced in the company of the Austrian General Count Neipperg, who was to dominate her life for the next fifteen years.

It has often been said that Neipperg was assigned to Marie Louise by Metternich. In fact it was the Emperor Francis who himself chose the man to look after his daughter. At the time General Neipperg was forty-two years old, of medium height and with an 'elegantly slim figure'. Having lost his right eye in combat (pierced by an enemy lance) he wore a black patch over it, tied with a black silk ribbon at the back, which 'attractively contrasted with his abundant blond hair'. Under an outward façade of languid disdain he nurtured considerable ambition.

One of his chief attractions was his voice, 'low and harmonious'; he was an accomplished musician, and this talent, combined with his reputation for gallantry and distinguished military career, made him irresistible to the ladies. Neipperg had just recently married an attractive Italian woman, who had been his mistress for the past fifteen years and had borne him five children, when he was unexpectedly summoned by the Emperor Francis and asked to accompany Marie Louise on her journey to Aix-les-Bains and then to Vienna. His instructions were to keep the Empress company and prevent her from rejoining her husband on Elba. Marie Louise was a silly, feckless and sensual woman: it did not take her long to fall in love with her dashing equerry and to become his mistress. She married him some years later, having first borne him two children.

Marie would certainly have heard Theodore's assessment of the situation before embarking for Elba. This may explain why she made tentative plans to remain on the island more or less indefinitely. Possibly she envisaged a Mediterranean Schönbrunn or Finkenstein, this time as a family unit and perhaps on a permanent basis? She was both loyal and constant, and even if her passionate love had now turned into mere affection, her compassion for the dethroned conqueror must have been overwhelming. Whatever the fine points of her feelings, she was determined to go to him and to stay if he expressed a desire to keep her.

Through the agent, Cipriani, in Florence, Marie promptly sent Napoleon a message announcing her early arrival; she would be accompanied by young Alexander, brother Theodore and sister Antonia, and would sail from Livorno on the evening tide on 31 August.

Back on the island, preparations were going ahead to receive her. Napoleon, much as he was looking forward to Marie's visit, was nevertheless anxious to keep it a secret. Unaware of his wife's treachery, and still very much the family man, he feared that news of Marie's appearance on the island might upset Marie Louise and delay their reunion. He would have felt differently had he known that, on the very day of Marie's departure for Elba, his wife was writing to her father, the Emperor Francis, in Vienna, 'I want you to know, dear Papa, that I have less than ever the desire to set off for Elba . . . you may rest assured that I will never undertake the voyage without first asking your permission.'

The situation was further complicated by the presence on the island of Madame Mère. Madame Letizia arrived in mid-August in time for the Emperor's birthday, bringing with her placid good humour, common sense and reserves of money she had wisely saved over the years. Alone among Napoleon's entourage, she was delighted with Elba, which of course reminded her of Corsica – the same stone-pines, fig trees and craggy coastline, the same houses among the vineyards, fishermen's nets, pride of clan. Here in this warm, peaceful place she was at last able to spend some leisurely hours with her son. No more ministers or officials or the tiresome pomp and etiquette of the Court, and she need not fear Napoleon's assassination or death on the battlefield any longer. They could talk, look at the sea, play cards together, at which 'Naboulione' cheated as usual.

What would Madame Mère have said of Marie's presence? The old lady had met her briefly at the Tuileries once or twice, and at the house of Napoleon's sister Pauline. She once remarked that the Countess looked 'graceful and good'; Court gossip must have told her the rest. Madame Mère, though old-fashioned, was no prude, but even though she was not overly fond of her Austrian daughter-in-law, she would not have condoned a visit from another woman while there was still a chance of a reunion between the Emperor, his wife and their son. So it all had to be planned in great secrecy.

As the August heat became stifling, Napoleon moved his mother and her small entourage from Portoferraio, where it was particularly humid and any new arrival was conspicuous, to Marciana Alta, a delightful village in the mountains where in past centuries the inhabitants of Marciana Marina, the fishing village below, had taken refuge from the Barbary pirates who used to swoop down the coast to kidnap their women and children. (On one ill-fated day in the early 1740s some six hundred children were rounded up and abducted.)

Time has by-passed Marciana; it remains what it must have been in Napoleon's day, a collection of picturesque houses painted in gay pastel colours, perched on cliffs with a breathtaking view of the mountains and the Gulf of Procchio below. Madame Mère was installed in the house of a certain Cerbone Vadi, assistant to the local mayor. It is today a modest trattoria, its terrace much enjoyed by sightseers. A marble tablet commemorates Napoleon's first exploratory visit and Madame Mère's later stay in the house. It reads:

In this house, the property of Giuseppe and Giovanni Paolo Vadi, their grandfather Cerbone Vadi, Mayor of Marciana, extended hospitality to Napoleon the Great from 21 August to 24 August 1814, and to Letizia Ramolino, His August Mother from 25 August to 5 September 1814.

This sign has been put up by the community of Marciana for the benefit of posterity – dated 1894.

There was no such easy solution for Marie's place of residence. One hour's climb up from Marciana Alta, following the old muleteers' track – the route of an ancient pilgrimage to the shrine of Our Lady of the Mountain, the Madonna del Monte – stands an old church and a hermitage which was then inhabited by six monks. It is a long climb up the hill, made worthwhile by the spectacular views all around and the feeling of absolute solitude it conveys. To the left rises Mount Jupiter – Mont Giove, as it is locally known – the highest point on the island; chestnut trees and little acacias gradually make room for the scented *maquis*. To the right, vineyards tumble down to the sea a mile away. The winding track, on which steps have been hewn out of granite, is marked by fourteen Stations of the Cross. Above the tree line, the scent of rosemary, thyme and mint rises from the earth warmed by the sun. The steps become steeper and higher, and there are fewer of them as one approaches the summit. At the top the road flattens onto a terrace bordered by a dilapidated wall. Venerable chestnut trees, their trunks gnarled in extraordinary shapes, shelter the ancient church. It has retained the original *campanile*, the look-out tower from which archers could direct their arrows at the enemy. Facing it is a semi-circular wall decorated with Doric columns with a seventeenth-century font; three Baroque masks spout water from an underground source. The hermitage on the right is a low house built on the side of the mountain, so that its first floor levels off with the terrace. It has remained unchanged since the days of the pirates. Its five small rooms, from which the monks have departed, are now empty, as spartan-looking as they must have appeared to Marie and her sister when they stayed there. But the view from the terrace is unparalleled: the wide sweep of the Mediterranean at one's feet, not only the entire coast of Elba, all ninety-one miles of it, with its innumerable inlets, spectacular rocky points and islands, but also Corsica, the islands of Capraia and Gorgona. the towns of Piombino and Livorno and the outline of the Argentario Peninsula on the Italian mainland.

Having installed his mother in her rustic summer residence in the village, Napoleon announced that he was off on a trip for a few days, and set off for the Madonna del Monte, accompanied by two valets, his ordnance officer, Bernotti, a Captain Paoli, the commander of Elba's police, and one of his former officers of the Guard, Mellini, a native of Elba, who had rejoined the Emperor's household on his arrival from France. 'It was hot that morning,' recalls Marchand, the valet. 'The Emperor, abandoning his usual day uniform, was dressed in a lightweight costume of white and blue cotton drill, worn by the Elba National Guard . . . even so he found the ascent arduous.' Napoleon was then forty-five years old and quite corpulent. He had put on even more weight since arriving at Elba. In the hermitage, from which the monks had temporarily departed (they went to live in the cellar), iron bedsteads were set up in the rooms. fires laid against the cold of the night. 'Send us some cooking utensils,' Napoleon requested of Bertrand, the Grand Marshal of his diminutive household, 'as well as a few buckets and spades.' He himself was going to sleep under a large chestnut tree in a tent on the terrace, with his back to the wall of the hermitage.

The only way to the mountain retreat was through the village of Marciana Alta, where Madame Mère was in residence. While for all outward purposes it would appear that Napoleon was with his mother, the sentries posted to guard Madame Mère would also stand guard over the Madonna del Monte and forbid all unauthorized access to it. In a sense Madame Mère would become the chaperone of her son's tryst.

As the sun set behind Mount Giove, the *Abeille*, in full sail, clearly came into view. One could now distinguish the features of the four people standing on deck: two young women, a tall man of about thirty, wearing a French uniform and gold-rimmed glasses, and a blond, curly-haired boy who 'kept dashing around excitedly'. His excitement must have been fully shared by his mother, as the ship edged its way into the bay of Portoferraio, and the spectaular panorama unfolded. To people brought up in northern climes, the sheer beauty of a Mediterranean landscape, the warmth, the intense light, the uncontrolled richness of vegetation, is always an exhilarating experience. For Marie, as she stood at the rail, enveloped in a navy-blue cloak with a long veil floating behind her in the breeze, the feeling must have been heightened by the prospect of being with Napoleon again, in circumstances so very different from their meetings in the past. She had come prepared to remain with him on this lovely island. She brought all her jewels with her, since she had heard that he was in financial need. Would he accept her offer to stay? Such thoughts undoubtedly crossed her mind.

At nine o'clock in the evening, as night fell, the ship cast anchor in front of the little hamlet of San Giovanni, in a secluded bay on the other side from Portoferraio. The Grand Marshal, Bertrand, bowed his head as Marie and her party stepped ashore on a beach in an olive grove. Captain Bernotti transported the passengers and the baggage to Napoleon's own carriage, the so-called imperial coach, driven by four sturdy horses; they immediately set off at a brisk pace. The air smelled of wild herbs; the mountain track was winding and rough – it was too dark to see the precipices on each side. Alexander promptly fell asleep while Marie and her sister talked together in low voices.

They had been driving for about two hours when suddenly, before Procchio, three riders carrying torches barred the road. Someone shouted, 'The Emperor'. Napoleon stood at the door of the carriage; he kissed Marie's hand and got in beside her. Bertrand mounted the Emperor's horse. They continued on to Procchio, which was then the end of the road. From there the carriage returned to Portoferraio with Bertrand. They transferred to a smaller carriage in which they ascended the track to Marciana Alta, where Madame Letizia was sleeping soundly. From there onwards, the little cortège had to proceed on foot up the mountain. Luckily, the far-sighted Bertrand, rightly guessing that Marie and her sister would not relish a long climb at such an hour, thoughtfully produced ponies and mules for the baggage. Napoleon rode ahead holding little Alexander in his arms. Four men carrying torches brought up the rear of the romantic procession. It was one o'clock in the morning when they arrived at the hermitage.

The night was still. Supper had been laid on a table beneath the chestnut trees under a dazzling canopy of stars. The Emperor, seated between Marie and his son, was in fine spirits, 'pinching the little boy's ears', as was his custom. Alexander, now fully awake, called him *'Papa Empereur'*. Louis Etienne St Denis, Napoleon's famous Mameluke Ali, whose eyewitness accounts are greatly valued by historians, has left us a charming picture of the occasion:

As the visitors arrived late we hurried to serve dinner. This being an informal occasion His Majesty himself carved the meats and poured the wines; he took great pleasure in serving the ladies himself; during the entire meal the Emperor was very gay, gracious and charmingly gallant. He was happy. Marchand and I attended to the service.

Madame Walewska must have been very beautiful in her youth. [Marie was then twenty–seven and Louis Etienne twenty–five.] Though nearing thirty she was still lovely, though her otherwise flawless complexion was somewhat marred by a few tiny red veins. Apart from that her skin was milky white with a pink cast – evidence of good health. She had a very nice figure, a lovely mouth, fine eyes; her hair was very light chestnut or dark blonde; there was great sweetness about her; she seemed to me like an excellent person. It was obvious that the Emperor found her very attractive.

Her sister looked charming. She must have then been about eighteen or nineteen and radiantly fresh. She had regular features, but was not as tall as Madame Walewska. The young boy looked a bit pale and his features were very like the Emperor's; he was rather serious for his age.

Theodore was to be lodged in Marciana Alta, and one of the valets conducted him down the hill, while Marie, who had changed into 'a dress of grey taffeta gathered high under the bosom', talked to the Emperor for a long time. Alexander had to be put to bed, and eventually Marie and her sister also retired for the night to the two cells which had been prepared for them in the hermitage.

The Emperor saw the ladies to their quarters and returned to undress in his tent [continued Louis Etienne St Denis]. It must be said that at Elba the Emperor was surrounded by people who were new in his service and did not know about discretion. What they saw they repeated. It is surprising that he, who had such a liking for secrecy, would have behaved in what seemed to me a rather incautious manner. Both evenings of Madame Walewska's visit he came out of his tent wearing a dressing gown and went to her room where he stayed until daybreak. It was obvious to all what was going on . . . Even the most humble of his subjects would have been more skilful at conducting a secret love affair than the Emperor. I have often noticed that in matters of love humble people are much better at preserving appearances than the grand seigneurs.

The next day was idyllic. In the morning the Emperor led his lady to the 'Seddia Napoleone' – a rock shaped like a chair, on which he liked to sit looking towards Corsica. He showed her the spectacular view from the summit. There was his native island to the left. One could almost see the town of Bastia on the west side of the island, where French warships had landed in 1768 and occupied Corsica just a year before Napoleon's birth – a fortuitous event, since it made him a French citizen. Nearby, only eight miles distant, was Pianosa, which he had annexed a few months earlier, and further right Capraia and the isles of Gilio and Gorgona. They walked among the fragrant bushes and the *maquis* 'looking contented'. They visited the church of the Madonna del Monte, where generations of Elban wives had prayed for the safe return of their men from the sea, and Marie knelt in front of the altar covered with countless votive offerings (it is still the same today). Time passed in the peace of a family reunion, with Napoleon delightedly playing childish games with his son and teaching him how to ride. They sat in the shade of the ancient chestnut trees, looking down on the island; 'only the murmur of the stream and the bell of a restless goat broke the silence.' Years later, Alexander Walewski, France's Minister of Foreign Affairs and Ambassador to the Court of St James, was to write about that day in his Memoirs: 'I was a small boy then [he was four], but I clearly recall the little house where we stayed. I remember the Emperor as he talked and played with me. I can still see his tent, and I remember the grenadier guards. . . .'

Alas for the happiness of the romantic idyll on the mountain. Back in Portoferraio, news spread that the Empress and the King of Rome had arrived. The gossip might have come from the ship's sailors, or from the coachman and the postilions, some of whom were old hands from the Tuileries. Marie was blonde like the Empress, and the men would have been unable to see her face through the veil. Alexander was only a year older than the King of Rome, and Theodore, tall and robust, was taken for Eugène de Beauharnais, Napoleon's stepson. As for the other lady, well, she must be a lady-in-waiting to the Empress. What other party of guests would have been greeted by the Grand Marshal of the Court himself? Before the day was out, the tale was generally accepted, and in the evening, without orders from anyone, the people of Portoferraio organized their simple, spontaneous salute, putting lamps and candles in the windows.

Early next morning Fourreau de Beauregard, Napoleon's local doctor (a former veterinary), donned his best Sunday clothes and rode his horse from Portoferraio to Marciana Alta, then climbed the muleteer's tracks to the top, to check personally on the news and present his respects to the Empress. What he saw was a pastoral scene: the Emperor sitting on a chair in front of his tent, holding a blond, blue-eyed boy on his knee, engaged in animated conversation. Marchand, Napoleon's valet, recalled that the following conversation took place: 'Well, Fourreau, how do you find him?' 'Sire, I find the King quite tall.' Napoleon did not bother to disabuse the doctor but asked him to keep the visit a secret. Fourreau, a shrewd man, had his doubts. Years later, in 1843, he wrote to Alexander Walewski, who was soon to become Minister of Foreign Affairs of France, 'It moves me to realize that you are the same pretty young Alexander whom I saw more than twenty-nine years ago on the knees of the Emperor at the Madonna del Monte on Elba.' No sooner had the doctor departed than a message came from a member of Napoleon's household in Portoferraio, telling of the general excitement in the town; an hour later the mayor of Marciana asked for an audience to 'present his respects to the Empress'.

Napoleon reacted with alarm. It was obvious that, as the news had got around on the island, it would be only a matter of time before it reached the mainland, the Court in Vienna and the Empress – and what then? Marie's visit might provide an excuse for further delay. Could he risk it? There may also have been another consideration. Napoleon had fostered his image as a family man, which evoked great sympathy among the traditionally religious and conservative population of Elba. His apparent anticipation of the arrival of the Empress and his son had won him the hearts of the local women. He must avoid a public scandal at all costs.

He made up his mind in an instant. The only way to stifle the rumour was for Marie to leave immediately for the mainland. Orders were sent down to the captain of the *Abeille* to get the ship ready to sail from Marciana that evening, and to Bertrand to send a carriage up for the party, for the horses and the baggage-mules to be ready.

One can imagine the effect the Emperor's sudden announcement would have had on Marie, who, serene and confident, was savouring the longed-for peace of their mountain retreat. She knew that General Count Neipperg, so irresistible to ladies, had by now replaced Napoleon in his wife's heart and thoughts. She was convinced that the Empress had no desire to come to Elba, but how could she tell Napoleon the truth? It was kinder to leave him to his happy illusions.

That morning Napoleon worked in his tent on a letter to Murat, King of Naples, regarding Alexander's estates, which he knew were about to be confiscated. (They were taken over on 15 September together with those of Fouché, Duke of Otranto and Count Regnier.) Marshal Murat's betrayal of his former commander and imperial brother-in-law still rankled with Napoleon. It was to him an odious act of ingratitude and a breach of the sacred honour of the clan. Madame Mère shared his feelings: indulgent by nature and always ready to smooth over family quarrels, she broke off all correspondence with her daughter Caroline, Murat's wife, and sent word that she never wanted to see her again. But since his arrival on Elba, Napoleon, knowing that Murat 'liked to operate on two fronts', had reinstated the correspondence.

While the Emperor worked on his papers and discussed the day's arrangements with Captain Bernotti, Marie and her sister sadly went for a walk on the hill, then returned to the house to pack. The general feeling of gloom was heightened by the ugly, menacing clouds which began to roll over the mountains from the south-east; the sky darkened; in spite of the altitude the air became breathless and sultry, and distant thunder was heard from the direction of Mount Giove. Rain was falling when the horses arrived.

Napoleon escorted the party down the mountain. It was now obvious that the sea was too rough for them to board the brig at Marciana Marina, and an order was sent to the captain to sail on to Porto Longone, an inconspicuous, well-sheltered harbour over twenty-two miles down the coast to the east of Porto-ferraio. The main port would have been easier to embark from, but the same obsession with secrecy still governed Napoleon's decision.

They said goodbye at the door of the carriage. By then the wind was so strong that conversation was virtually impossible. Contemporary memoirs suggest that earlier that morning Marie had offered Napoleon her jewels, because she had heard from Peyrusse, the treasurer, that he was short of money; but he refused to accept them.

The journey to Porto Longone was a nightmare. As they climbed into the hills on a newly made road, not everywhere completed, they lurched about in murky twilight and implacable rain. Here and there the rain had washed away great lumps of the road, and they had to halt the horses and dismount. Alexander and Antonia cried with fright. There is no record of Marie's reaction, but she was probably too unhappy to care.

Finally, at about midnight, they arrived at Porto Longone (today's Porto Azzuro). The commandant of the port was Captain Jerzmanowski, who, at the head of 120 Polish Lancers, had followed Napoleon to Elba. He vainly tried to persuade Marie to wait until the storm passed. So did the harbourmaster and the mayor. But the Polish girl was undaunted. She thanked them all but insisted that the Emperor's orders were explicit – they must embark at daybreak. They sailed in a mountainous sea under a single topsail; it is doubtful whether any of them had the strength to take a last look at Elba, where Marie had expected to live.

The ship was clearing the bay when a messenger, who had

ridden furiously through the night, arrived with an order from the Emperor expressly forbidding the sailing. But by then it was already too late. As the agitated harbourmaster pointed out, the *Abeille* was now only a tiny speck on the white-flecked, boiling sea.

There are those who maintain that the Emperor, by now bitterly regretting his mistake, had ridden through the night to Porto Longone to prevent Marie and her party from sailing. His 'furious ride through the mountains amid the rain and the lightning' has, it is being said on the island, 'inspired an opera or two'. That may be, but there is no tangible evidence to show that it took place. What is certain, however, is that Napoleon, rent by guilt, spent a long, anxious week worrying about the fate of his 'Polish wife' and his son. At last came a message from Livorno, from the ship's captain, announcing their safe arrival on the mainland. But there was no word from Countess Walewska.

12
THE HUNDRED DAYS

For six years prior to Marie's arrival in Naples, the most beautiful kingdom in Europe had been ruled by Napoleon's energetic younger sister Caroline and her flamboyant husband, Marshal Joachim Murat.

The kingdom had had a turbulent history: after the Normans and the Hohenstaufen came the French of the House of Anjou, then the Spaniards. For over two hundred years Naples' affairs were handled by a succession of Spanish viceroys, who paid little heed to its welfare. In the early-eighteenth century an Austrian army had conquered the kingdom, and Spanish rule came to an end; thirty years later it acquired a sovereign of its own in the person of Don Carlos of Bourbon, son of Philip v of Spain who, following the tradition set by the Normans, united Sicily with Naples to found the independent Kingdom of the Two Sicilies. Since 1759, and again after the fall of the Napoleonic Empire, Naples' sovereign was the simple-minded Bourbon King Ferdinand IV (he was kept ignorant on the theory that study might damage his brain). He was called 'Il Nasone' ('the Big Nose'), ascended the throne at the age of eight, and nine years later married the sixteen-year-old Maria Carolina. daughter of the Austrian Empress Maria Theresa and sister of Marie Antoinette of France.

Thus it was the strong-minded Maria Carolina who effectively ran Naples with the help of Sir John Acton, a distinguished

British naval commander and man of letters. It was he who persuaded the Queen to forsake France and Spain and instead turn to England and Austria for support. The Queen's best friend was Emma Hamilton, the wife of the British envoy to Naples, Sir William Hamilton. In the wake of the French Revolution, following a wave of republican feeling and the unpopularity of the English and Austrians, King Ferdinand and his queen, together with Sir John Acton and the Hamiltons, had to flee Naples to Palermo; they were restored to power by Admiral Nelson and his fleet – a moment of supreme triumph for the 'divine Lady Hamilton'.

Early in 1806, after Austerlitz, Napoleon had sent an army under his brother Joseph to occupy the kingdom and again forced Ferdinand and Maria Carolina to take refuge in Palermo – this time until the fall of the Empire in 1815, when they were reluctantly accepted back in Naples.

Meanwhile when Joseph became King of Spain in 1808, Marshal Murat succeeded him as King of Naples. He was popular with the Neapolitans, and so was his handsome wife, with her classical good looks and fair complexion, who spoke Italian with a pure Tuscan accent – a great improvement on the former queen. From their splendid residence in the Palazzo Reale in the centre of Naples, the Murats reigned over their subjects with a benevolent hand. 'They are like children,' Caroline used to say, 'content with little, adoring spectacles, and they have the Italian capacity of adapting to circumstances.' King Murat worked hard: like King Joseph, his brother-in-law, before him, he introduced reforms based on French law, restored order in the administration, reorganized the judiciary, brought in strict measures against the brigands and tried to heal divisions between the royalists and the republicans by returning sequestrated lands to former partisans of the Bourbons. As everywhere under the rule of the Bonapartes, his administration favoured the local people of the country, and he conferred numerous appointments on Neapolitans. Caroline took great interest in the excavations of Pompeii, trebling the number of workers on the sites.

Marie, with Alexander and sister Antonia (Theodore had gone back to Paris), sailed into the beautiful bay of Naples on board a ship from Livorno. After the heartbreak of Elba it would not have been surprising if she had sworn never to see any of the Bonapartes again, but there were important considerations at stake – she had a son to look after, whose future financial well-being was entirely in the hands of King Murat. Soon after their arrival, Marie, bearing Napoleon's letter, called on Queen Caroline at the Palazzo Reale to give her news of her brother. Caroline, who was strong-minded, logical and consistent, was convinced that Napoleon's career was at an end; her objective was to safeguard the future of her children, and this meant preserving the kingdom of Naples for Murat at all costs. Schooled in the art of diplomacy by Talleyrand and Metternich, her long-time lover, she contrived to keep on excellent terms with the Austrians, and, conscious of the network of spies circulating all over the Italian mainland and the islands, she confined her communications with Elba strictly to family matters, such as birthday greetings and news of the children. At the time of Marie Walewska's arrival, Pauline, Princess Borghese, was also in Naples, residing at the Villa Favorita at Portici by the sea, preparing to leave shortly for Elba, where she was to stay with Napoleon through the winter. Pauline was all fun, loveliness and affection; it was impossible to dislike her. She alone of all the three sisters was genuinely attached to the Emperor and willing to remain by his side. In this she had much in common with Marie, whom she liked, though in the past she had found the Polish Countess's 'total commitment' to her brother and her fidelity 'quite old-fashioned'. As for Marie, even with her Paris-acquired worldly polish, she was too romantic and too earnest in matters of love ever to get really close to Princess Pauline, whose amorous attachments were legion. But this time Napoleon was the unifying link between the two women.

The Murats received the Countess Walewska with great

warmth. It is not known whose arguments were the most persuasive. Was it Marie's beauty and grace, or Pauline's urging, or Caroline's well-known strong maternal feelings, stirred by the sight of little Alexander, apparently so 'like Naboulione at that age – only fair'? Mother and son must have woven quite a spell, for on 30 November 1814 the confiscatory decree was annulled and Alexander's estates were returned to him, together with back-payments for the past two years and an advance on the first five months of 1815, with interest a total of nearly a million francs. This was a considerable sum, and it must to some extent have allayed Marie's fears for the future and added to the pleasures of life in beautiful Naples.

'I well remember Naples,' wrote Alexander in his Memoirs. 'I can still see Vesuvius and the sea – and I remember King Murat and the queen, who used to give me so many, many toys.' A quarter of a century later, when Count Walewski, by then an influential politician, was travelling to Corsica on a French government mission, the ex-Queen Caroline Murat, widowed and living in Florence, while sending him letters of introduction to family friends in Ajaccio, wrote at the end of a long letter, 'I leave you with regret, Alexander, for writing to you brings me so many memories of your dear mother for whom I have always had such affection.'

In the winter of 1814–15 Naples was full of visitors, mostly English, who, deprived for so many years of their 'grand tour', were now pouring onto the Continent in droves. Even before Sir William Hamilton's splendid days, Naples – the warm, luxurious playground of the ancients – had been their favourite city, and now, added to the theatrical setting, the Pompeii excavations and Vesuvius, there was also 'Boney's sister' and her swashbuckling husband to add to the famous sights. No wonder it became so popular. Among the distinguished visitors was Caroline of Brunswick, Princess of Wales, the estranged wife of the Prince Regent, who, tired of her years of neglect in England, arrived just before Christmas. The Bonapartes were great snobs, and snobbery knows no family loyalties. Even

Lucien, Napoleon's 'egalitarian' brother, delighted with the title of Prince of Canino, recently conferred on him by the Pope, went to great trouble to entertain the English Princess in Rome and passed her on to his sister in Naples for a series of splendid festivities. Queen Caroline's delight at being hostess to 'the future Queen of England' (she did not know about the Princess's equivocal marital status) was slightly marred by the Princess's falling madly in love with King Murat, 'a passion she did not even bother to disguise'. Finding that she was not loved in return, the Princess turned against poor Queen Caroline 'as the cause of her failure' and did everything 'to trouble the peace of the royal ménage'.

Naples was gay that winter: there were boating and hunting parties, military reviews, *tableaux vivants*, dances, a Court ball for over a thousand guests and even a fancy-dress ball, at which the Princess of Wales appeared 'immodestly dressed as a Sultana'. It was carnival time, a season traditionally gay and carefree, with splendid floats proceeding down the Corso and along the waterfront, to the wild applause of the public. The flowers and the sunshine, the music and the spontaneous gaiety of the people, obscured from the passing visitor the dismal poverty of the population.

Marie enjoyed her winter in Naples. It was a much-needed rest, and the sunshine was a welcome boost to her health, always delicate. The warmth of her reception, the beauty of her surroundings, helped to soften the shock she had suffered at the abrupt departure from Elba. She did not, at least not for the present, relish the prospect of returning to Louis xviii's Paris. Poland was in turmoil: the so-called 'Congressional Kingdom' (created after the Grand Duchy of Warsaw had been dismembered), with the Tsar of Russia as head of state, was still the subject of acrimonious negotiations between powers currently meeting at the Congress of Vienna. Anthony, her elder son, now almost ten, had rejoined his ailing father at Walewice; why not linger on for a bit in this enchanting corner of Europe, ruled by the last of the Bonaparte dynasties? But the privilege of living in peace, even for very short periods, was not in the pattern of her life. The year 1815 was to be a sad time for Marie – a year of partings and many sorrows.

In January came the news of Anastase Walewski's death. 'It was during our stay in Naples that my mother received the letter, announcing that my father had passed away,' recalled Alexander Walewski in his Memoirs. They were written for the benefit of posterity, so he omitted to mention that at that particular time of his life it was Napoleon to whom he referred as his father. Marie could not have been surprised by the news, given Anastase's age and state of health, and Walewice must have appeared extraordinarily remote when viewed from Naples. What it meant was that she was now truly a free woman, able to marry again, if she wished, according to the rites of her Church. Did she contemplate a new future? She did not leave us any means of ascertaining what her thoughts were at that particular period of her life, but it would have been only natural if her attachment to Napoleon had suffered as a result of his selfish behaviour on Elba. He had inflicted a wound more profound than when he married Marie Louise just a month before his 'Polish wife' brought his son into the world. Marie was weary of constant sacrifice and longed for a strong, masculine arm to lean on. And yet one did not lightly sever links with Napoleon. For years now not only her own destiny but that of Poland and of innumerable people in Europe had centred on this one man: he was their sun and their glory and constant hope. It was hard to imagine that he would not return to the stage of history and again fill everything with his presence.

In February came a letter from the deposed Emperor to Murat, brought from Elba by the Chevalier Colonna, a shadowy historical figure who has sometimes been confused with Marie's brother. In fact there was no connection between them. Colonna had been Madame Letizia's Chamberlain in Rome and became one of Napoleon's secret agents, circulating between Rome, Naples and Elba.

The letter, dated 17 February 1815, thanked Murat for

restoring the Walewski entail and went on: 'I entrust her [Marie] to your care, as well as her son, who is very dear to me.' It ended with the cryptic communication: 'Colonna will inform you about a number of very important developments, and I count on you to act with utmost speed. My best to the Queen and the children. All yours, Napoleon.' What it meant was that Napoleon was ready to leave his place of detention and expected Murat's help in his future plans. Napoleon wanted Murat and his forty-thousand-man army to wait in a state of 'apparent neutrality' until he had landed in France, and then march on Milan, to attack the Austrians from the rear. But the impetuous King of Naples spoiled the plan by embarking on a wild attempt to conquer all Italy and declaring war on Austria without consulting with the Emperor. His move convinced the allies that Napoleon's reappearance was the signal for a renewed war on the Continent and shattered whatever slim hopes Napoleon might have had of concluding a negotiated peace with his enemies; it greatly contributed to his final defeat.

On Wednesday 1 March the frigate *Inconstant*, followed by four smaller craft carrying a thousand troops, landed in the Gulf of Juan between Fréjus and Antibes. Napoleon had left Elba on 26 February, profiting from the absence of his guardian, Commander Neil Campbell, who was visiting his mistress in Florence. Having successfully evaded the watch of the British cruisers patrolling the Mediterranean, they disembarked, spent the night on the beach and next morning began to march north. Napoleon, 'wrapped in his blue Marengo coat', rode ahead.

Of all the reasons for his leaving Elba, one of the most pressing was his dismal financial situation. Louis XVIII refused to pay the yearly indemnity stipulated by the Treaty of Fontainebleau, and Napoleon found himself unable to provide for his contingent of soldiers and his own household expenses on Elba. Separation from wife and son, and fear of being deported to some distant place such as the Azores or St Helena, had also been preying on his mind. Through his numerous spies the Emperor was kept well informed of the growing dissatisfaction of France with the Bourbons; he had also heard rumours that Fouché (his former Minister of Police) was planning to over-throw the monarchy and set up a government from which he would be excluded. These were all powerful reasons, so when the opportunity presented itself, he acted on it and escaped.

It is possible that if the powers assembled at the Congress of Vienna had honoured their undertakings and given him back wife and child, if Louis xviii had paid him his pension, if France was happy and had forgotten him, he would – in the opinion of many historians – probably have remained on Elba. He might have, but it did not happen this way. The epic of the Hundred Days, glorious adventure though it was, only led to further tragedy and exile.

Living in close proximity to the Court at the Palazzo Reale, Marie was undoubtedly aware of Napoleon's plans. We do not know on what date she left Naples, but there are indications in the Murat Correspondence at the Bibliothèque Thiers that lead one to believe that by mid-January both King Murat and Queen Caroline were anxious to get her out of their kingdom to avoid any potential embarrassment with Austria. There was also the matter of her personal safety if she happened to be on Austrian-controlled territory when news came of the Emperor's escape. Pauline Bonaparte, after her departure from Elba a few weeks after Napoleon, was arrested by the Austrians and held prisoner at Viareggio. The most likely guess is that Marie left Naples a couple of weeks before the Gulf of Juan landing and travelled across the length of Italy to Bologna, where she stayed with Elisa Bonaparte, arriving in Paris in early April. Napoleon in his triumphal progress through France reached Paris on 20 March and was carried into the Tuileries on the shoulders of his Old Guard – a moment of 'supreme happiness'. Louis xviii and his government folded up like a house of cards and fled abroad.

There is no record of Marie's visit to Napoleon either at the Tuileries or at the Elysée before 11 June, the eve of his departure for the Waterloo campaign. We know that she communicated with him through Queen Hortense, Josephine's daughter, who was one of the first to welcome the Emperor back to Paris and acted as his hostess during his brief stay at the Elysée. Hortense would have told Marie of Napoleon's bitter disappointment at his wife's infidelity, the details of which he learned from Méneval's correspondence, and of his longing for his small son. This could have been one reason why she did not immediately ask for an audience, but there might have been other, more personal considerations. Nevertheless, Napoleon's return to the historical stage stirred her deeply, and it also revived hope for the restoration of Poland. From the moment of her return to Paris, Marie found herself surrounded by excited compatriots, spinning dreams of another war for Polish independence. It was almost like being back in 1806, but not quite : too much suffering had accumulated in the intervening years.

In the meantime the Allied forces, determined to finish off Napoleon once and for all, were massing at the frontiers of France. There were the English, the Belgians, the Dutch and the Hanoverians all under the command of Wellington and 120,000 Prussians under Blücher. The Austrians and the Russians did not get to the theatre of war until July. Rather than await the avalanche that was about to fall on the country, Napoleon decided to go and meet it. Only a victory, followed by peace on favourable terms, could maintain him on the throne. The game had to be played to the end.

On 11 June, before his departure for the front the next morning, the Emperor summoned the Countess Walewska to the Elysée. According to Marchand's account, 'they talked for a very long time.' Judging from notes left by Marie's solicitors, discovered some years ago by Jean Savant, Napoleon gave Marie some sound financial advice on that occasion. He suggested that she 'sell out' and convert the money from her shares on the canals of Loing and Orleans into Dutch bonds. This she did, and in years to come Alexander, who appreciated money and knew how to spend it, had reason to be grateful to his parents for their foresight.

On Sunday 18 June Napoleon was defeated by Wellington at

Waterloo. He was so tired at the end of the battle that he had to be held on his horse as he escaped with the remnants of his army to Charleroi.

Back at the Elysée Palace three days later, on the eve of the signing of his second abdication, he received Marie and Alexander for a brief moment. 'The mood was lugubrious,' recalls Marchand. 'It was raining, the Emperor was burning state papers and I was packing his personal effects.' Marie, Queen Hortense and Madame Bertrand were the only women allowed to keep him company on that day. Alexander played with Hortense's son, young Louis, the future Napoleon III, whom he was to serve as Foreign Minister some forty years later. Outside the crowds still cheered Napoleon. *'Vive l'Empereur! Ne nous abandonnez pas'*. But by then the decision was out of the Emperor's hands.

On a hot Sunday in June, just a week after the débâcle of Waterloo, the deposed Emperor drove out to Malmaison, which now belonged to Hortense, to await the completion of arrangements for his departure to the United States or to England. He arrived at the house where he had spent the happiest years of his life on a perfect summer evening, when the gardens were suffused with light, and the air was filled with the scent of roses and lime trees. Though Josephine had been dead for over a year, three gardeners took meticulous care of the grounds and kept the gardens as she would have wished them to be. 'The roses were everywhere,' recalled one of the visitors to Malmaison in that week, 'every conceivable kind from the humble églantine [cottage-rose] to the Empress's favourite Maréchal Niel rose.'

It was the peaceful sight of this beautiful garden in the full glory of summer which must have greeted Marie and her son, as they drove out to Malmaison on the afternoon of Wednesday 28 June, for their final farewell to the Emperor.

'The atmosphere was very sad,' recalled Alexander Walewski some years later. 'I can still see the Emperor . . . every single feature of his face. . . . He took me in his arms and I remember a tear ran down his face. . . . But I cannot recall what exactly he said to me on that occasion.'

Marie and Napoleon talked alone for over an hour. We shall never know what was said. According to Marchand, 'As the time came to leave, she fell into his arms and remained there for a long time. . . .'

'The young Countess Walewska was crying, when I came across her that afternoon,' wrote Queen Hortense in her Memoirs. 'Her obvious distress touched me deeply; I insisted that she remain and have dinner with me; I could not let her go in such a state.'

As Marie and Alexander drove back to Paris that evening they saw Prussian soldiers erecting barricades at the Place de Neuilly. They were not stopped and continued down the Avenue of the Grande Armée, past the unfinished Arc de Triomphe, back home to the rue de la Victoire. The sentries let them pass, but it was evident that time was drawing short for the Emperor.

Next day Napoleon said good-bye to his mother and to Hortense. Madame Letizia, sensing that she was never going to see him again, was stricken with grief. Hortense sewed a diamond necklace into a cloth belt, insisting he take it with him. Finally – as at Fontainebleau a year earlier – he got into a waiting carriage with Bertrand and drove off in the direction of the coast.

The heroic epic had ended; the curtain came down on the last act. Left behind on the stage was a twenty-eight-year-old woman, alone in a Europe convulsed by violent changes, and her five-year-old son – the image of the departed Emperor. What was she expected to do with the rest of her life? She had offered to follow the defeated Emperor into exile, but he had refused. She still had – or so it seemed at the time – a long life stretching ahead. Like her country, she had staked everything on one man : she had given him nine years, nearly a third of her life, and was left with glorious memories, not much else. Was she to spend the rest of her days nurturing the Napoleonic legend – alone?

General Ornano had been hovering in the background for a long time; for years he had been determined to marry the Countess Walewska, and each time he was sent away thoroughly discouraged; he felt he was fighting against impossible odds. But earlier that year, following the news of Anastase Walewski's death and with Marie still smarting from Napoleon's brutal conduct on Elba, the General had finally extracted a promise from her to 'consider' giving way to his persistent requests. Acting on the principle that it is the duty of a soldier to serve the legal government of his country, Ornano had remained in the army to serve the King after Napoleon's abdication at Fontainebleau. At the time of Marie's stay in Naples he was commanding a corps of the Royal Dragoons at Tours; they corresponded now and then. It is likely that Ornano first heard of old Count Walewski's death from Theodore, even before the news reached Marie, for he immediately wrote to her in Naples, pressing his suit. Marie's answer must have been fairly encouraging, for, according to records in the files of the War Ministry in Paris, a letter from General Ornano, dated 11 February 1815, advises his military superiors that he plans to apply for a month's leave, 'sometime in the near future', in order to marry.

Had Marie really made up her mind, or was much of it the General's wishful thinking? Whatever understanding might have existed between them, Napoleon's sudden return from Elba changed everything. How could any man, no matter how young, rich and glamorous, compete with Napoleon's magic presence? How puny would the problems of every-day life have appeared, when measured against the continuation of the epic or perhaps the beginning of a new one? Marie's suppressed love, loyalty and concern for the future of Poland blazed anew – the old magic again took possession of her.

After Napoleon's triumphant return from Elba, Ornano was one of the first to cast off his allegiance to the Bourbons and to rejoin the Napoleonic eagles. He was sent to organize the recruitment of volunteers in the south. As it became increasingly plain that the Allies were determined to open hostilities at the earliest possible moment, Napoleon's immediate concern was to raise an army and to rally the nation behind him. Conscription was extremely unpopular, and he resorted to it only on the eve of the Waterloo campaign. What he thought to bring about was a revival of the spirit of 1793, which had spontaneously produced a nation under arms. Ornano was moderately successful in enlisting a number of volunteers in the south and returned to Paris a few days before Waterloo. There he became involved in a duel with a rival cavalry officer – General Bonet, following an exchange of heated words about who was to command the cavalry corps. Whenever an officer's code of honour was involved, a duel apparently had to be fought. In spite of efforts of friends and Marie's fervent entreaties – she considered fighting a duel a mortal sin and knew that those who took part in it were automatically ex-communicated by the Church – the two participants decided that there was no other way out. It was unfortunate, in the circumstances, that the two generals were such excellent shots, for they inflicted serious wounds on each other and put themselves out of action on the eve of the most important of all battles. The duel was fought near Paris, probably in the Bois de Vincennes, the traditional site for such encounters. Marie, though distressed at what she called a 'stupid and unworthy incident', paid a call on the wounded general the day before she went to Malmaison for her farewell visit to the Emperor.

The shock of Napoleon's departure and the accumulated strain of the last months was too much for her fragile constitution. For days she remained cloistered at home, refusing all calls. She emerged only once, to request an audience with Tsar Alexander, who by then had arrived in Paris, to ask him to intervene for Madame Mère, who was being held in custody on the orders of Fouché, the head of the provisional government. The démarche, which she undertook at the request of Queen Hortense (who, in contrast with her position in 1814, was now out of favour with the Tsar because of her support of Napoleon after his return from Elba), cost her all her remaining strength. She came down with a serious liver complaint and remained in bed for several weeks, refusing to see visitors, including Ornano. As soon as she had recovered her health, she left for Holland, where her presence was urgently required by her financial adviser. She returned to Paris in late October, but even then she did not communicate with Ornano. Her descendants attributed the reason for this course of action to her unwillingness to 'ruin Ornano's career'. Marriage with someone as close to the deposed Emperor as Marie, was certainly not the best way to further a general's career.

Marie continued to live quietly at the rue de la Victoire with Alexander. Theodore and her sister had by then returned to Poland. Matrimonial plans, if any, appeared to have been definitely shelved when in January 1816 Ornano, who by then had for the second time joined the service of the Bourbons, found himself suddenly arrested in Paris. The reason for it was his outspoken condemnation of the recent trial and execution of an old comrade-in-arms, the heroic Marshal Ney. After the second Restoration, Marshal Ney, Prince of Moscow, was tried by the House of Peers, condemned to death by a firing-squad and shot on 8 December 1815. Ornano's outburst at a private gathering was reported to the Bourbon police, and he was arrested at his house. He thus found himself in the Abbaye prison. There had lately been so many trials and so many executions in Paris that there was every reason to fear for his life. Marie interceded on his behalf with her old friend Talleyrand and went so far as to write to Fouché. Neither Talleyrand nor Fouché was willing to help. Eventually, due to the intercession of old friends, Ornano was released from prison and advised to disappear from the scene for the time being. After a short stay in England, he moved to Belgium.

In the course of his peregrinations, Ornano again proposed to Marie. She finally said that she would marry him. On 23 May she wrote to Mercey, Queen Caroline's business adviser in Naples, asking him to submit a claim for restitution of

Alexander's estates. 'I am about to leave Paris for a protracted absence and will be communicating with you from Belgium later this year.'

They were married on 7 September at the church of St Gudule in Brussels. After a short honeymoon at the watering-resort of Spa, they took up residence in Liège at 326, rue Mandeville, a large, comfortable house surrounded on three sides by a garden.

In January 1817 Marie, who by then was expecting a child, decided to travel to Poland to consult her old friend the eminent gynæcologist Dr Ciekierski. Why she, in her delicate condition, decided to undertake such a long and extraordinarily tiring journey at the height of winter, and her husband allowed her to go, is a mystery. Marie had always been strong-willed, even obstinate, and it can only be assumed that her husband was too weak to stop her. Accompanied by her newly-engaged secretary, Carité, and a maid, she arrived in Walewice on 24 January 1817 and a few days later went to Warsaw to see her doctor. Ciekierski found his patient in a very precarious state of health. He diagnosed a kidney disease – acute toxæmia, aggravated by pregnancy – which had been sapping her strength for some time now. Seven years before, at the time of the birth of Alexander, the doctor had forbidden Marie to nurse her baby, a warning she immediately disregarded. This time her condition was far more serious, and the doctor went as far as to inform her that, if she insisted on nursing the new baby, she would pay for it with her life. There is a curious note of fatalism and depression in the letters Marie wrote to her husband from Poland. It is as if she knew that, no matter what she did, nothing could prevent the illness from killing her. She returned to Liège in February, and on 9 June 1817 Rodolphe Auguste Ornano, a healthy, good-looking baby, was born. In spite of her doctor's strict orders, she insisted on nursing her son. She never recovered her health.

In the course of the summer, lying on a chaise-longue in the garden of her house in Liège, she dictated to her secretary, Carité, what was supposed to be her memoirs, a touching, highly subjective and at times confused version of her life, in which her romance with the Emperor was described as a 'sacrifice for her country'. It is understandable that at this stage she would have been tempted to present it in such a way. She was writing for the benefit of her new husband and her sons. Perhaps she wanted to 'justify herself' in their eyes. If so, it was a touching effort on the part of a woman who knew she had only a few more months to live.

As the autumn set in, it became evident that Marie's life was drawing to a close. She was in constant pain, plunged into a depression which was a symptom of her illness, plagued by nightmares and constantly shivering from cold, though she lay swathed in blankets. She begged her husband to apply for permission for them to return to France. She wanted to die in France, for after Poland France had always been the country she loved most.

After a slow and painful journey from Liège, the Ornanos arrived in Paris in November. Marie was glad to be home once again, but after the journey her health began to deteriorate rapidly. At seven o'clock in the evening of 11 December 1817, a day of squally snow showers and gusty winds, as her husband and her three sons gathered around her bed, Marie Walewska's heart stopped beating. She was just thirty-one years and four days old.

'The entire household was plunged into terrible despair,' wrote Alexander years later. 'I cannot even begin to describe the deep suffering of General Ornano. My mother was one of the most remarkable women that ever existed. . . . I can say so myself from this distance without family prejudice, for enough time has now passed to make this judgement.' Ornano, who survived Marie by forty years, never remarried.

It had been a long journey for the shy little Polish patriot from the manor house of Kiernozia to the palace of Schönbrunn, to the Tuileries, Elba and Naples. She had traversed life in the wake of history's most glorious epic, when the life of all Europe was centred on one man. This man had loved her. And when it came for him to die in a distant place, it was the image of Marie next to his graceful wife Josephine's that came to comfort him in his last days, as his companions in exile have noted.

Napoleon, who earlier that year had learned of Marie's marriage to Ornano, was never told of her death. The mail to St Helena was slow, and sometimes entire shipments were re-routed because of adverse weather conditions. Ornano's letter bearing the news only reached St Helena after his death.

In article 37 of the Emperor's last Will, under the heading: 'Instructions for my executors', codicil 8 states: 'I wish Alexander Walewski to serve France, preferably in the army.'

EPILOGUE

In her last Will Marie expressed the desire that her heart remain in France but that her body be transported to Poland to the family grave at Kiernozia. In accordance with her wish, an urn containing her heart reposes today at the cemetery of Père Lachaise in Paris in the Ornano family vaults, bearing the simple inscription: '*Marie Laczynska, Comtesse d'Ornano, décédée le 11 December 1817*'. Her body remained at Père Lachaise until it was taken to Poland four months later.

At the time of her death, Marie left her two elder sons in the care of her brother Theodore and made him a legal trustee of Alexander's estate. It was a surprising move, considering her esteem of and the confidence she reposed in her husband. She may have felt that she had no right to burden him with children who were not of his own blood. Though she clearly stipulated in her Will that her brother should keep in frequent touch with her 'dear husband' in all matters concerning Alexander, ask his advice as to the boy's upbringing and in later years place him at a school where 'his stepfather will be able to supervise his education', by investing Theodore with all legal rights to the boy she effectively removed him from Ornano's guardianship during his childhood. In spite of this Alexander remained fond of his stepfather and in later years always kept in close touch with him and with his half-brother Rodolphe.

Theodore arrived at the house at 48, rue de la Victoire, which was now Alexander's property, shortly after his sister's death. He does not appear to have acted in a very tactful manner in the bereaved household, for he immediately 'and loudly' demanded the sale of the house and insisted on taking Alexander back to Poland with him. Worse still, in spite of General Ornano's strong objections, he instantly addressed a petition to the French Minister of the Interior for a permit to transport his sister's body to Poland. The petition was filed in the name of himself, Marie's elder brother Benedict and her two sisters, Antonia and Honor. As Poland was then under Russian control, the family's application was duly supported by the Russian Ambassador in Paris, a formality that Marie would have greatly resented.

On 22 March 1818, after overcoming a number of complex administrative regulations, Theodore arranged for a funeral cortège to escort his sister's body from the cemetery of Père Lachaise, through Paris to Senlis, Bonavy and Hal, by-passing Brussels and then all the way on to Poland. Later that year the charming Hôtel St Chamans was sold, with a large proportion of the money going to pay mortgages on the Walewice estate. General Ornano, in a kind and magnanimous gesture, relinquished, in favour of his two stepsons, the sum of one hundred thousand livres left to him by Marie as part of their marriage settlement.

At the time of his mother's death, Alexander was seven and a half years old. He returned to Poland with his uncle Theodore after the house in Paris had been sold and settled down with him and his elder half-brother Anthony in the Laczynski family house at Kiernozia, surrounded by mementoes of Napoleonic campaigns. He later reminisced of this period in his Memoirs:

In almost every conversation my uncle Laczynski paid homage to the memory of my mother – his sister. As a result, from a very early age, we two boys learned to love and admire her, realizing the enormity of our loss.... Uncle Theodore told us much about the Napoleonic Wars and always expressed his unbounded admiration for the Emperor.... It is needless to say that we listened to him spellbound. . . . My uncle's greatest wish was to take us on a visit to St Helena, but he thought we had better wait until we were older.

Alexander had his first lessons at home with a tutor and later went to a Jesuit school in Warsaw. At the age of ten he was sent to a school in Geneva, from which he kept in touch with his stepfather. His elder brother Anthony, to whom he became very attached in Poland, remained in Warsaw. (He died in his early twenties.) It was in the summer of 1821, in Geneva, that Alexander heard of the death of the Emperor on St Helena. It made a tremendous impression on him.

He returned to Poland when he was almost fifteen, a handsome, serious-looking young man, well spoken and bearing a striking resemblance to the Emperor, though much taller. His appearance on the scene provoked much interest among the Russian authorities in Warsaw. When he was seventeen, the Tsar's brother Constantine, the much disliked commander-in-chief of the Polish forces, decided that as a conciliatory gesture to the Poles it might be politic to appoint Alexander Walewski his ADC. But it was an appointment Alexander could not possibly have accepted. Following his refusal, the Russian police made his life in Warsaw extremely disagreeable. As his application for a passport and exit-permit was turned down, he decided to escape to France on board an English vessel from Saint Petersburg. He eventually arrived at his stepfather's house in Paris in the autumn of 1827. Surrounded by an aura of romance, he became an immediate social success in the drawing-rooms of Charles x's Paris.

In 1830, at a time when the Napoleonic legend was reviving under the liberal reign of King Louis Philippe, Alexander was sent on a diplomatic mission to Poland by the then Foreign Minister, General Sebastiani, a former cavalry-commander under Napoleon. He found Poland in a state of armed insurrection against the Russians. As he was crossing the border from Germany, he was arrested by the Prussian authorities near Posen but escaped and managed to get to Warsaw, where he decided to enlist into the Polish army and join in the fighting.

He remained in Poland for almost two years, taking part in the abortive campaign for independence. He advanced to the rank of captain and also won several decorations for valour. At the end of 1831 he travelled to London to enlist British sympathy for the Polish cause. There he met and married Catherine Montague, daughter of Lord Sandwich. They returned to Paris early the next year. His happy marriage did not last very long, for on 30 April 1834 Catherine Montague Walewska died while giving birth prematurely to a baby daughter, who survived her by only a few months.

Soon after, Alexander formally applied for French citizenship and entered French military service, as Napoleon had desired. After serving in the French North African Foreign Legion, he returned to Paris and dabbled in journalism and politics; he also conducted a tempestuous love-affair with Rachel, the famous Comédie Française actress, by whom he had a son, Alexander. When the affaire with Rachel petered out, Alexander, by then thirty-six years old and one of the most attractive men of his day, married Marianne Ricci, the daughter of the Marquese Ricci, a Florentine, whose mother was a Poniatowska, a first cousin of the heroic Prince Joseph. Marianne was gay, elegant and a wonderful hostess – a perfect wife for a diplomat.

With the ascent to power of Louis Napoleon Bonaparte – the son of Hortense and Louis Bonaparte, King of Holland – first as President of France and later as Emperor Napoleon III, the pace of Alexander's diplomatic career gathered momentum. After a spell as minister in Florence and Naples, he was made ambassador to London in the summer of 1851, and four years later, by then a senator, he took over the post of Minister of Foreign Affairs of France. One of his first duties as ambassador of France to London was to arrange the formal recognition by Queen Victoria's government of the Second Empire, ruled by Napoleon III, his cousin. A less agreeable duty was to represent France at the funeral of the Duke of Wellington, his father's victor.

Ever since Napoleon's death on St Helena, his Testament had been kept in the Canterbury archives. It fell to Alexander

247

Walewski to obtain for France his father's last Will. In a moving letter to Edouard Thouvenel, the Permanent Secretary of the French Foreign Office, he wrote, 'The restitution to France of this precious document is for me the greatest possible honour; nothing in my present or future diplomatic career could ever bring me greater happiness.'

Alexander and his attractive, elegant wife, who became a celebrated hostess and a personal friend of the Empress Eugénie, were as much of a success at the Foreign Ministry as they had been at the French Embassy in London, where Alexander had become a great favourite with Queen Victoria.

The new era of friendship between France and Great Britain, so successfully fostered by Walewski's embassy in London and strengthened by Queen Victoria's and Prince Albert's state visit to Paris, owed much to the diplomatic skill of Alexander and the elegant, if somewhat brittle, Countess Marianne Walewska. Contemporary diarists all mention the prevailing rumours of a liaison between Marianne and Napoleon III, conducted under the very eye of the Empress Eugénie, who always used to refer to Marianne as her 'best friend'. It is an interesting footnote to history.

Throughout his entire life Alexander's resemblance to the Emperor provoked frequent comments. It was mostly the expression in his eyes, people said, and his voice. Once, in Paris, Alexander was asked to speak at the funeral of a prominent politician. As he talked, an old man in the audience covered his face with his hands, crying. 'I did not know you were such a friend of the deceased,' said a neighbour. 'Oh, no,' answered the veteran of the Napoleonic campaigns, 'I know this voice. I have loved it, and I never thought I would hear it again.'

Walewski's last years were spent in Paris in a succession of important government posts; he was in turn Privy Councillor, Minister of Arts, Member of the French Academy and President of the Legislative Assembly. He died at the age of fifty-eight from a heart attack in Strasbourg. He was survived by six children of his two marriages, two sons and four daughters, and

a son, Alexander, the child of his liaison with Rachel, whom he
adopted and brought up with the rest of his family. There are
no direct descendants of Marie in Poland at the moment, but
the French branch of the family, Alexander's and Rodolphe
d'Ornano's great-grandchildren, are enjoying a prosperous
existence in France. It is thanks to their kind assistance that this
book has been written.

MANUSCRIPT SOURCES

Archives Walewski, Paris (family papers)
Archives de la Bibliothèque Thiers (Fonds Masson), Paris
Archives of the Quai d'Orsay, Paris, volumes on Poland, 1807–14
Archives Nationales, Paris
Archives de la Seine, Paris
Belgian State Archives, Brussels (documentation on Ornano's marriage and purchase of a house in Liège)
Vienna State Archives
Naples State Archives
Archives of the Casa Mulini at Portoferraio, Elba
Polish Church records, regarding Marie's birth, marriage and divorce
Adam Mauersberger – the Walewski divorce proceedings; published in Poland, 1939
Excerpts from birth certificates of the Laczynski family; Alexander Walewski's birth records – as registered in Poland, 1810

BIBLIOGRAPHY

Polish
Askenazy, Szymon, *Ksiaze Josef Poniatowski*, Warsaw, 1910
  Rosya-Polska, Lwow, 1907
  Dwa Stulecia, xviii and xix, Crakow, 1903
Brandys, Marian, *Klopoty z Pania Walewska*, Warsaw, 1969
  Kozietulski i inni, 2 volumes, Warsaw, 1967
Canaletto, *Malarz Warszawy*, Warsaw, 1954
Dembowski, Leon, *Mes Souvenirs*, Warsaw, 1834
Dmochowski, Francis, *Wspomnienia od 1806 do 1830 roku*,
  Warsaw, 1959
Fredro, A., *Pamietniki*, Warsaw, 1837
Kicka, Natalia, *Pamietniki z roku 1807–38*, Warsaw, 1972
Konarski, Szymon, *Herbarz Polski*, Warsaw, 1909
Kukiel, Marian, 'Prawda o Pani Walewskiej', *Wiadomosci
  Literackie*, London, 1958
Lubienski, Tomasz, *Pamietniki*, Warsaw, 1830
Nakwaska, Anna, *Pamietniki*, Warsaw, 1852
Niemcewicz, Julian Ursyn, *Pamietniki*, Warsaw, 1830
Nieswieski, Kasper, *Herbarz Polski*, volume vi, Leipzig, 1841
Oginski, M. K., *Pamietniki*, Warsaw, 1837
Skarbek, Frederic, *Memoirs – Pamietniki*, Paris, 1821
Trembicka, F., *Les mémoires d'une Polonaise*, Paris, 1847
Uruski, *Herbarz Polski*, Dresden, 1805
Wasylewski, Stanislaw, *Zerwana Kokarda*, Warsaw, 1967
Wybicki, Jozef, *Pamietniki*, volume iii, Poznan, 1840
Zaluski, Jozef, *Wspomnienia*, volumes i, ii, iii, Poznan, 1841

Polish Periodicals
Mauersberger, Adam, in *Atheneum*, 1939, no. 2
Gazeta Warszawska (*Gazette de Varsovie*) throughout the first six months of 1807 and throughout 1808; also June to December 1812
The calendar of the royal Court has been established through contemporary Polish papers

French
Abrantès, Laure Junot, Duchess of, *Mémoires*, Paris, 1831 and 1893
Avrillon, Mademoiselle, *Mémoires sur la vie privée de Joséphine*, Paris, 1833
Bausset, Louis, F. J., *Mémoires anecdotiques sur l'interieur du palais*, Brussels, 1827–9
Begouen, Count, *Une Polonaise à Spa*, Archer Publications, Brussels, 1939
Bernardy, Françoise, *Comte Alexandre Walewski*, Paris, 1974
Bertrand, Marshal, *Les cahiers de Ste Hélène*, Paris, 1828
Bignon, Louis, *Ambassade de France à Varsovie, 1808–12*,
Boigne, Comtesse de, *Mes mémoires*, London, 1907
Bonaparte, Caroline (Murat), *Mémoires*, Paris, 1840 (and New York, 1910)
Bonaparte, Lucien, *Mémoires secrets*, Paris, 1818
Broglie, Duke of, *Souvenirs*, Paris, 1886
Campbell, Col. Sir Neil, *Journal de 1814 et 1815*, Paris, 1873
Castelot, André, *Napoléon*, Paris, 1967
Caulaincourt, Duke of Vicenza, *Mémoires*, annotated by Jean Hanoteau, 3 volumes, Paris, 1945
Chastenay, Victorine de, *Les mémoires de Mme de Chastenay*, 2 volumes, Paris, 1870
Christophe, R., *L'Empereur de l'Ile d'Elbe*, 1959
Clary et Almedingen, Prince de, *Trois mois à Paris lors du marriage de Napoléon et Marie Louise*, Paris, 1914
Fain, Baron, *Mémoires du Baron Fain, premier secrétaire du Cabinet de l'Empereur*, Paris, 1908

Fleischmann, H., *Dessous des princesses et maréchales de l'Empire*, Paris, 1909

Godlewski, Dr Guy, *Trois cent jours d'exil*, Paris, 1961

Halévy, Ludovic, *Notes et souvenirs*, Paris, 1889

Handelsman, A., *Napoléon et la Pologne*, Paris, 1897

Hortense, Queen of Holland, *Hortense*, ed. Jean Hanoteau, published by the Prince Napoléon, Paris, 1927

Iwaszkievicz, J., *Vie de Chopin*, Paris, 1949

Kielmansegge, Comtesse de, *Mémoires*, Paris, 1849

Las Cases, Comte de, *Memorial de Ste Hélène*, Paris, 1823

Lévy, Arthur, *Napoléon intime*, Paris, 1893

Marbot, General Baron de, *Mémoires*, Paris, 1844

Marchand, Louis, *Mémoires*, ed. Bourguignon, Paris, 1932

Masson, Frédéric, *Napoléon et les femmes*, Paris, 1897
Napoléon et sa famille, Paris, 1895

Meneval, Baron de, *Mémoires*, ed. Sherrod, volume II, Paris, 1894

Montesquiou, Anatole de, *Mémoires*, volumes I and III, Paris, 1846

Montholon, C. J., *Mémoires*, Paris, 1857

Ornano, Philippe d', *La vie passionante du Comte Walewski*, Paris, 1953

Oudinot, Marshal, *Mémoires*, ed. Gaston Stiegler, Paris, 1894

Palewski, Jean de, *Dernier roi de Pologne*, Paris, 1946

Potocka, Countess Anna, *Mémoires, 1794–1820*, ed. K. Stryjenski, Paris, 1897

Pradt, Abbé, *Histoire de l'Ambassade à Varsovie*, Paris, 1819

Remusat, Claire de, *Mémoires*, Paris, 1880

Robiquet, Jean, *La vie quotidienne au temps de Napoléon*, Paris, 1938

Rulhière, C., *Histoire de l'anarchie en Pologne*, Paris, 1787

Savant, Jean, *L'affaire de Marie Walewska*, Paris (privately printed), 1963
Napoleon raconté par lui-même, Paris, 1954

Schuermans, Albert, *Itineraine général de Napoléon Ier*, Paris, 1908

Segur, Comte de, *Memoires: la campagne de Russie*, 2 volumes, Paris, 1901

Sieburg, Friedrich, *Napoléon: les cent jours*, ed. Robert Laffont, Paris, 1938

Stendhal (Marie Henri Beyle), *Promenades dans Rome*, Paris, 1826

Tour, Jean de la Tour, *Duroc, Duc de Friul*, Paris, 1897

Tulard, Jean, *Napoléon*, Paris, 1978

Valynseele, Joseph, *La descendance naturelle de Napoléon Ier*, Paris

Wairy, Constant Louis, *Mémoires de Constant, premier valet de l'Empereur*, Paris, 1830–31

Italian

Pasquale, Luigi de, *Napoleone all'Elba, 1814–15*, Cronaca Retrospettiva, Lecco, Editione Stefanoni, 1972

English language

Aretz, Gertrude, *Napoleon and his women friends*, translated from the French by E. and C. Paul (Allen & Unwin, London 1927; Lippincott, New York 1927)

Bain, R. Nisbet, *The last King of Poland and his contemporaries* (Methuen, London 1909)

Barnett, Corelli, *Bonaparte* (Allen & Unwin, London 1978)

Bear, Joan, *Caroline Murat: a biography* (Collins, London 1972)

Bearne, Catherine, *A Leader of Society at Napoleon's Court* (Fisher & Unwin, London 1904)

Bernard, J. F., *Talleyrand: a biography* (Collins, London 1973; Putnam, New York 1973)

Breton, G., *Napoleon and his ladies*, translated by F. Holt (Robert Hale, London 1965)

Cole, Hubert, *Joséphine* (Heinemann, London 1961)

Cooper, A. Duff, *Talleyrand* (Jonathan Cape, London 1932; Harper, New York 1932)

Coxe, William, *Travels into Poland, Russia, Sweden and Denmark*, I, London 1792

Cronin, Vincent, *Napoleon: an intimate biography* (Collins, London 1971; William Morrow. New York 1972)

Dixon, Sir Pierson, *Pauline: Napoleon's favourite sister* (Collins, London 1964; McKay, New York 1965)

Dodds, Dennis W., *Napoleon's love child: a biography of Count Leon* (William Kimber, London 1974)

Geyl, Peter, *Napoleon: for and against*, translated from the Dutch by Olive Renier (Jonathan Cape, London 1949; Yale University Press, New Haven, 1949)

Greer, Walter *Napoleon and his Family* (Allen & Unwin, London 1928)

Herbert, A. P., *Why Waterloo?* (Methuen, London 1952)

Herold, J. Christopher, *Mistress to an Age: a life of Madame de Stael* (Bobbs-Merrill, Indianapolis 1958; Hamish Hamilton, London 1959)

Hobsbawn, E. J., *The Age of Revolution* (Weidenfeld & Nicolson, London 1962; World Publishing Company, New York 1962)

Ludwig, Emil, *Napoleon*, translated by E. and C. Paul, (Boni & Livewright, New York 1926; Allen & Unwin, London 1927)

Kemble, J., *Napoleon Immortal: the medical history and private life of Napoleon Bonaparte* (John Murray, London 1959).

Knapton, E. A., *Empress Josephine* (Harvard University Press, 1963)

Macdonell, A. G., *Napoleon and his Marshals* (Macmillan, London 1934; Macmillan, New York 1936)

Markham, Felix, *Napoleon* (Weidenfeld & Nicolson, London 1964; New American Library, New York 1964)

Palmer, Alan, *Alexander I: Tsar of war and peace* (Weidenfeld & Nicolson, London 1974)

Petre, F. Loraine, *Napoleon's Campaign in Poland, 1806–7* (John Lane, London 1901)
Napoleon at bay, 1814 (John Lane, London 1914)

Richardson, General Frank, *Napoleon: bisexual Emperor* (William Kimber, London 1972; Horizon Press, New York 1972)

Russell, Jack, *Nelson and the Hamiltons* (Blond, London 1969;
Simon & Schuster, New York 1969)
Yale French Studies, *The Myth of Napoleon* (Yale University
Study Center 1960–1)

INDEX